CW01271667

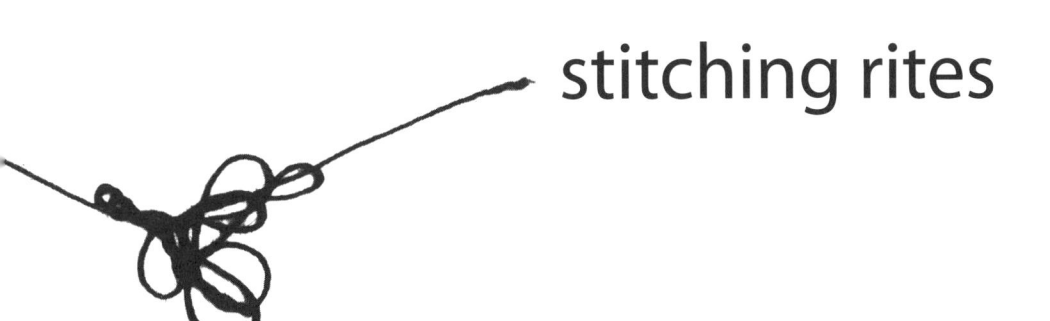

stitching rites

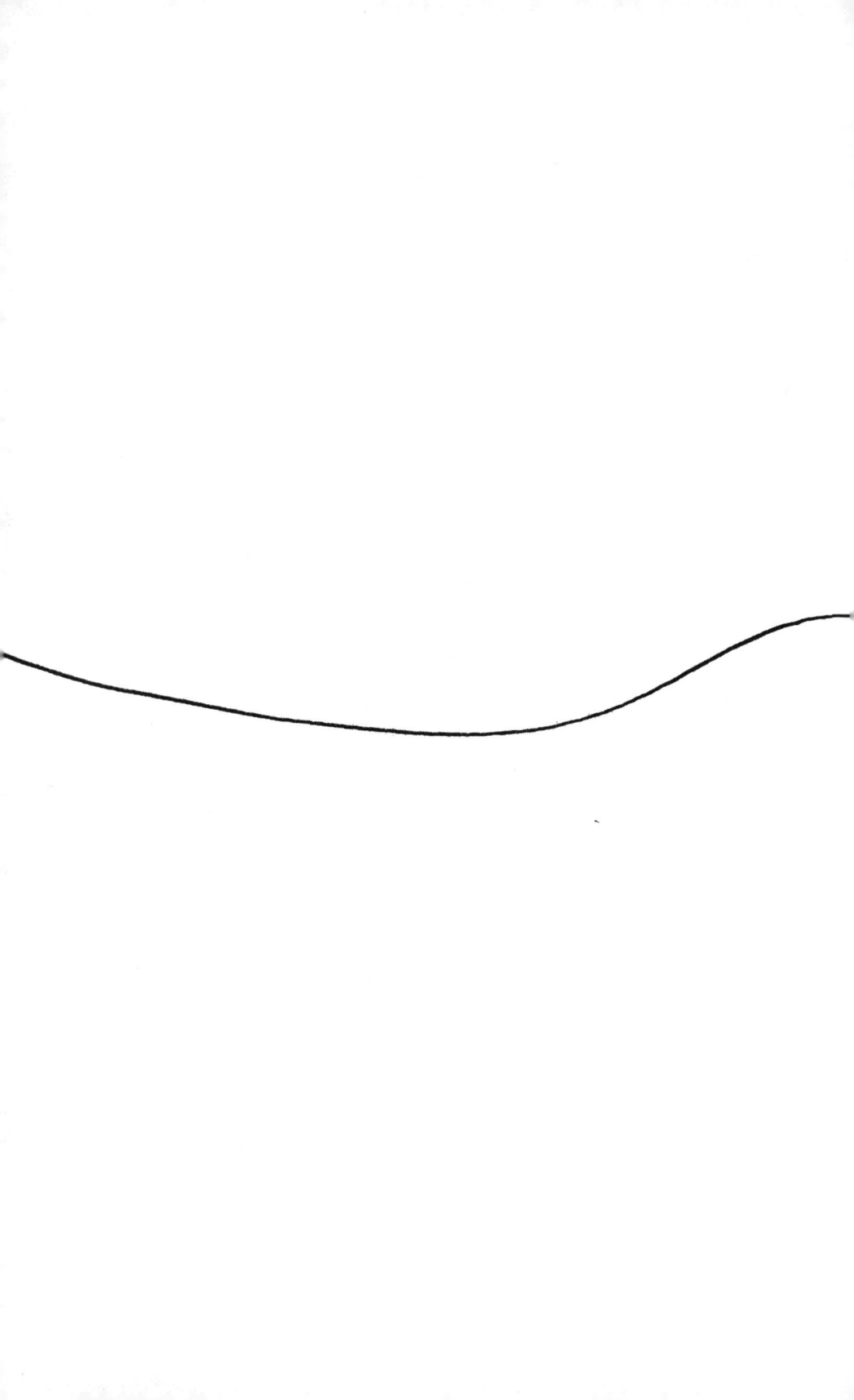

suzanne p. macaulay

# stitching rites

colcha embroidery
along the northern
rio grande

the university of arizona press   tucson

First printing
The University of Arizona Press
© 2000 The Arizona Board of Regents
All rights reserved
∞ This book is printed on acid-free,
archival-quality paper.
Manufactured in the
United States of America
05 04 03 02 01 00  6 5 4 3 2 1

Library of Congress
Cataloging-in-Publication Data

MacAulay, Suzanne P. (Suzanne Pollock)
Stitching rites: colcha embroidery
along the northern Rio Grande /
Suzanne P. MacAulay.
p.  cm.
Includes bibliographical
references and index.
ISBN 0-8165-2029-1 (cloth: alk. paper)
1. Embroidery—San Luis Valley (Colo.
and N.M.)  2. Coverlets—San Luis
Valley (Colo. and N.M.)  3. Hispanic
American decorative arts—San Luis
Valley (Colo. and N.M.)  I. Title.
TT769.U62 S256   2000
746.44′08968078—dc21
00-008200

British Library
Cataloguing-in-Publication Data

A catalogue record for this book is
available from the British Library.

Publication of this book is made
possible in part by a grant from
Wanganui Regional Community
Polytechnic.

Para las bordadoras de San Luis

"A lo dado no se le da fin."

(What is given has no end)

## contents

List of Plates ix
List of Figures xi
Preface xiii

1. *Tierra Nueva* 3
2. Josephine Lobato as Cultural Commentator 13
3. Change and Tradition in Historical Colcha Making 53
4. Embroidery Revivals 75
5. The Ladies Sewing Circle of San Luis 109
6. Stitches of Myth and Memory 153

Notes 159
Bibliography 171
Index 181

## plates

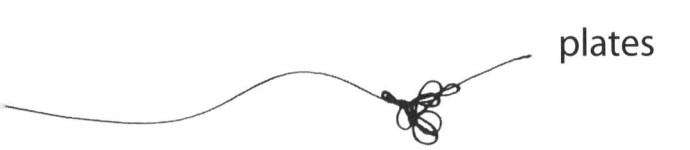

following page  46

1  An embroidered map of the San Luis Valley by Tiva Trujillo
2  *Mis Crismes,* by Josephine Lobato
3  *Los Penitentes,* by Josephine Lobato
4  The wool embroidery *El Milagro de San Acacio,* by Josephine Lobato
5  A nineteenth-century colcha embroidery with geometric and floral design elements
6  A nineteenth-century floral colcha embroidery
7  A detail of the wool embroidery *Las Misiones,* by Josephine Lobato
8  The wool embroidery *El Rancho Grande,* by Sostena Cleven

# figures

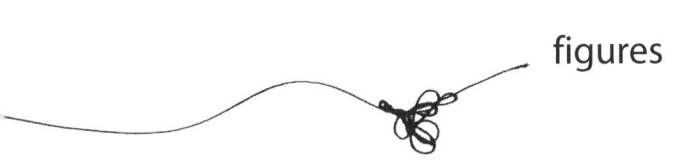

Map of San Luis, Colorado, and vicinity   2

following page   46

1  A floral detail showing the distinctive colcha couching stitch
2  *La Entriega de los Novios,* by Josephine Lobato
3  A nineteenth-century colcha embroidery inspired by Rio Grande Saltillo-style weavings
4  The 1930s "Carson Colcha," attributed to Wayne Graves
5  *Haciendo Ristras,* by Filomena Gonzales and A. Chavéz
6  *Old San Acacio,* by Julia Valdez
7  *La Vega,* by Evangeline Salazar
8  *La Casa de Piedra,* by Sally Chavez
9  *Magpie,* by Pacífica La Combe

# preface

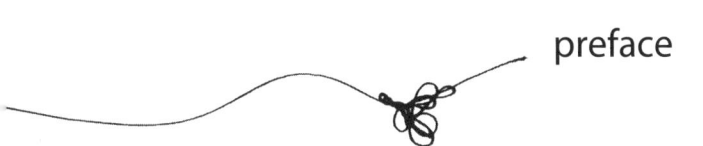

"You express and you remember."

"My life.... It's a true picture and a real picture. They were alive sometime.... Oh, once upon a time."

"So it's coming out in bits and pieces in my mind as to what was important. But the point of the whole thing is . . . not to lose something that is going to be lost."

Words melding yet crossing over, pronounced by three stitchers from the San Luis Valley, as personal testaments to the kinetic interplay between stitching and reverie. The thoughts of these artist storytellers reveal the eternal round of inspiration and creative action, the circularity of imagination feeding off experience arising from biography and inclination. Women who by their careful and attentive way of embroidering, observing, and narrating inspired me in my fieldwork practice to keep looking until I could really see, which is probably the simplest yet most radical effect of participant observation. It is this observant looking and seeing that gradually sensitized me to all the inconsistencies and anomalies present throughout the history of colcha embroidery, but most particularly in its vitalized and revitalized contemporary forms.

The voices of the artists, their comments and attitudes, are central to this book. In the early 1990s when I first visited San Luis and immersed myself in that rural town in southern Colorado, I determined that I would start at the local level in order to begin to question the relation between stitching acts and culture politics. It did not take long to realize that I could also use this microstudy as a framework to investigate larger historical concerns. Over the next two years I found this method useful whenever I reached an impasse in working with relatively undocumented textile collections of colcha embroideries, because I could always rely on the residual imprint of stitchers' words and actions to ground me in the practicalities of the craft. No matter the paradox or the enigma, pondering the pragmatics of stitching in one way or another always provided a different, often a more productive way of coping with the latest conundrum.

By working from the inside out I started to understand how the notion of ethnoaesthetics or folk aesthetics, art and aesthetics as practiced and interpreted by the artists themselves, is vital to maintaining internal creative expressiveness in order to deflect some of the more powerful forces of the external art worlds. In this study ethnoaesthetics, inclusive of the multiple viewpoints surrounding colcha embroidery, delineate the extent of negotiations, accord, and disagreements among ethnic artists, entrepreneurs, collectors, and others. These disagreements revolve around the meaning and application of authenticity, cultural and aesthetic autonomy, self-representation, and outside influence. But it is the experience of being the *outsider within* that really orients our discussion on art, aesthetics, and community, because the state of "being within" raises such familiar classic ethnographic questions as "What is it like to be an embroiderer in San Luis?" "How does it feel to live in a culture such as this one?" And the ultimate "outsider" quandary, "Can we ever know how it feels?"

My arrival in San Luis in 1990 was in its own way a kind of revival. Although I was there to begin folklore fieldwork for my doctorate after returning to graduate school in 1988, I had initiated a documentary project on folk artists and folk art revivals in the San Luis Valley in 1979 when I was teaching art history at a Denver college. During that time I had come to know colcha embroiderers from the other end of the valley and a few in San Luis. Regrettably, I gave up my involvement before the project ended. Returning to San Luis ten years later in order to combine folklore with art history in another folk art project on colcha embroidery seemed like destiny.

This book treats colcha embroidery in its discrete form as a traditional Spanish colonial textile, bed covering or wall hanging dating from the early to mid-nineteenth century, and in its modified contemporary version as a stitched pictorial narrative, which is usually framed and hung on walls. Colcha is often ranked with weaving and woodcarving as an important representative of Southwestern Hispano culture and history. Despite this cluster of material culture artifacts symbolizing ethnic identity in perpetuity as cultural icons, colcha embroidery is frequently regarded as somewhat minor in relation to the other two genres. To counter this, our discussion foregrounds colcha embroidery as critical to the interplay of aesthetic and social interaction. Throughout this book colcha is taken as a means to explore issues of creativity, contentions over colcha making held by insiders and outsiders, and reflexivity as a form of meditative feedback flowing between art and life.

The first chapter begins with the social and religious revitalization of San Luis in the mid-1980s. This reform was catalyzed by the charismatic Father Patricio Valdez, who, wary of acting on faith alone, believed that the town's spiritual resurrection had to be accompanied by an economic miracle as well. The Ladies Sewing Circle was formed as part of Father Pat's economic revival. This group is discussed extensively in chapter 5 as a microcosm of San Luis because of strong links to the community through lineage, kinship, and parish membership.

Stitcher Josephine Lobato is introduced in chapter 2 as a "cultural commentator" (a tour guide to her own culture) in terms of her colcha imagery and her biographical legacy of being both an insider by birth and an outsider by circumstance. Josie Lobato is the subject of a separate chapter because her work differs from the majority of stitchers in San Luis and she is not a member of the Ladies Sewing Circle—the often self-appointed arbiter of colcha aesthetics for the community. This chapter derives its impact, tension, and pace from the complexities associated with Josie's interpretation and use of colcha embroidery, the utilization of art as autobiography, and her imaginative manipulation of memory—societal, familial, and personal. The majority of Josie's embroidered images and narrative scenes derive from her memories of the post–World War II 1940s, a transitional period in the valley. Thus, her imagery and diverse subject matter provide clues to evaluating acts of remembrance and cultural transformation in relation to tradition, change, and discontinuity.

The image of Josie Lobato privately communing with a nineteenth-century colonial style colcha embroidery in the local museum where she works leads into the third chapter, which is a historical treatment of colcha embroidery. This section questions historical precedents, not only investigating the myriad definitions of colcha but examining the implication of the colcha art form as an emblem of Hispanic ethnicity and as a tangible record of the forces of cultural and artistic transformation.

In order to measure and evaluate the impact of the revitalization methods implemented in San Luis in the 1990s, chapter 4 traces previous private and government agencies' agendas and efforts to revive Hispanic colcha embroidery in New Mexico and Colorado from the 1920s onward. Its content is a colorful mix of opinion and contradiction culled from interviews with people outside the San Luis area and from archival material in regional museum collections. Interestingly, the picture that emerges, of stitchers interacting with entrepreneurs, appears to be primarily conditioned by mutually effective cultural forces in contact—rather than simply one group (outsiders) dominating and subordinating the other (villagers). Authenticity and tradition are the principal signposts here. Their value and meaning, of course, depend on which individuals are charting the cultural landscape.

Toward the end of the chapter, expectations concerning tradition and authenticity are upended and dramatically turned around once again in terms of a subgenre of embroideries, New Mexican Carson colchas. These textiles have posed something of a puzzle since their appearance in the 1930s, when they were originally intended to replicate nineteenth-century historical colonial colchas. Surprisingly, Carson colchas developed into a distinct genre of their own and have confused and exasperated museum curators and collectors ever since.

Chapter 5, on the San Luis Ladies Sewing Circle, demonstrates how colcha creation and societal forces are inextricably bound by a perpetual round of cultural commentary and self-reflexivity. Much of this exchange is subject to another force, a type of cultural inversion, which helps to explain the often subtle reactions and adjustments occurring within San Luis and outside it—relative to the external marketplace. The analysis of how all these components fit together underscores a central issue concerning the linkage of power to community self-representation in San Luis, and possibly in other traditional Hispano groups.

Memory offers one of the most effective ways to evaluate the power structure and culture of San Luis, both artistically and politically. Furthermore, the pictorial narrative genre of colcha is an ideal form to explore the conditions of possibility and continuity by weaving together the different strands of past, present, and future within one frame. Chapter 6 continues the theme of memory. In the end memory in tandem with ethnoaesthetics becomes crucial to interpreting the historical and iconographical dimensions of colcha embroidery from any era, Spanish colonial to contemporary. Throughout the discussion definitions are as open-ended and fluid as appropriate. My main intention in writing on ethnic art is to offer a notion of art making as a creative space where boundaries are continually redefined with respect to alterations between insiders and outsiders, shifts in tradition and change, and individual versus collective creative expression.

This book has been a long time in the making. Many people have accompanied me along the way. The naturalist John Muir wrote, "Whenever we try to pick out anything by itself, we find it hitched to everything else in the universe." Muir's words pertain not only to the patterns of research, but also aptly describe the following configuration of individuals. Although several are unacquainted, many are inadvertently linked together by their association with my study of colcha embroidery.

At the University of Pennsylvania, Roger Abrahams first pointed out the perfect match between investigator and subject when he asked, "Why not study colcha embroidery?" As if in response to this somewhat oracular question, Evangeline Salazar, Sally T. Chavez, and women of the Ladies Sewing Circle warmly welcomed me to San Luis—a great distance from Philadelphia, and now, of course, even farther from my home in New Zealand. Daisy Ortega taught me her "signature" stitch, the Lazy Daisy. Mary Taylor and Frances Martinez considerately shepherded me to Holy Week processions and special events. Julia and Abie Valdez generously shared their lives and views on family issues and increased my understanding of the San Luis community, as did *mis compañeros,* Sally and Salomón Chavez. Stitchers Sostena Cleven, Teresa Vigil, Mary Martinez, and Paula Cunningham spent time unraveling the intricacies of their involvement with colcha embroidery. My collaboration with Josephine Lobato sensitized me to the subtleties of creativity and colcha making. Accordingly, Eugene Lobato's interest in Josie's work and in local history helped to amplify my own experience. Much of the richness of chapter 2 derives from Gene's stories and jokes.

Father Pat Valdez, Charles Manzanares, and Maclovio Martinez contributed greatly to the sacred and secular aspects of this study. Throughout this time I always appreciated Sangre de Cristo parishioners' friendly acceptance of my presence. I also credit much of my interpretation of vernacular architecture and community planning to open discussions with Maria and Arnie Valdez. During my visits, John Ortega frequently provided sustenance—cultural and culinary.

My analysis of Carson colchas would have lacked dimension without Frances Graves's voice. Her niece, Maria Fernandez Graves, and different New Mexico embroiderers and artists, including Helen Thompson, Lorraine Varela, Teresa Archuleta-Sagel, Maria Vergara Wilson, Victoria Mascarenas, and Isidora Madrid de Flores, spoke freely about their own work and helped me to conceptualize the scope of contemporary colcha revitalization and vitalization movements.

Carmen Orrego-Salas's opinions and cooperation have been vital to this study and help shape some of my analysis. I am also indebted to the following individuals and organizations who encouraged and facilitated my museum research: Kathy Reynolds and former curator William Wroth, of the Taylor Museum, Colorado Springs Fine Arts Center; Judy Sellars and former curator Helen Lucero, of the Museum of International Folk Art in Santa Fe; Guadalupe Tafoya of the Millicent Rogers Museum, Taos, New Mexico; and Jenny Gurule of the San Luis Cultural Museum. I am grateful to Helen Lucero for her diligent reading and valuable insights regarding colchas and Hispano ethnicity. Anthropologist Richard Hirshberg offered encouragement and lively critiques along the way. I appreciate art historian John Hoag's support for my conviction that folklore and art history are compatible. The map of the San Luis Valley was prepared by Brian Smith. Unless otherwise noted, all photographs are my own, and, of course, any errors in interpretation and content are my own.

Since writing the dissertation upon which this book is based, I have moved to the opposite side of the earth, to New Zealand, where I teach and pursue the myriad ways of being a long-term guest in another country. The Wanganui Polytechnic, particularly the Research and Ethics Committee, has generously supported my writing with allocations of time and funding. Thanks to Christine Szuter of the University of Arizona Press for her initial encouragement and abiding commitment to this project.

Finally, the hospitality and continued support of good friends sustained me through the throes of fieldwork and, later, during the aftermath of research and writing. It was always a pleasure to admire Mt. Blanca (Sisnaajini) with Pat and Blaine Sloan. Spanish language sessions with Cristina Baud were not only critical to my fieldwork but enlightening for my investigations of Spanish antecedents for colchas. Despite our physical distance, my conversations and friendship with Joan Saverino and Ruth Olson have continued to bolster my spirit from the inception of this project. Of course, I acknowledge my family, Brigid Pollock, Allan, Lazrus, and Heather as integral to the realization of this book.

stitching rites

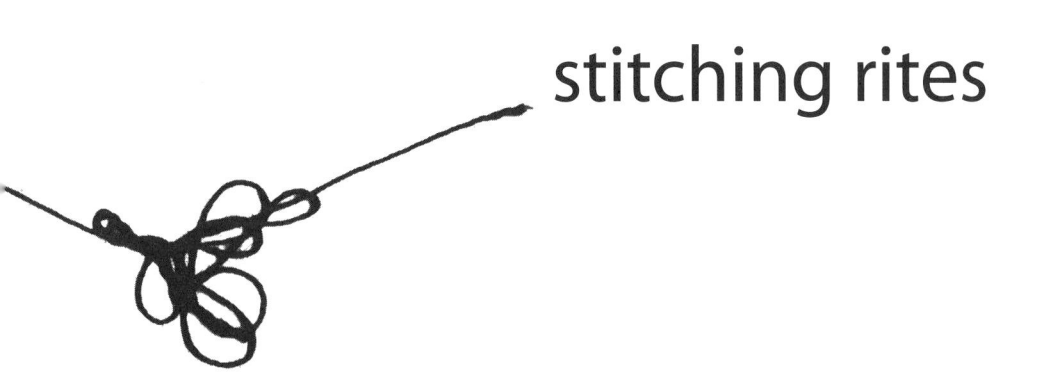

San Luis in south central Colorado located near New Mexico border. (Map prepared by Brian Smith)

# 1

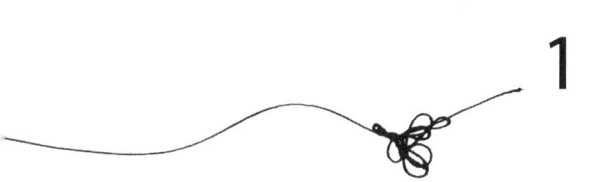

*tierra nueva*

"Our town was just sad. You know? . . . So many people out of work. Everybody's children would leave and they never came back . . . we felt hopeless." [In a few words Esther Romero summarized the bleak mood in San Luis before Father Patricio Valdez arrived and went door-to-door actively recruiting help from his parishioners.] Señora Romero, now in her eighties, opened her door: "Yes, Father, I'll bake some cookies. . . . Yes, Father Pat, I'll stuff envelopes. . . . Before I knew it, I was out of my house and I didn't feel so lonely anymore."

—Terry Mattingly, "San Luis Bears a Cross of Its Own"

Doors opened all over San Luis. Father Patricio Valdez's timely arrival in 1985, and his personal magnetism, energized the people of this Hispanic community in south central Colorado, not far from the New Mexico border. His appearance heralded change, but his actions (from encouraging organic farming ventures to supporting a craft revival) also forcefully rekindled traditions and cultural connections within the community. Father Pat was an insider turned outsider who had come home again. Raised in another part of the San Luis Valley, he had sufficient family connections to be considered a "local" in the eyes of San Luis; but as a member of the Theatine Order, he had lived, trained, and been educated in Denver.

The revitalization of the economy and, essentially, the spirit of San Luis was primarily catalyzed by Father Pat; wary of acting on faith alone, he believed that the town's spiritual resurrection had to be accompanied by "an economic miracle" as well. He was transferred from the Denver Diocese to the San Luis Parish after successfully battling alcoholism. Thus, his social campaigns to bring the community of San Luis out of a lengthy financial and emotional depression actually dovetailed with his own struggles for personal redemption. Esther Romero's words could also reflect Father Pat's thoughts when she said, "But I don't feel lonely and hopeless anymore. I feel like I belong to a living community again. We are trying to make new lives, with the help of God."[1]

As part of Father Pat's economic revival, the Ladies Sewing Circle began as a stitching group ostensibly to learn to create "ethnically identifiable" colcha embroideries for sale. Most of these women still stitch and, as artists, continue to conform to what they would recognize as their community ethics tempered by personal initiative and individual drive. This is a story about colcha embroidery as a textile in dispute—as an arena in which key concepts like authenticity, tradition, creativity, aesthetics, and memory are actively questioned, possibly transformed, and constantly realigned by embroiderers, entrepreneurs, art consultants, and cultural interpreters. Women have been embroidering patterns and ripping out stitches for years. Whether they are creating new forms or eradicating mistakes in order to recover original intentions, they are engaged in both fabrication and deconstruction—a dual process of "trying to get it right." This study follows a similar method of accretion but also snips away at extra details in order to track all the activity that crisscrosses over colcha making like so many threads securing the shape of life's designs.

I have entered this story in midstream, so to speak. It began several years before my arrival in San Luis and, I am certain, has continued in the years since my departure. My arrival, in the early spring of 1990, coincided with another burst of economic and cultural reinvigoration—once again instigated by Father Pat. At the same time, San Luis colcha embroidery practice had become more established, internalized, and distinct. Colcha in its pictorial narrative format had emerged from externally generated craft workshops in 1988 (promoted by outside art consultants and artist facilitators) to become an internally shared artistic expression. Among different factions of San Luis stitchers there was ample opportunity within the creative reach of this genre to embrace themes ranging from memories and cultural enactments (appreciated by outsiders) to popular images of raccoons climbing out of trash cans (admired by stitchers) literally lifted from mainstream craft magazines. I was captivated by the reemergence of San Luis in the early 1990s and chose a microstudy of colcha making, with its claims to authenticity marked by dissent and individualism, as a way to understand the complexities involved in the self-realization of this "reawakened" community.

Committed to my fieldwork, I spent the next few years traveling to San Luis and crossing over the mountains in dust and wind storms in which the headwinds were so strong that I thought there was something wrong with the clutch in my car. Other times I navigated blizzards like a pilot fish with a convoy of semi trucks cautiously following in my wake. The conditions were often so extreme and I was snowed in so frequently that some of the stitchers came to view me as a harbinger of bad weather.

Some of those moments traveling alone through severe storms were also the most poetic. They are memories made from dreams—like the time I crossed the New Mexico border in a virtual whiteout just as the moon emerged from behind clouds that were moving so fast that I felt a sudden new comprehension of the idea, "the speed of light." Almost at the same time I gradually became aware that my car was flanked by two groups of wild horses galloping on either side of me. I detected movement and snow shadows before I could make out shapes. It was eerie yet comforting to be escorted through the night by these spectral chaperones, like stories of tired swimmers brought to shore by benign dolphins.

La Veta Pass is the gateway through the Sangre de Cristo mountain range from the Colorado plains to an extensive intermontane basin, the San Luis Valley. At the nine-thousand-foot summit of this historic pass are two signs. One marks the entry to Costilla County; the other informs the traveler that this crossing occurs at the uppermost eastern reach of the valley's vast boundaries. Every time I drive over La Veta Pass from the east on my way south, I am conscious that I am moving in a direction counter to the original exploratory campaigns of the Spanish *conquistadores*. I am also aware that this boundary is more than a geographical demarcation. It signals a cultural separation as well.

The valley is an area of spectacular vistas, but also one of the most impoverished regions in Colorado. A land of contrast and dichotomy, the topography and politics of the valley actually meld diversity into combination rather than polarity. Ringed by an impressive cluster of fourteen-thousand-foot peaks, the highest dunes in the United States sift their desert sands not far from one of the most abundant aquifers on the continent—a site of acrimonious contention over water rights between water boards and Denver corporations desiring to disburse the water to other parts of the state and local valley farmers, who believe their crops and land will vanish along with the water. Their anguish is simply stated: "Sin agua es destroso para El Valle" (without water, destruction for the valley).[2]

Exploitation from outside its boundaries eats away at the valley's natural resources and their access (e.g., minerals, lumber, water rights), and drains revenues from the native populace. In the southern part of the San Luis Valley, particularly in Costilla County around San Luis (population slightly over eight hundred), unemployment is high, by some estimates as high as 25 percent.[3] Despite the poverty level, most residents in Costilla County engage in subsistence farming and own their homes and land. In some cases poverty figures for San Luis may offset or obscure the fact that a few community families enjoy a generous economic solvency through agriculture, ranching, or commerce. Thus, their revenues and consequent lifestyles are solidly middle-class.

Tracts of land have been deeded to and maintained by the same families through several generations, for almost one hundred and fifty years since the founding of San Luis in 1851. Many of these homesteads are the enduring remains of the Spanish, and subsequent Mexican, practice of bestowing land grants to Hispanic settlers in order to populate the northern frontiers of the Spanish Colonial Empire. The names of these original grantees of the lands along the Culebra River live on in the surnames of their descendants and as street markers outlining the dim tracery of former plazas and placitas: Salazar, Gaspar, Valdes, Gallegos, Jacquez, Vigil.

The geographical isolation of the San Luis Valley, with mountainous barriers on all sides except in the south, historically reinforced notions of community solidarity through a naturally occurring topographical insularity.[4] Since World War II these culturally homogeneous village enclaves have been eaten away, eroded and altered by an attrition of younger people moving to Colorado's Front Range cities seeking greater career and educational opportunities. They are also enticed by the easier, more sophisticated and materialistic lifestyles. An interesting facet of these migrations, however, is that they are not final. Family connections endure despite distance, separation, and cultural dilution. A strong sense of attachment to cultural roots and an equally strong sense of place frequently induce some of these emigrants to return home as they approach middle age.

## San Luis's Cultural Landscape

Driving south on State Highway 159 through the center of San Luis, one is attracted by a mural on the left-hand side of the road about midway through town. A Denver artist, Carlos Sandoval, originally a native of San Pablo just a few miles from San Luis, finished painting it in autumn 1988. The mural is partitioned into panels depicting themes the residents regard as important segments of their culture: the era of nomadic Indians; a dynamic foreshortened view of the upper portion of the crucifix suspended from clouds out of which emerges a cluster of galloping Spanish conquistadores; an allegorical rendering of the bounty of Mother Earth; and other panels depicting settlers, deer hunters, farming, and adobe making. The background of sky-filled and limitless distance suffused with an unshaded bright light successfully melds these visual elements into a cohesive artistic and cultural vision.

The mural's prominent position at the heart of San Luis invites the speculation that for both residents and travelers its presence advertises, like a billboard, a symbolically constructed glimpse of the community's belief system with respect to the primacy of Catholicism, ethnic heritage and pride, and connectedness to the earth through hunting and agriculture. Unlike a billboard, these images are rendered on a mythic rather than a commercial scale.

Within the mural's pictorial scheme, one of the most binding elements around which the San Luis community coheres is land—its use, its constancy, and the power exercised through its acquisition. The linkage between the belief in land as a God-given birthright and the Spanish conquest of the region in the name of God and religion is apparent in the interrelationship within the iconic arrangement of conquistadores, Christ, and cultivation.

At a time like this, when ethnic solidarity emerging in the face of historic Anglo dominance is invigorating self-esteem and community pride in Hispanic villages, the issues of land and birthright are crucial. The people of San Luis view the history of the Sangre de Cristo Land Grant as intertwined with issues of heritage and self-reliance that depend on the communal right to use resources, though not necessarily to own them. This is clearly stated in the 1863 Beaubien Deed, which established the Plaza of San Luis de la Culebra: "As such, everyone should exercise scrupulous care with the use of water without causing harm to their *vecinos* [neighbors] with the water, nor to anyone; all of the inhabitants shall have with convenient arrangement, the enjoyment of the benefits of the pastures, water, wood and lumber, always being careful not to prejudice one another."[5]

The Sangre de Cristo Grant was one of the last in a series of large tracts of land granted to petitioners in the final years of Mexican governance of the Southwest. It encompassed more than a million acres in the southeastern section of the San Luis Valley. It was realized through *la merced,* the land grant, a practice initiated by Spain and, after independence in 1821, continued by Mexico to encourage settlement in frontier areas. The importance of these historical developments and some of the unique communitarian practices associated with land grant tenure, such as the right to the use of *ejido* or common lands in perpetuity (for pasture, lumber, and access to water), are directly relevant to the actions and attitude of the San Luis Hispanic community that persist into the present—particularly the corporate cast of local behavior. The Spanish tradition of usufruct rights in common is just one of the many links to Iberian culture San Luis residents still cite as significant in situating their historic roots in Spain rather than Mexico.

In the mural's upper central panel, Spanish conquistadores are depicted as the cultural progenitors of this part of the Hispanic Southwest. This relationship is proudly recognized and claimed by the majority of San Luis citizenry even though historical narratives do not corroborate the facts of organized Spanish occupation of the valley during the era of the conquistadores. The first indication of Spanish association with this area was on April 30, 1598, when Don Juan de Oñate, in the name of his king, Philip II of Spain, claimed all the land drained by the Rio Grande (including the San Luis Valley), "from the leaves of the trees in the forest to the stones and sands of the river," Rio del Norte. Thus, Tierra Nueva, the Spanish New World, became the possession of Spain and the people in it were all considered King Philip's subjects.[6]

At the time of Oñate's proclamation, the only "King's subjects" residing in the San Luis Valley were nomadic Native Americans—migrating bands of Ute, Apache, Arapaho, Comanche, Cheyenne, and Kiowa. Even if they could have heard Oñate's words borne on the winds of change, they would not have fathomed the notion of owning "the leaves of the trees" or "the stones of the river." In south central Colorado, the seventeenth and eighteenth centuries were periods of exploration, reconnaissance, and maintaining control over Indian populations rather than an era of settlement. Colonies such as San Luis were founded either long after 1821, during the Mexican period when Spain's political dominion in the New World had ceased, or subsequent to the Treaty of Guadalupe Hidalgo, which officially ended the Mexican War in 1848 and deeded these lands to the United States.

In present-day San Luis, the persistent sense of Spanish ethnic heritage and ancestry transcends the ordinary interest in the genealogical remnants of early colonists' emotional attachment to the parent country. The prevailing attitude involves an identification with a cultural legacy from Spain rather than Mexico—past or present. At the fiesta of Santa Ana in the summer of 1990, I was informed by an older resident that the San Luis townspeople label themselves as Spanish—not Spanish Americans or Mexican Americans. "Somos españoles" (we are Spanish).

On numerous other occasions I have witnessed San Luis friends proudly declaiming their Spanish heritage to visitors and emphasizing as evidence of their Castilian bloodlines the prevalence of European characteristics (blonde hair, aquiline features, light-colored eyes) rather than stereotypical Native American or Mexican traits (dark hair, dark skin, dark eyes). These residents pointedly distinguish between their physical appearance and that of the more *mestizo* populations in communities to the west such as Antonito or La Jara. When I visited San Luis with a Spanish friend from Madrid, she experienced a sense of familiarity and expressed a feeling of "homecoming." Indeed, the physical resemblance between her and a number of San Luis residents was striking.

Advocacy of an untainted Spanish blood connection is a two-way street. Outsiders such as journalists, marketing consultants, and tourism agencies join locals (artists, the regional Economic Development Council) to promote a vision of San Luis as a romantically conceived, picturesque enclave of intact Spanish culture. Never mind that such a promotional scheme prolongs a sense of residual colonialism. Its appeal is principally based on marketing logistics that want to recognize exotic cultural ties to a dominant European power rather than accepting origins in the Western Hemisphere, such as links to "Third World" village societies in Mexico and Latin America.

In San Luis some individuals also choose certain ethnic labels that perpetuate belief in Spanish descent. As described above, community members' cultural understanding of heritage honors the endurance of Spanish lineage apart from the vicissitudes of time and birthplace. The terms Hispano, Hispanic, and Spanish are used interchangeably by residents of San Luis, with Hispanic being the most frequent. Evangeline Salazar and Sally Chavez, two active colcha embroiderers, prefer "Spanish" or "Hispanic" but were quite negative about "Chicana." When advising me on the proper terminology, they took turns expressing their ideas.

Evangeline begins: "Just don't use *Chicana*. I hate that word. Hispanic or Spanish, I mean, Spanish is your . . . from Spain, you know? I like to be considered an American with an Hispanic surname or an Hispanic descendant of . . . you know. I don't like Mexican and I don't like Chicano." Sally agrees and continues to embellish the predictable stereotype through her own interpretation: "To me Chicano is . . . I get these visions of graffiti and stuff like that on the walls . . . just the way it's used . . . the headband thing and the militant [aspects]." Evangeline refocuses the conversation on her personal sense of pride cast in the light of prejudice: "It's an Hispanic community. I'm very proud . . . you know, we are proud. I've always carried a chip on my shoulder. Not because of what I am, but because of how people treat it. It used to be.... It's not so long ago that we'd go to Alamosa and discrimination was high. It's still high in Montevista [a town nearby]."[7]

## Tourists and Pilgrimages

The central image of the San Luis town mural is Christ on the cross. The belief in ethnicity rooted in Spanish soil is usually equated with the perpetuation of Catholicism. The intertwining of sacred and secular Spanish hegemony at the heart of the mural's symbolism also represents the combined forces (ethnicity and religiosity) behind the revitalization of San Luis. Despite the presence of other denominations in San Luis—there is a Presbyterian congregation, and a group of Jehovah's Witnesses operates a successful alcoholism recovery program—Father Pat believes that regardless of religious affiliation, everyone in town essentially shares Catholic roots. "The whole culture, I think, is so Catholic, anyway . . . whether they've converted to other religions or not. They're still basically Catholic. It's kind of hard to change . . . in spite of what our head says. It's hard to change. We're brought up with what we learned as children . . . so, the whole place is Catholic."[8]

From her perspective as a parishioner, Mary Jo Manzanares personalizes Father Pat's statement by echoing the belief that faith, hope, and communal solidarity are intertwined and inseparable: "For me, I can't separate what it means to live here and what it means to be a Catholic. The faith and the culture are all mixed up together in my heart. . . . We've all done so much work here and so much praying here. Now, I'm happy to see our dreams come true."[9]

Father Pat's belief in the fruition of a religious and economic miracle manifests itself in a variety of ways. His main focus is the creation of a shrine on the mesa above town featuring bronze sculptures of the Fourteen Stations of the Cross that symbolize Christ's journey to Calvary and His ultimate resurrection. Situated on a hill above San Luis—the same promontory overlooking an arrangement of white painted stones announcing, "Welcome to San Luis Oldest Town in Colorado"—this shrine is one of the latest in a series of *sacro montes*, artificial Calvaries dating from fifteenth-century Franciscan shrines in Italy.

Huberto Maestas, a native of San Luis who returned from the Front Range to work with Father Pat, finally completed the prodigious effort of sculpting and casting fifteen groups of figures. Maestas has included a fifteenth sculpture, of the Resurrection, which is part of the Penitente Brotherhood's interpretation of the Via Crucis. The Brotherhood is quite active around San Luis and was heavily involved in Father Pat's projects helping to reclaim the soul and vitality of San Luis. Father

Pat envisions the shrine for local use and as a pilgrimage site or tourist attraction, which could create jobs and improve the lives of residents. Within the tradition of Spanish colonial secular and religious authority, Father Pat's program for his community's revitalization continues to connect spirit with action.

While the shrine (now designated La Mesa de la Piedad) was being completed, San Luis's visibility as a dedicated religious community extended all the way to Rome. In May 1991, twenty-nine parishioners accompanied Father Pat and Huberto Maestas on a visit to Pope John Paul II. During the papal audience on May 8, Father Pat and Huberto Maestas presented the Pope with a set of miniature bronze replicas representing the Fourteen Stations of the Cross. These miniatures were created by Huberto Maestas especially for this occasion. Excerpts from letters published in the parish newsletter a few months after this event attest to the transformative experience shared by all participants: "Seeing and touching the Pope is such a wonderful feeling . . . probably like being in heaven for awhile," and "Father Pat entered . . . walked slowly to the altar and faced us with a radiant glow on his face. Then it happened! An indescribable . . . feeling overcame everyone in that small but humble chapel . . . gathered around the altar with our 'Padrecito de San Luis!'"[10] People inside San Luis and beyond were convinced that the Pope would return the visit when he traveled to Denver in the summer of 1993. During that time rumors abounded and people lined the sides of the San Luis highway below the shrine for days in anticipation of a papal appearance that never happened.

Under Father Pat's tutelage the Sangre de Cristo Parish is experiencing an impressive renascence that stimulates communal spirituality, inspires artistic creativity, strengthens economic programs, and forms alliances with a group historically on the periphery of the institutional reach of the church, the Penitente Brotherhood; the parish itself has received the Pope's blessing. Thus with a link to the Vatican, the hope implicit in revitalization is to establish an international pilgrimage center, not merely a local shrine:

> La Mesa de la Piedad already bears the signs of heavy use by area residents. Worshipers have strung hundreds of votas [offerings], or rosaries, scapulars and medals around statues of the Virgin Mary and at the foot of the full-size crucifixion tableau at the mesa's crest.
>
> [Ruby] Payne [a resident] said, "We pray that people from all over the world will come here and leave their own votas on La Mesa."[11]

# 2

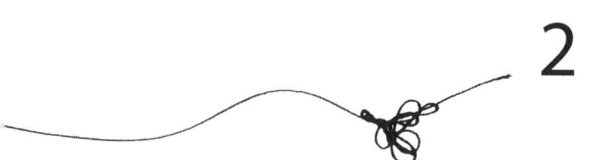

## josephine lobato as cultural commentator

I am only half finished with *La Entriega* and already my thoughts are on the next one. Already my thoughts are racing, you know, "what am I going to do with this?" "What am I going to do after I finish this one?" So I never stop. And it's not like I have a whole lot of time. I'm still going to classes, and I am taking a full load this year. I'm taking twelve credit hours. Full morning, because I managed to squeeze it all into a morning, don't ask me how. This [embroidery] isn't something I do . . . as work. I may put two or three threads, and sometimes I do as much as one section in one evening. It just depends on how I am feeling. It's almost . . . for me it's almost like a stress reliever.

—Josephine Lobato

As she speaks, Josephine Lobato pokes the needle in and out of her embroidery, pacing her thoughts to the fluid rhythm of her stitching. In just a few words she pinpoints the artistic and conceptual forces behind the ideas linking one of her colcha embroideries to another—each activated by a chain of successive creative actions and spirited responses. Even as an embroidery is being stitched, the process of its creation is gestating the shape and form of the next one.

These creative shifts and embryonic ideas occur internally in Josie's imagination. They materialize first as words in a dialogue with friends and family to kindle interest and savor the anticipation of what is coming. Then these thoughts start to cohere as shades of artistic intention, generating new plans and more research. Josie uses this tactic of creative leapfrogging to sustain her interest in—or sometimes to curb her impatience with—the embroidery she is currently working on while her mind restlessly moves ahead to the enticing possibilities of future work. She describes the drive behind this kind of creative momentum: "Sometimes even before I'm finished with this one, I'll come up with a new design. If you really get into something that you're doing, you start feeling like, 'That's waiting for me!'"[1]

I heard Josie using similar phrases time and again as I witnessed the kinetics of embroidery yielding up fertile new ideas that inspired a vigorous progression of eloquent pictorial narratives from *Los Penitentes, El Milagro,* and *Los Misiones* to the votive image of *Santa Rita*. When I first listened to Josie talking animatedly about the resolute forces that drove her from one creation to the next, I understood that this was what I wanted to hear. Although I had arrived in the San Luis Valley armed with some fairly straightforward objectives relating to investigating the revitalization of Hispanic colcha embroidery, and perhaps a bit more obliquely to the notion of cultural politics, in my heart I knew that I sought evidence for the power or precedence of the creative act over academic concerns with style, refinement, originality, tradition, and aesthetics. While I did not fully register the impact nor comprehend the implications of my personal response to what Josie was saying at the time, I did realize encountering her just then and seeing her art work was a great stroke of luck.

It has been said that the people we choose to collaborate with during fieldwork probably pick us as much as we pick them. I had been working with other stitchers in San Luis months before I met Josie. With some of the women our relationship was quite clearly defined from the outset. In fact, my motives underlying our proposed collaboration were immediately questioned during one of the initial meetings when one stitcher asked me, "You are going to get a dissertation out of this, but what are we going to get?"

However disturbing the question, I was somewhat relieved to face this test straight away in order to minimize the discomfort of ambiguity and clear the air at the very beginning. Nevertheless, echoes of this challenge (both negative and positive) persisted and set the tone for my relationship with some of these women for years to come.

Josie probably wondered the same thing about my goals. But it did not take long for our interactions to become naturally reciprocal, as our professional and personal rhythms intertwined through mutual interests in art, culture, history, and documentary work. And there was another profound—almost mystical—connection between us that revealed itself right away, at our first meeting.

Josie had learned colcha stitching at a workshop sponsored by the San Luis Sangre de Cristo Church in 1988. At the time Josie was fifty-two, had been hired as a supervisor for the Fort Garland Museum under the aegis of the Colorado Historical Society, and was earnestly trying to complete an associate arts degree at Adams State College in Alamosa, about half an hour from the Fort. She attended the workshop as a local museum employee in the role of observer intending to take notes and record the event for the Historical Society archives. Instead, Josie fell in love with colcha embroidery through the dynamism of the instructor, Carmen Orrego-Salas. But perhaps more significantly, she was affected by the work and words of another embroiderer, Tiva Trujillo, who was featured on a videotape Señora Orrego-Salas showed prior to one of the stitching sessions.

Initially, according to Josie, the report was paramount on her mind, no matter how Carmen kept chiding her for her apparent lack of interest. As a result of her excited reaction to the videotape, however, Carmen then urged Josie to put her notes aside and embroider.

> I was there to do a report. I really didn't know . . . In fact [Carmen] had to look at me a few times, very sternly, and say, "Aren't you paying attention?" I was, but I wasn't and . . . until I went to see . . . until we saw the video. I think Tiva sort of struck me . . . Tiva? What was her last name? Trujillo. She sort of . . . I never met the lady. In fact, she was dead by the time I saw some of her colchas at an exhibit that I put up at the San Luis Museum. But it didn't affect me. [Laughs] I just thought, "*colchas!*" Probably that's how some people feel when they look at mine [today]. Okay. But to me [referring to the video] what I saw was feelings. There was something there that touched me. And, I thought, well I have so much of that, and . . . working with history and then having so much in my background of the period of time when there was transition [1940s] and when there was . . .

when things were happening. I began to think . . . I've always thought, well, someday I will sit down and write. But I will never sit down and write. [Laughs]²

I listened to Josie recalling circumstances that literally changed her life and realized that her emotional intensity was matching mine, although not entirely for the same reason. Mine was influenced by memories—even loss—but there was also the stirring of a sense of the inevitable. Tiva Trujillo, who had died in 1980, had been central to my earlier project on Hispanic women folk artists of the San Luis Valley. The videotape and an exhibition resulted from it, but regrettably I had to relinquish my involvement around the time of Tiva's death, before the project was fully realized.

My feelings remained painfully unresolved concerning my withdrawal from that work until I witnessed Josie passionately forging a connection between her artistic inspiration and what she perceived as Tiva Trujillo's spirit as revealed in the video. Tiva's "presence" had become Josie's muse, cast in the role of a kind of supernatural confidante or guide frequently invoked throughout the process of creating her embroideries. As for me, I instantly understood that I had met another woman who was as artistically driven as Tiva had been, and who was equally responsive to the disquieting effect colcha stitching could have on her life. Thus, with a sense of something predetermined, Josie and I began our work together.

The significance of Josie Lobato's epiphany in the 1988 stitching workshop, and her subsequent devotion to creating colcha embroideries, recalls Henry Glassie's observation that "medium is a biographical accident."³ Josie's discovery of colcha was the perfect confluence of craft with an innate desire to express herself artistically. She had always wanted to write about her life and other historical aspects of the valley but had never done so. The insights Josie experienced when viewing Tiva Trujillo's work on tape suddenly offered a different creative possibility for the expression of her ideas. At that time her artistic awakening marked a critical entry point into an imaginative world colored by her own biography and her hunger for cultural history.

Consequently, Josie conceived a series of pictorial embroideries more or less on the same scale, depicting different cultural enactments as a means of teaching her children about Hispanic traditions and providing a legacy of remembrance. This was a way of tying them into her past, because none of Josie's children had been raised in the San Luis Valley, and ensuring that her work would have a perpetual audience—one that would last for generations. Since she began stitching, Josie has always tried to complete a colcha by Christmas Eve to give to one of her eight grown children, with the eventual goal of giving each of them an example of her work. This practice has, in turn, become a family ritual. As a process of double "traditionalizing" (recording cultural themes and inventing a new cycle of cultural action), Josie not only creatively and aesthetically constructs her children's heritage through her art work, but she also concurrently regenerates her own cultural legacy.

Josie describes a particular piece in this series:

> So, this is sort of a story. But it's sort of a legacy. I started to think about it and I thought, well, what do I want to leave my children? They'll never know much about Hispanic life... about the Hispanic traditions because they weren't raised with the Spanish traditions. They were raised in Denver, Colorado, and we lost a lot of our traditions when we went to the city—both my husband and I.[4]

Josie Lobato's life story oscillates between two alternating positions: looking out from the inside of her culture and looking in from outside it. She was born in the predominantly Hispanic town of San Luis in the late 1930s. Her memories of those early years, however, are permeated with recollections of living with her Mormon grandmother of English and German descent. Josie's grandmother had arrived in San Luis from nearby Chama with six children after having been abandoned by her Mexican husband, who was originally from Chihuahua, Mexico. He was a carpenter by trade, but colorful and restless. Family stories simply speak of his disappearance and imply that he chose music over paternity, eventually going off to play with a band called The Bluebirds.

In an era of large families and little money, it was a traditional family practice among Hispanos for certain children to live with their grandparents. During interviews with San Luis stitchers, many women cited the importance of their grandparents' influence over that of their parents. In several instances these grandparent memories are especially revered and cherished for the binding continuities that appear to explain aspects of the narrator's adult character or personality and some of their abiding interests. Josie's love of history originated in her grandmother's stories about her birthplace in Georgia and her adventures as a child following Mormon leaders westward by train, then by wagon. But Josie's determination to listen to "a different drummer" also stems from her grandmother's difference and status as an outsider in San Luis. "She was interesting to me. I was more inquisitive, you know, [asking] 'why?'. She was intriguing because she was different. And I could see the difference totally."[5]

This difference was sometimes stubbornly maintained in the face of local customs, particularly food. Josie wryly recalls her grandmother's variation on tortillas:

> [They were] wonderful mouth-watering biscuits! This was funny because one day I got home from school and she's pulling this sheet out of the oven.... She had flattened them out as well as she could and put them on this sheet. And

when she pulled them out they were that thick [demonstrating with her fingers]. They were thick, thick. And she was cooking them in the oven. We made different tortillas . . . puffier and larger. They tasted great but that was her version of tortillas.[6]

Thus, some aspects of her childhood were experienced as if she were a native "outsider." The twenty years of her married life that were spent in Denver further sensitized Josie to her own cultural difference. "It took me a long time to realize that I was different. [In the city] my traditions weren't like anyone else's."[7]

Her subsequent return to San Luis from Colorado's Front Range, plus her taking the job as museum supervisor of the nearby small historical museum, Fort Garland, intensified Josie's outsider status in the eyes of the San Luis community. Josie recasts her feelings of difference and the experience of otherness into the colcha art form as an artistic reconstruction of her personal biography. The dual perspective of insider/outsider, acquired through the vagaries of her life experience, orients her direction as a colcha artist. The self-conscious synthesis of internal and external viewpoints within the context of her art work validates Josie's artistic mission to serve as a type of cultural commentator or tour guide to her own culture.[8] Despite the artistic or conceptually creative advantage of this kind of liminal position (i.e., in-between, neither here nor there), actually living and experiencing it is often isolating and painful. This theme of estrangement emerges as a kind of *leitmotif* for Josie, experienced in different contexts but referred to occasionally throughout our work together.

As a cultural commentator and artist-as-social-actor, Josie Lobato not only conveys information about the past with didactic precision (titles and labels are integrated into the stitched compositions, and written essays usually accompany her exact and complicated scenes), but she also reaffirms her ethnicity through the act of artistic representation. Josie, a San Luis native who returned to her birthplace after an extended absence, adopts the pictorial narrative genre associated with the revitalized form of colcha to reestablish her ethnic roots and reconnect with the local Hispano community.

Historically, to perform certain actions, to live in a particular manner, and to identify specific symbols defined traditional Hispanic culture in the eyes of the people involved. Now, from the external viewpoint of consumers and collectors—the museum world or the marketplace—to stitch scenes of ethnic cultural performance using specific formal devices is considered "Hispanic" behavior. In this manner, Josie's artistic style (in terms of colcha needlework and naive representational devices), coupled with the content of her work, reinforces the academic and entrepreneurial aesthetic perception of Hispanic folk culture. This becomes the colcha standard as supported or authenticated by stitching workshop facilitators and economic development officials as the touchstone for this type of folk expression. Aware of these dynamics but involved in a personal journey of self-discovery, Josie Lobato's artistic efforts not only represent "sanctioned" visualizations, but (as noted before) also serve to ease her own relocation into the San Luis community.

**Techniques and Artistry**

Before discussing Josie's embroidery with reference to the cultural context, it is useful to examine some of the distinctive technical features of her work. She always completes her figures first, before tackling the background, because she depends on the visible markings she draws on the ground fabric to guide and help shape her embroidered forms. Application of the background typically obscures these outlines. Josie also considers the background more difficult than individual figures: "Hardest is the background. It's tedious; that's why I like to leave the background until last."[9]

Unaffected by the concern with virtuosity and the mastery of a comprehensive stitching vocabulary as advocated and practiced by other San Luis stitchers, Josie prefers to embroider only with the traditional colcha stitch (fig. 1), a stitch that has persisted unaltered since frontier days. It is a fairly classical version of the basic couching stitch, with one stitch anchored to the ground fabric and a shorter one placed perpendicularly across it. Occasionally she will add different stitches such as the turkey clip or the "worm" (an elongated French knot), or even leave short strands of yarn dangling out of the picture plane as in *Mis Crismes* (e.g., Santa Claus's reins or the end of the whip held by the character wearing the deer mask).

Josie uses these technical devices to create accents and to achieve textural contrast, as well as to playfully heighten visual interest. But she feels that the distinctive dimensional and tactile qualities associated with colcha embroidery are primarily attributable to the presence of the colcha stitch: "It's the most necessary stitch. You can do miracles with that colcha stitch." The aesthetic byproduct of a simplified stitching palette imbues her embroideries with a distinctly molten, almost geologic quality evidenced by large areas of luxuriant undulating, curvilinear colcha stitches.

Whenever Josie is stymied by a technical quandary or needs to refresh her memory, she examines the nineteenth-century wool-on-wool colcha bed cover in the Fort Garland collection. Because of her job at the Fort Garland museum, she has easy access to this piece and has used it over the years as a personal resource, not only for technical aid but also for inspiration. Despite the differences in format and function (bed cover with a decorative floral design versus a pictorial narrative art work), Josie feels there is enough correspondence between her work and the nineteenth-century colcha that she can learn from it in order to develop her own critical attitudes toward colcha needlework.

The image of this mute object being lovingly handled and scrutinized by this earnest woman is an arresting one. Josie's consultations have often eased her confusion, and occasionally they have corroborated her method of virtually self-taught colcha embroidery. One site of contention among dedicated stitchers in Colorado and New Mexico is the appearance of the back of a colcha. The reverse side of a Josie Lobato colcha is just as distinctive as the front. When her colchas are turned over, they appear to mirror the designs on the front of her pieces. This effect results from Josie's primary use of the colcha stitch, which consequently produces a dense yarn coverage on the back of the embroidery. The practice of creating lush areas of stitchery on an embroidery's reverse side is contrary to the general San Luis method of uncluttered colcha backs with little "waste" of wool thread. However, Josephine Lobato feels that her technical choices are often validated by their appearance on the historical wool-on-wool Fort Garland colcha, the double thickness of which was also no doubt an effective protection against the penetrating cold of the frontier zone.

Searching for ideas, professional and personal interests inspired Josie to choose an image of her workplace, historic Fort Garland, for her first colcha embroidery, executed during Carmen Orrego-Salas's 1988 workshop. Fort Garland and its prominent position in the history of the valley provided a familiar historical context from which to develop her visual concept. This composition marks the first of many to contain certain narrative elements that herald the appearance of a constant theme in Josie Lobato's work—transition and cultural change.

Historically, the Fort's establishment in 1858 presaged change, as it was the farthest extension of Anglo-American sovereignty in the San Luis Valley. In her embroidery Josie portrayed old Fort Garland as the nexus for the Anglo military, Hispanic settlers, mountain men, and resident American Indian bands. Josie's own mixed background inspires her need to represent this diversity artistically: "Almost everything I do, I do in the multicultural sense. Because if you are working with history in this corner of the world, you can't do anything else. You can't separate it. There's just no way. It's intertwined so badly and [it's] so diverse here in the valley."[10] Although she has illustrated this scene as if it were one of the contemporary historical pageants staged annually at the Fort (a festival in miniature), Josie is really chronicling the imminent passage of native cultures in the face of such encroaching Anglo commercial interests as the railroad and cattle ranching. The Anglo soldiers also left their legacy throughout the valley in the perpetuation of certain surnames still found among Hispanic families: Taylor, Martin, McCarty, Burns, Carson. Thus Josie documents the past with an eye to its impact and lingering effect on the present.

Josie's passion for history is tempered by her desire for exactness and precision. For several months I watched her amassing various historical objects to include in a military teaching kit she was assembling as an instructional aid for valley teachers. She had chosen 1866 as the focal year because of the greater ease of acquiring items from within that time frame instead of the Fort's founding date, 1858. Her approach to this project seems to parallel the way she conceptualizes her embroidery content—a mixture of discovery, literality, and sympathy for a neglected subject not mentioned in conventional histories.

> It's going to consist of a [private infantryman's] uniform and all the accouterments. Now they may be in photograph form or in actual form. The idea came to me . . . well, almost everywhere you go there's officers. Officers are everywhere; officers are commonplace. The private you never hear of, what was his life like? I think this will focus on that, what was the private's life like at Fort Garland?[11]

This striving for historical accuracy in her characterization of frontier military life extended to Josie's concern for realistic particulars in rendering the scene of old Fort Garland with both factual and embroidered detail. This methodical approach was critical in her subsequent colchas as well. According to Josie, Fort Garland "is all dirt." She wanted to represent this major feature of the landscape as realistically as possible.

> If you wanted it to be lifelike, you almost had to look at the real thing. For instance, if you're working on the sky, look at the sky. If you're working on the grass, look at the grass. You could almost see the different shades of color. So, Fort Garland was entirely all dirt, and I wasn't sure just what I was going to do, because I'd never done anything like that in my life. And I began to look around me and I could almost. . . . Well, I would look at photographs because it was winter time, I couldn't see the real thing. (This [colcha scene] was in summer). I would try to envision what different colors were in the dirt and try to come up with the colors that I saw. That was the most difficult thing I had to do. I think if I had to do it, you know . . . when anybody's starting at the beginning, I think if I had to tell them what was the most difficult thing it would be the design and the selection of color. It almost takes an artist's feel. Well, somebody that's an

artist. I'm not an . . . but these people [teachers] do become like artists, eventually, like say for instance, Carmen.

And like I say, I never took art. So you realize that this is an extremely difficult thing for me. It's taken a lot of thought and a lot of imagination. I would think imagination is the word for it. Because I don't consider myself so creative that I can make it [look] real.[12]

The question of who is an artist and who is not is often debated among stitchers in the valley. They commonly measure their efforts against external or outsider notions of art and art work, and generally conclude that "they are not artists." Most of the time this disavowal is so personally convincing that even someone as observant and articulate as Josie will describe her stitching methods and aesthetic choices in detail but will fail to credit her kind of creative activity as artistic practice. One might interpret this attitude as indicative of a society that does not differentiate between art and craft. The idea of the singular nature of the artist is simply nonexistent. This is partially true, but the unease of these generally self-effacing women belies a discomfort with labels or categories such as art and artist, which originate in another realm of experience. Whatever the reason, our counterperceptions of clashing art worlds signify the long reach of difference between stitchers and outsiders.

No matter how prodigiously Josie worked on her embroidery, when she experienced difficulty controlling the "flow" of her stitchery she might eventually resort to drastically pulling out a number of stitches, but she never gave up:

I took out the stitches. The most difficult thing was for me to go in the right direction so that it will look like dirt. I've never been a painter . . . and I never took painting. It was an extremely difficult task. Ah, at the beginning I was very overwhelmed. I would throw it [the colcha] away. I'd pick it up again. [Laughs] I'd put it away just as far as I could. But I was intrigued and I'd pull it out again. I'd say, "What the heck?" you know, and I'd pull it out again.[13]

Josie Lobato's vividly expressed frustration was mitigated by her willingness to rectify mistakes through the painstaking and repetitive processes of removal and recreation. After the completion of "Old Fort Garland," she became totally absorbed with colcha embroidery's artistic challenges and personally satisfying rewards. The intensity of feelings generated by a state of ongoing creative restlessness continued to drive Josie to begin a new colcha while still in the midst of embroidering its precursor. Countless times she has lamented over the telephone, "It's so weird. I get so *obsessed* with doing these colchas. I have so much to do, but I must work on them at least two hours a day."[14] Those two hours are frequently around midnight. Reminiscent of the lives of frontier women who seized time away from chores, work, and family duties to embroider, Josie Lobato stitches late into the night, relishing the solitude and release of tension that colcha making has brought into her life.

### Mis Crismes

Following the "Old Fort Garland" embroidery, *Mis Crismes* is the second in Josephine Lobato's colcha sequence representing tradition and change. She has temporally situated this piece just after the Second World War, in the mid-1940s, during a period of profound transition in San Luis. As Josie describes it, "This colcha is a combination of the old and the new—the old that I remember and the new that was in my life at that time. So, it's a memory."[15] It is also a complex representation of a particular cultural enactment, *Mis Crismes*, which is barely remembered by many residents and is no longer performed in the San Luis area.

Josie has stitched her memory of this almost forgotten Hispanic Christmas custom, which is similar to the Anglo practice of "trick-or-treating" at Halloween. The scene is set in the magical predawn hours when the stars begin to fade—at the time of *La Misa del Gallo,* the rooster mass that was celebrated around five or six in the morning. An eight-year-old Josephine Lobato takes her younger siblings from house to house on a sled while singing "En Belén Nació Jesús." As she recalls, this verse celebrates Christ's birth in Bethlehem and finishes with the joyous shout, "¡Mis Crismes!" At the song's climax the hosts of each house usually responded by showering the children with homemade treats.

Juxtaposed with this scene of expectation and reward is the mysterious, possibly disturbing spectacle of the *luminaria,* the bonfire, in the lower right. The focal point is the masked *abuelo* or *abuelito* figure in the guise of an antlered bogeyman with black whip in hand. With face averted from the viewer, he stands squarely, flanked by two boys (Josie's brothers), one on either side. One boy dutifully kneels in prayer (perhaps with a shade of apprehension), while the other conveniently warms his hands by the bonfire, stitched as realistically as possible to capture the flames' flickering quality: "fire, fire tends to fly away."[16] The metaphorical import of the abuelo image resides in his mystery and in the strength of his power over the behavior of young boys who neglected their prayers. As a sinister character who menaced these errant children with his whip, the abuelo's punitive capability surpassed the Anglo Santa Claus's fabled practice of leaving lumps of coal in the stockings of bad children. Both the Hispanic and the Anglo figures are positioned on the right side of the picture in an interesting balance between airy, buoyant cheerfulness (Santa Claus) and earthly enigma (the abuelo).

The ritualistic interaction with the abuelo was a rite exclusively for boys. By recreating this scene in her colcha, Josie Lobato artistically appropriates these images from her brothers' life stories as her own. Through the creative act she "co-experiences" some of the drama of past events that were virtually inaccessible to her, as a young female. In this instance, the visualizing process of converting her imagination into a pictorial narrative broadens the scope of Josie's actual biographical experience to incorporate some of her younger brothers'.

Her artistic action amplifies Josie's power of memory and recall as she claims these recollections for herself and offers them to us, the viewers, to deepen our understanding of and involvement in the cultural dialogue of San Luis. This idea also underscores the potency of the artistic narrative voice, expressed through the stitching act, imaginatively to reshape life's events, a power that is "integral to leading that life rather than being led through it."[17] Since the occurrence of this childhood event, the sum total of Josie's life experience also serves to reshape her recollections and add a different dimension to memory.

The concept of a dual perspective extends to the formal compartmentalization of the composition—i.e., the explicit division of *Mis Crismes* into symbolic and realistic zones. The upper, primarily symbolical realm provides the backdrop for the nativity scene, Santa Claus with his reindeer, the carolers, and the illuminated cross. By populating it with symbols, Josie transformed the sky into a repository of images signifying the eminence of the Catholic Church; the religious mysteries of Christ's birth, suffering, and resurrection (the cross); community fellowship and traditional singing (a visual reference to the song "En Belén Nació Jesús"; and munificent gift-giving personified by the rather commercially conceived Anglo Santa Claus. According to Josie, the inclusion of Santa Claus was Father Pat's suggestion: "And Father said, 'Where's Santa Claus?' And I said, 'Santa Claus, Father?!' And he said, 'Yes, where's Santa Claus?' And I got to thinking about it . . . I thought maybe . . . Well, he is right. I need a *contrast*."[18]

Along with Tiva Trujillo's spirit, Father Pat and Josie's husband, Eugene Lobato, also play muse to her art work. Josie was frustrated by the amount of undecorated space remaining in her composition, especially when Father Pat questioned her— "You have a lot of empty space. Don't you have any other ideas?" Believing that she needed an objective viewpoint, Josie promised to consider it, and then asked Gene for his opinion, since "we both have the same memories." The result was her addition of many of the allegorical elements she personally calls "symbols."[19]

Despite the iconographical weight of the upper half of the picture, Josie Lobato considers the concrete symbolic elements in the sky secondary to the more interesting allegorical nature of the landscape setting. Josie regards many of the natural elements in the lower, earthly zone as "symbols," or more appropriately, allegories. For example, the *horno*, the cone-shaped oven for baking bread and drying corn, is a familiar icon in the Hispanic cultural landscape, and embodies nurturing and hospitality. The wagon is a relic of the frontier and represents the agrarian foundation and self-sufficiency of this society. The dormant apple orchard in the foreground also signifies the eventual return of spring and the promise of fecundity.[20]

In order to achieve the appropriate visual effects, Josie often awoke early to observe the changes in the predawn sky.

> I'd get up at five o'clock in the morning and look at the sky. In the winter time you can see the different clouds stretching out. Before the sun rises there are still stars out. If I had done it [the sky] solid, it wouldn't have caught your eye—if it had been entirely like it is at night [opaque]. So, I tried to catch the dawn. As I looked at the dawn, I wanted [the embroidery] to almost look like the Santa Claus was interrupting the cloud formations.[21]

Josie also struggled with one of art's greatest challenges—the rendering of faces, especially as they clustered together as a choir in the sky:

> For instance, I have worked quite a bit on faces ... I got myself into this, right? When I worked with the first one [Old Fort Garland], I had one, two, three, four ... five faces [laughs]. Believe me that was no joke, because I had never embroidered a face. I had outlined a face but I had never embroidered a face. And believe it or not, faces have a certain line that you have to follow, too. And I'm not kidding you that when I worked with one that has a lot of faces, I've had to learn that, for instance, if you're doing the forehead, the forehead [stitching] goes in one direction. The [rest of the] face goes in another direction.
>
> For instance, my choir needed to show up really ... sharp. And that is hard. That, I did have to take apart a few times. Working with anything that has real intricate detail, you almost have to take it apart until you get the right thing. You do it and you look at it. You do it and you look at it ... and you almost have to take it apart and redo it until it gets the right effect. It's a totally different thing, trying to embroider in an outline ... than it is to fill in.[22]

The colcha's lower zone is a realistic reconstruction of Josie's childhood neighborhood in San Luis. Her choice of form, content, and stitching technique was determined by her interest in detail and historical correctness. The rendition of the central row of houses was probably the most pronounced manifestation of change occurring in her pictorialization of this 1940s cultural landscape. Josie Lobato has very consciously delineated the structural and temporal differences between the connected line of indigenous adobe dwellings, *chorreras,* and the newer vernacular interpretation of free-standing, Anglicized homes with pitched roofs, gables, and dormer windows.[23] Despite their modern appearance, these particular homes were often adobe structures overlaid with whitewashed cement or concealed by pastel colored siding.

Josie has also emphasized the natural irregularities of terrain and architecture by subtly placing the houses at slightly different heights and by angling the muddy paths that extend out into the snowy field. Her manipulation of the arrangement of these buildings was critical to her conception of a familiar and neighborly atmosphere. In describing her intention to convey the significance of an important social pattern through an elaboration of realistic detail, she asserts, "To me, the houses on my block weren't straight. And they didn't sit on a flat plateau, either. One house was a little lower, one was a little higher. [In my picture] I wanted to get the feel of community . . . and a sense of street."[24]

As she has chronicled the concept of communality, Josie Lobato has also illustrated her neighborhood on the cusp of change. Her representation of a 1940s setting is located in a specific period of burgeoning receptivity to Anglo influence (e.g., architectural style, and of course Santa Claus). In the conversation with Father Pat cited above, she emphasizes that she included the depiction of Santa Claus as a contrast to the more integrated Hispanic imagery present in the rest of her composition, just as the Anglo-style houses contrast with the traditional adobes.

Besides these thematic shifts from indigenous emblems to transitional Anglo influences, Josie Lobato's picture purposefully heralds encroaching technological developments. This is especially apparent in her rendition of manufactured architectural ornamentation used to modify the adobe structures. In varying ways, her conceptual framework for *Mis Crismes* appears to differ from the academic or entrepreneurial notion or expectation of a timeless, unchanging, nontechnological era in an isolated Hispanic village.

Many of the iconographical elements in *Mis Crismes,* however, are consonant with the notion of colcha embroidery as a hallmark of ethnicity. These include the depiction of dramatic or theatrical ethnic practices, the use of a Spanish title and a traditional verse, the Hispanic rural setting for background, and the predominant theme of the actual cultural enactment.

Carmen Orrego-Salas urged San Luis stitchers to embroider their names on the front of their pieces. Signed art works are common to the fine art world of museums and galleries for which the creative products of the stitching workshops were originally intended. To sign one's work also counteracts the prevalent notion of the "anonymous" and interchangeable folk artist, an idea that still circulates among some academicians and museum personnel. Being an artist herself, perhaps Señora Orrego-Salas encouraged the women to embroider their signatures as a gesture of pride and as a declaration of ownership and individuality.

Josie Lobato not only signs her work, but also boldly stitches titles across the field of her embroideries. These literary signals recall her initial and basic interest in "writing her stories," before she learned how to create colcha embroideries. According to her, however, her titles alone cannot provide a total understanding of her work. Although she adds labels to a few culturally specific images in her work (e.g., *la morada, el banquéte*), Josie considers her stitched presentations of cultural enactments too complicated for viewers to understand without written explanations. Typed narratives accompany each colcha as adjunct forms of verbal communication that explicate the cultural background and help to unravel the symbolic meanings. This information is compiled from the original research material she collected during the early stages of planning each composition. Her belief is that the "essay is essential, because most people wouldn't know what my thoughts were."[25]

Josie Lobato's colcha embroideries differ from the early 1930s and 1940s pictorial Carson pieces of New Mexico in the complexity of her multilevel, semantically rich compositions. It has already been emphasized that Josie's colchas are usually so intricately detailed that they require essays to accurately convey the range of meaning. The many cultural allusions and elements in her pictures, plus the comprehensive explanatory texts, further distinguish Josie Lobato's work from the type of tourist art creations usually promoted by economic development projects. According to Paula Ben-Amos, one of the objectives of tourist art is to "operate as a minimal system which must make meanings as accessible as possible across visual boundary lines."[26]

The desire to teach that is so evident in Josie Lobato's art work strengthens and complements her role as cultural commentator. On a descriptive level her embroideries teach about facets of her cultural background, as is apparent from the foregoing analysis of *Mis Crismes*. Her embroidery series also function as a cultural critique (e.g., the *luminaria* scene with the abuelo). But Josie's use of written narratives as a form of cultural commentary operates on still another level—to expand perceptual sensitivity by verbally translating abstract imagery and symbolic systems into concrete terms for the viewer.

Josie's life history of being both inside and outside her culture enables her successfully to assume the interpretive role of instructor and commentator. This position, supported by her penchant for historical research and written explanations, might appear to be at odds with the popular or marketplace perception of a native storyteller-artist whose narratives are grounded in spontaneous oral presentation. But an objective appreciation of Josie Lobato's intense personal engagement and her sincere aesthetic transmutation of local Hispanic history leave no doubt concerning her competency and authenticity as a culture bearer.

> There is more than one way to do history. This is my history . . . the history that I grew up with. So, it's coming out in bits and pieces in my mind as to what was important. But the point of this whole thing is . . . not to lose something that is going to be lost. And my children would never know about La Entriega, if I didn't do this.[27]

### *La Entriega de los Novios*

*La Entriega de los Novios* (fig. 2) is the second in Josie's series of cultural enactments. After Fort Garland's historical content, she was excited to pursue folkloric themes, first exploring local Christmas customs in *Mis Crismes* and then looking at religious sacraments (such as marriage, baptism, and first communion). Again, she traces her creative impulse back to a gentle but persistent prodding from her inner muse, Tiva Trujillo's spirit, which Josie interpreted to be supportive of the artistic direction in which she was heading. "I was just beginning to think of folklore, and the idea of folklore had bitten . . . me since Tiva. But at the same time I wasn't exactly sure what direction to take, you know? What do I want on this? What do I want to see on it?"[28]

The *entriega* is a little-known ritual, rarely performed today, that translates as "to turn over."[29] Josie's scene depicts a critical point in this rite—the point in the Hispanic wedding ceremony when the *padrinos*, the godparents, bless their godchildren and relinquish their responsibility as caretakers, thus turning the bridal pair over to each other, to their new in-laws (more frequently, the emphasis was on the transference of the daughter), and to the community. This was a fragile moment of passage in Hispanic nuptial rites. According to custom, the bride and groom could be kidnapped and held for ransom anytime before the entriega was actually performed.

> Up until the time the parents bless the children, the bride or the groom may be kidnapped. The padrinos are responsible for the bride and groom and they have

to try to keep them from being kidnapped because it's their responsibility. And they are very paranoid about it . . . but they still get stolen. And the point of it is the bride and groom are the ones that will get the money that is collected because you need to ransom them out. Sometimes they can even put the bridegroom in jail or take the bride and keep her for the whole day, whatever . . . you know?

So, the sooner she's ransomed the better. So everybody participating in the wedding ceremony or the reception puts out money for it. The padrinos are responsible for getting it out there. And I think in the very early days they were much more paranoid about it because a lot of times they had to put out the bulk of the funds. But it's always been a very big responsibility to be a godparent among Hispanics. It's not just being the best man or anything. It's almost as much responsibility as when you baptize a child.[30]

The padrinos in Josie's own wedding in 1954 were selected especially for that occasion by her parents. The male padrino actually doubled as a best man for Gene Lobato, although they had never met before. Josie's *madrino* was her sister. According to Josie these roles were usually kept within the family,

In the early days, it was almost always family. And they were always couples. And it was somebody older than you [referring to the bridal pair]. A lot of times I think the parents had a lot to do with it in the early days. For instance, when I got married, which was 1954, my mother chose my madrino, which ended up being my sister, of course. But it was her husband who was the best man, and he . . . had no knowledge of my husband. It's not like the best man thing of today. It's totally different.[31]

The performance was accompanied by the singing of at least twelve verses describing the passage of responsibility from one set of adults to another. Mixed into the content of these verses were blessings, surrender, allusions to marital obligation, and innuendoes concerning the future of the marriage. For example, the following stanzas proclaim a convergence of the two contradictory actions of receiving and letting go, poetically concentrated into a single intense moment that alters forever the lifelong connections of parents and children alike.

Padres, reciban sus hijos,
Con gusto y con alegría,
Y que cumplan con su estado
Como San José y María.
Padres, reciban sus híjos,

Y échenles la bendición;
Se van sus híjos queridos,
Nacidos del corazón.

Parents, receive thy children,
With joy and happiness.
May they comply with their duties
As did Mary and Joseph.
Parents, receive thy children
And give them your blessing.
They are parting from you,
Thy loving children, born from your heart.[32]

Josie was quite concerned with visually rendering both the realistic moment of transference and the import of the message or moral tone buried in the verses' rhythms. Part of her research entailed finding people who accurately remembered the words and proper sequence.

> Some people just know them. My husband knows some. My brother-in-law who is almost eighty knows a few. So I get them from people who know them. I do oral history among people I know. I say, "What did they sing? How did they sing it?" The main idea is just to get the wording. Because the wording for that one I knew [Mis Crismes]. I mean I could never forget THAT one. But this one, the verses . . . I wasn't really familiar with the verses. Although I remember hearing them. I hear them in my mind, you know? They were singing and playing. To me, I knew how to speak Spanish, so I caught some of the wording, so I remember some of the wording but I could never repeat them. Among the Hispanics it was a very familiar thing, they sang verses for the entriega that said from this day on you're a married man and it was sort of a reminder . . . "Okay, you're a married man and your bride is so pretty." It all went together with the ceremony, everything clicked with one thing or another and of course the priest was ever present.[33]

One of the black figures framing the bridal couple is Father Mortarell, who now stands in back as a witness (perhaps also as a religious protector) after having already performed the actual wedding ceremony (fig. 2). Apparently, the memory of Father Mortarell serves as a ubiquitous clerical symbol for this era in the imagination of local artists. Josie picked him because she worked for him as a teenager "and knew him a little better."[34] He has been characterized before in the work of San Luis stitchers Julia Valdez and Daisy Ortega, who also depict scenes from different decades of the priest's residency in San Luis (fig. 6). We will discuss their work in a later chapter.

The spatial composition of *La Entriega* resembles a shadow box with its edges peeled back to expose inner space. Conceptually, it is a composite spatial arrangement of many viewpoints intersecting simultaneously. The way space is treated not only reproduces the sense of scale of an expansive inner room but indicates a portion of exterior space as well. When Josie Lobato conceived this scheme of intersecting multiple planes (an almost cubist design incorporating different views), her requirements were, "You need to see part of the floor, part of the ceiling, and the back of the building, and yet you need to see a little bit of the outside on the corner to know that he [the figure in the lower right] is going out the door. But I almost have to use quite a bit of imagination for that."[35]

The juxtaposition of the basketball court of the Mercy High School gymnasium with the sacramental rite of *La Entriega* staged beneath the slogan, "Go, Wildcats" wonderfully represents a union of the sacred with the secular (fig. 2). The local gym, with its panoply of regalia and totemic imagery (school insignia), is temporarily converted into the backdrop for this version of the post-wedding celebration. Specific memories of the gym in this context date the scene to the 1940s. But its aesthetic appeal and symbolic potential also coincide with Josie Lobato's artistic vision of, and interest in, scenes of cultural transition.

Furthermore, consonant with Josie's chronicling change and cultural practice, the school setting for the illustration of *La Entriega* accentuates the multipurpose nature of the school gym space. The quotidian experience of mutable public space is also common to scores of villages and small cities beyond San Luis. The everyday reality of instantaneous conversions of athletic arenas to ceremonial halls and auditoriums is typical of small town life in the United States and is universally recognized by anyone who has ever lived in such a community. While *La Entriega* is represented as a unique cultural performance, the reason behind its rather incongruous setting is understood by most viewers.

On the far right of the composition is Josie Lobato's self-portrait as a little girl in pink. The performance is seen through her young eyes as if all were enchantment and evanescence. This transitory quality extends to the predominant themes of vulnerability and change at the heart of the precarious rite of passage, the *entriega*. The ephemeral nature of this scene is visually underscored by an illusory atmosphere suffused with shades of pink, purple, and blue highlighted by startling red accents placed here and there.

Josie's early struggles with color in the Fort Garland composition move to another level of competency in *La Entriega* when she begins to portray volume, shading, and shadows. She recalls her first confusing introduction to the concept of shadow and her bewilderment over the depiction of something she considered next to invisible:

> I remember hearing Carmen and it didn't hit me until much after she was gone. In fact, what she said didn't even make a dent at the time that she was saying it. She said, "You need to think of shadows." And I thought, "What does she mean think of shadows? I can't even think of the . . . the thing, you know? How am I going to think of shadows?" As I began to work with the pieces, I began to realize the darker thread is your shadow. You can almost outline anything with your shadow. Your lighter thread brings it out. But there is a shadow in almost anything that you've got. As you're stitching you begin to realize, "Well, I need shadow here. I need to bring this out."
>
> For instance, on the entriega when I finish outlining that bride, she'll show up. Right now she's all white . . . when I do the background on the wall and the background on the floor, she'll pop out. So that's what we're talking about when we say shadow. But if you had asked me in 1988 when I worked with the Fort Garland one, I would have said, "What shadow? Where?" [Laughs]. But that's what shadow is all about![36]

Whether she is manipulating shadow or contending with spatial perspective, Josie's growing artistic awareness is not only shaped by increasingly sophisticated creative action; it is also conditioned by a kind of meditative feedback process of questions and answers with a lot of hard work invested in their resolution. Reflexivity and greater skill now become constant elements in her colcha making. Both of these factors will continue to figure in Josie's tendency to self-scrutiny and to extension of her aesthetic experience through interrogation and observation.

Earlier Josie detailed how she had conceived the arrangement of internal and external views in order to show a figure retreating from the ceremony. The image of this man leaving by the side door with bottle in hand interjects a humorous note, but also hints at a prevalent social concern. He obviously exits because drinking is forbidden inside, especially since the gym has been transformed into sacred space. On the underside of behavioral restraint and respect for rules are alcoholism, isolation, and ostracism. Although the seriousness of the widespread drinking problem in this region is downplayed in the benign, humorous treatment of the fellow tottering outside for a drink, this is a visual reference to a social issue that profoundly affects the community.

In both *Mis Crismes* and *La Entriega* Josie Lobato presents the contrast between ritualized action and individual spontaneity. In each picture there is one figure who deflects the seriousness of the occasion by some action that is either irreverent (the drunken man) or touchingly human (the young boy warming his hands before the luminaria). The tenor of the two compositions also suggests uneasy undercurrents. As a rite of passage *La Entriega* is traditionally "fraught" with danger and degrees of paranoia because of the possibility of (ceremonial) kidnapping. In this ritualistic context the possibility of disruptive, potentially abusive action still carries a threat. The kidnapping risk adds a frisson, a bit of thrill, to the event through a sense of impending danger, intimidation, or extortion similar to the disturbing or invasive menace implicit in other cultural practices worldwide like *charivari,* mumming, or even some kinds of clowning. Despite the bright colors, the almost auditory sense of music, and the feeling of fiesta, the entriega festivities apparently overwhelm the drinker and he escapes.

Likewise, in *Mis Crismes* Josie has created an image of her brother concerned with his own comfort while menace in the form of the abuelo threatens to engulf him. These narrative devices immediately engage the viewer's interest through self-identification, empathy, a hint of mystery, and an overview of circumstances—much like privileged members of an audience apprised of more than just the plot's outlines.

*La Entriega de los Novios* is conceived primarily from Josie's own childhood memories. But her husband Eugene, who is slightly older, also contributed to it. The "Go Wildcats" slogan was his addition to historical precision with a humorous edge. As mentioned before, Josie claims that he is an effective collaborator "because we both have the same memories!"[37]

## Los Penitentes

Gene Lobato collaborated with Josie again to create *Los Penitentes*, the popular name for La Hermandad de Nuestro Padre Jesús Nazareno or Society of the Brotherhood. This name derives from the penitential practices associated with communal religious activities performed during Semana Santa, Holy Week, by groups of devout lay Catholic Brothers. These usually occur in the outer boundaries of remote villages or in the surrounding hills. The locus of penitential observances is the *morada,* the chapel or meeting place, where the Brothers or *Hermanos* (locally abbreviated to *Manos*) congregate to fast and pray. The word *morada* can also signify the Brotherhood itself.

Symbolically, the morada represents the guardianship of community mores and values through the Brothers' exemplary behavioral codes and social action. In the eyes of the Hermandad, the ultimate achievement of penance is to try to surmount worldliness by transforming the heart and spirit. Their religious integrity is further underscored by the enduring network and support system of the *cofradías*, the confraternities. During Lent, and intensely during Holy Week, the Brothers sequester themselves in their moradas and fast and pray for the welfare of all Catholics in the area—as if their prayers uphold the delicate balance of the community's spirituality. Therefore, to most manos the concept of the morada is more abstract than a building's boundaries. Mano Juan Estévan Medina, an eighty-nine-year-old member from Fort Garland, interprets it in terms of sacred space: "Any place you pray is *morada*. Any place you pray Rosary or a prayer or . . . something, that's a *morada*. Even your own home."[38]

Josie based her artistic conception almost entirely on Gene Lobato's memories of his religious experience as a young boy joining in penitente activities. Although women could form a kind of auxiliary group within the morada, *Hermanas Piadosas*, in the past they were restricted from participating in many of the Brotherhood's penitential practices during Holy Week recreations of Christ's Passion. Because Gene had more direct experience of Penitentes, Josie depended on the density of detail from his youthful recollections, but she also retained the flavor of her own set of childhood memories stemming from when she occasionally attended services in the morada with her father.

Due to her greater reliance on Gene's memories for thematic material and detail, Josie maintains that her colcha depicting the Brotherhood's reenactment of Christ's journey to Calvary, *En Calvario*, was the most difficult one to create. She is a very empathic person, and her inability to identify completely with her subject troubled her from the start: "It was in Eugene's head and not in my head and I had to take his ideas, put them down on paper, and then try to *envision* it. 'What are you seeing? What are you seeing?' You know? I was trying to see it through someone else's eyes."[39] Throughout its creation Josie complained of her lack of closeness to the subject. In a letter dating to autumn 1991, she wrote me: "My penitente piece is three-quarters done and my classes and work leave me very little time. I hope when winter sets in I may find the time to continue. It has been a harder piece for me to relate to since it's basically my husband's memory more than mine, but it is progressing."[40]

Sometimes her frustration would surface around technical dilemmas, and she would agonize over her stitches until she had achieved the right effects. In August 1991 I was interviewing stitchers in Taos, New Mexico, who were associated with the Carson colcha era (described in a subsequent chapter). On my way back through the valley I often spoke with Josie about my discoveries. Consequently, she became intrigued with the Carson use of what those stitchers termed the "lazy stitch" (long stitches tacked down with cross stitches at intervals), and decided to use rows of these long stitches along the bottom of her penitente embroidery because "it goes quickly, fills space fast, and extends from one end of the piece to the other or . . . as far as the thread goes, anyway."[41]

There were several instances like this when I would convey some new material about an aspect of colcha that I had discovered and Josie would happily experiment with it. I never felt I compromised my role as researcher because Josie's insatiable curiosity was wide-ranging and I provided just one of many different sources of new inspiration. In essence, we often collaborated in a genuine exchange of information while Josie continued to enjoy the same freedom of choice and creative action as other contemporary artists, thus implicitly calling into question (for us scholars) the myth of the untutored folk artist "hermetically sealed off" from life's changing richness.

A few weeks after the "lazy stitch" conversation, Josie became upset with the middle ground stitches in *Los Penitentes* and ripped them out to rework the problem area until she was satisfied that she was on the right track with the embroidery "progressing steadily and the stitches flowing into shape."[42] Again, in what had become a rite of consultation and reorientation, she took the old traditional colcha out of its case at the museum and examined it. "I take it out and feel it. They weren't trying to fill every space. There are loose threads and lots of space. [Despite] its fragile appearance, it holds together amazingly well. But it's lost its dimensionality."[43] In this instance Josie uses that term to indicate the loss of tactility and lack of visual clarity in the old piece. Nevertheless her concept of dimensionality in the penitente composition encompassed movement through space, an idea that will be addressed later on in this section.

*Los Penitentes* is a composite picture of the San Luis morada (now abandoned) with the setting inspired by the colors and shapes of the foothills and mountains near Josie's home in Chama, a village not far from San Luis. Basically, *Los Penitentes* is the most poetically compelling of all her embroidered narratives. Her emotional and artistic expressiveness are conveyed through her dramatic colors and the manner in which the harsh landscape envelops the Brothers as they climb the steep grade to the place they have designated as Calvary. The manos undertake arduous climbs over rough ground strewn with loose sharp rocks to test the power and efficacy of their penitential acts. Gene Lobato told me that it was common to add rocks to these trails to intensify the Brothers' pain and make these ascents even more agonizing.

In order to capture the impression of the barren landscape suffused with the imminence of seasonal regeneration and spiritual renewal, Josie spent many hours walking through nearby hills and observing the light, the subtle colors of the vegetation emerging from winter, and the shadows on the surrounding peaks at different times of the day. Sometimes we walked the foothills together noting the colors, the mood, and the odd stares from this society of cowboys who were more at home in trucks than on the ground. Often, if one attempted to walk alone for any distance, people would stop and offer rides, incredulous at the preference for solitude and dust.

I returned every year during Holy Week for the Good Friday pilgrimage procession that traversed the eleven miles from the village of San Francisco to San Luis. Again I moved along back roads, noticing the raw elements of the landscape that inspired Josie's artistic visions. There were a few times when Josie joined the procession as far as Chama. Then we matched our pace to the regular rhythms of the procession, compressed into a group—yet separately registering the sonorous prayers and recitations of the Rosary and observing how our presence *en masse* spooked the horses and cattle so that they fled to the far ends of the fields.

In 1991 I was invited to attend *El Encuentro* at the El Rito morada nestled in the foothills of the Sangre de Cristo mountains. El Encuentro is a penitente observance staged on Good Friday commemorating the Fourth Station of the Cross—the point where Christ meets His Mother on the way to Calvary. I was particularly interested in witnessing this rite because of its dramatic connection to the theme and setting of Josie's colcha.

I arrived in a heavy snowfall and pushed through the door into a stiflingly hot chapel where women sat near a wood stove gossiping together in the midst of restless and fidgety children. The Brothers had secluded themselves in an adjoining room, from which the sounds of intermittent prayers and strains of singing could be heard. The chapel scene felt surprisingly secular, like an informal gathering or play group covertly monitored by ranks of plaster holy figures staring out from behind the altar railing.

Shortly thereafter the *Hermano Mayor* emerged from the side room and summoned us to join the procession up the hill behind the morada where El Encuentro would be staged. He considerately invited me to remain in the warm room next to the fire. Thoughts of months of planning to get there and actually missing the opportunity to participate at the last minute because of my own politeness and ingrained tendency to always honor the protocol of my hosts raced through my mind. These internal debates, however, were masked by outward efforts to be convincing without appearing too eager.

I pointed to my hiking boots, implying that I came prepared for the weather. He looked nonplused but graciously led me out to the start of the procession, whereupon I instantly understood his concern. Much of the hour-long ceremony was spent inching slowly up the hill and abruptly dropping to our knees to pray wherever we happened to be standing at that moment. The discomfort of repeatedly landing on piles of sharp mud-encrusted rocks caused me to start surveying the ground ahead for softer areas where I could quickly kneel less painfully. Although the cumulative effect of switching from spiritual absorption to physical awareness finally interfered with my concentration on the liturgy, I was still captivated by its ancient cadence and by the palpable intimacy that bound this group to each other in honoring death as much as life.

At the end of the ceremony when the Brothers and their relatives had caressed and cherished the plaster image of the Virgin and kissed the crucifix, we turned around to begin our descent and faced the San Luis Valley ringed by fourteen-thousand-foot mountain peaks. Just then thunder rumbled in the middle of the snowstorm, shaping all that emptiness with sound—augmenting and prolonging it in an overlay of echoes as we, in our imagination, registered the auditory beat of Christ's passing. For that is precisely what everyone meant afterwards when they responded to the extraordinary weather by affirming, "Of course, something always happens on Good Friday."

In *Los Penitentes* Josie conveys some of this spirit when she melds vision with technique by spatially telescoping the foreground of her picture into the background so that the compactness of space and form accentuate the density of features in the landscape. This method consequently heightens the emotional intensity of the re-enactment of the climb to Calvary. Thus, the principal elements and the ritual action are pushed up against the picture plane, which increases the work's dramatic effectiveness. This treatment of space differs from *La Entriega,* where the viewer is quite removed from the focal point and the ceremony appears to occur at the far end of the room.

Color was another means of expressing atmosphere and mood. Josie Lobato's rendition of the local topography, using shadow and color to suggest subtle contours and a sense of place, is masterful. She introduces purple and blue tones of color frequently, especially in the hills. The window frames of the morada are also composed of shades of purple. According to Josie, purple was "the color of penance." Thus, even the formal elements in her composition are layered with symbolic connotation and allegorical import.

In addition to portraying mood through the natural setting, Josie wrestled with her interpretation of "dimensionality." Her artistic aspirations exceeded the ideas of dimension normally bound to static spatial concepts (that is, the conventional rendering of the third dimension within a two-dimensional framework or bounded by the limitations of a flat surface). Josie is just as enthralled and plagued by the rendering of dynamic movement within a static format as other artists before her have been. From her own experience, however, she wanted to utilize the visual capabilities inherent in the embroidery medium "to give the dimension of walking"—probably to emulate the manner in which she herself moved through the landscape, encountering it sequentially as the scenes unfolded one after the other. Basically, Josie is expressing the notion of movement through space. However, she might be reaching beyond this to suggest the pictorialization of walking or progressive movement as it extends into the viewer's space. This is consistent with her other work, since she frequently mentions outlining her embroidered figures with a series of stitches so that "they pop out"—not only from the background or picture plane, but also into space.

Ostensibly, it was Josie's quest for pictorial accuracy that compelled her to pursue her investigations during her vigorous walks through the countryside. But these solitary walks were also Josie Lobato's means of strengthening the connection to the spirit of her colcha, which in her imagination was still conditioned by the power of Gene Lobato's memory. Although the opportunity to "claim these recollections for herself" through the process of artistic reconstruction was available to her in this embroidery, the efficacy of this method was not as instrumental as in her previous colchas.

Since it was difficult for Josie to identify personally with the Brothers' religious activities, she tried to effect the same experience of transference that had empowered her earlier renditions of *Mis Crismes* and *La Entriega*, by endowing each of the men in the scene with a real name and a distinct personality. Through the course of stitching, Josie warmly bonded with these figures as imagined friends. As she had in her previous colcha embroideries, she once again personified the characters as they performed mundane activities. Two men fraternally greet each other while another walks along the ditch in back. These modest vignettes enacted on either side of the morada are in contradistinction to the somber liturgical drama occurring on the hill above them. Their appearance in the visual narrative softens some of its emotional intensity and affords us an imaginative entrance into the composition through our curiosity about casual human action.

When Gene Lobato told stories, he interjected similar touches of informality and comic drama imbued with a flavor of the trickster. One of his tales that matched Josie's gesture of "naming" her penitente characters to make them seem more familiar and affable illustrates the typical San Luis penchant for nicknames. Gene described how one man is called "Dr. Johnson" not because he is in medicine nor because he is related to a family named Johnson, but because he looks like a person from the past with that same name. Another anecdote mentioned a remote mestizo uncle of Gene's with traces of American Indian ancestry, who was called "Tablet" because he resembled the popular Indian image on the covers of the old grade school tablets.[44]

Directly associated with pranks that undermine sacred practice, Gene and his friends used to pinch off the crystallized ends of *panocha*, a sweet Lenten sprouted wheat pudding, and put them in their pockets to nibble on later during the long penitente fasts of Holy Week, especially at *Las Tinieblas* toward its end.[45]

Gene and Josie's stories and art reproduce complementary sacred and secular behavior alternating between glimpses of veneration and revelations of customary irreverence. Their narrative and visual repertoire relies on anecdote and images of human foibles to humanize, yet acknowledge, the spiritual forces behind Catholic practice. I also heard other stories and listened to jokes from different members of this small community detailing similar thematic ideas or concepts in which the profane segues into the profound in surprising ways.

Back in 1988 one of Josie's first reactions to colcha embroidery was her excited response to what she perceived as pictorial narrative's potential to depict themes of historical transition and change. Her artistic interest in documenting various elements dating to the late 1930s and early 1940s is also present in the *Los Penitentes* composition. Again, the gabled roof denotes Anglo influence and is more common to southern Colorado moradas than those in New Mexico. The shingles on the roof are also uncharacteristic of the early twentieth-century vernacular adobe style, but were favored during this era. Another indication of change is the use of cement mixed with plaster for the morada's exterior walls.

Most notable, however, are the Brothers attired in jeans and work shirts. Blue jeans harmonized easily with the modest and subdued wardrobes of the Penitentes. The ubiquity of jeans was due to their association with notions of humility (the worker's attire), informality, function, and the growing popularity of manufactured goods. Today, the Penitente Brothers still dress somberly, but during Good Friday rites where there is a crowd of worshippers they usually wear their best suits. Many of the spectators, however, are more casually dressed. During one of these gatherings, another stitcher in attendance lamented over this development, recalling how they all "used to get dressed up fancy like Easter eggs."[46]

With respect to embroidery, Josie found this restricted palette of dark, somber colors quite challenging. Normally, darker shades are consigned to background and shadow. The problem with foregrounding them in the frontal plane is that they can lessen or conceal highlights and contrast. This effect erases modulations of tone, thus requiring transitions between darker and lighter shades to be very subtle and complex. In the 1940s not only Penitentes, but most men, did not wear loud colors. These limitations in color choice forced Josie to manipulate color, tone, and hue carefully, in addition to all the other formal difficulties she faced with this particular colcha embroidery.

Perhaps Josephine Lobato's personal estrangement from the subject of the Penitente Brotherhood was painful to her, but it provided the emotional detachment necessary for her artistic creation of *Los Penitentes*. This feeling of detachment, however, amplified Josie's sense of loneliness. My field notes from this period indicate a concern for Josie's personal and emotional isolation—apparent even within a circle of supportive family and friends. It was as if the colcha's subplot, the theme of Calvary, engaged her so intensely that it also triggered an equivalent sorrowful response on some level of her own consciousness. Despite the sensations inherent in this process, Josie's colcha series continued to function as an opportunity and an artistic license (or occasionally as a steam valve) to contend with the residual emotions or loneliness that resulted from her twenty-year absence and subsequent return to the valley.

Another aspect of this experience of dislocation was Josie's sense of difference and pride in her individuality, which, she believed, gave her art work purpose and special meaning. Painful as this becomes at times, Josie perseveres with her passion for quest and creativity. In frontier societies this type of individualism for its own sake was constrained by the necessity of everyone working and surviving together communally in the face of great threats. Thus, prescribed practices of conformity and solidarity endure into the present and continue to curb individualism where vestiges of frontier behavior still persist. Over time "in the face of great threats" has been supplanted by a social contract of conformity requisite for—or characteristic of—living in a small village society with its dynamics of dependency, compulsory cooperation, and even compromise.

Notwithstanding all the typical objections and almost taboo connotations, Josie chose the theme of penitente rites because of her intellectual curiosity for history and the challenge implicit in depicting this mysterious cultural enactment of Christ's Passion. Her choice of the Penitentes as a colcha subject was controversial because of its long association with secrecy and because it was considered the "domain" of particular male members of San Luis society. Excluded because of gender, Josie had the advantage of some degree of objectivity, because penitente involvement was not directly related to her own experience. But this subjectivity, which Josie considers essential for her artistic involvement in colcha embroidery, is really the final determinant of the depth of her artistic expressiveness. During the creation of her colcha, this condition was both the source of her painful frustration and the element that permitted her to transcend the limitation of her alterity, her sense of otherness and estrangement, to create an expressively unique and subjective vision of the Penitente Brotherhood.

### *El Milagro de San Acacio*

The colcha that followed *Los Penitentes* was *El Milagro de San Acacio,* based on a local folktale relating to the miracle of San Acacio. It has all the necessary elements for a popular and enduring frontier legend—familiar setting, potentially life-threatening cultural clash, and a dramatic denouement resolved in miraculous action. Actually, Josie had characteristically begun researching this topic long before completing the penitente piece. *El Milagro* was much easier for her. It was the kind of subject she loved: historical, folk-based, with many human elements embedded in the storyline.

The story itself revolves around the brave actions of two appealing main characters, an old man and his twelve-year-old grandson (the "eyes and ears for grandpa"), who figure prominently in local families' genealogies—that is, everyone wants to claim descent from these two heroes. Josie's version depicts the legend as it was recounted many years later by the Ute Indian chief who was also a principal actor. This account was later incorporated into a body of local legends and written down. Josie portrays the miraculous moment of holy intervention on behalf of the Hispanic settlers from the viewpoint of the Ute Indian chief who "halted in his tracks": "According to legend [the chief] was the teller of the story. It was not like a Hispanic was telling the story. . . . I've heard the legend ever since I was very small. The legend of San Acacio is . . . a fireside type of story which has been told over and over and over again. And it's a pass down thing, too."[47]

Josie's version sets the scene for narrative action around the middle of the nineteenth century in the small village of San Acacio, slightly south and west of San Luis. On this particular clear and cloudless day, San Acacio was virtually deserted, with most of the able-bodied male villagers away hunting or tending their gardens outside the village walls. The young boy notices a cloud of dust rapidly rising on the horizon and warns his grandfather and the women and children left behind in the unprotected village that a band of Indians is speeding towards them. As the raiding party of Ute Indians approaches, the villagers huddle together in the middle of the plaza for protection and begin to pray fervently to their patron saint, the Hispanic San Acacio (Anglicized, St. Acatius). Just as the Indians prepare to attack, they stop "dead in their tracks," turn around and flee as fast as they can. Puzzled but jubilant, the villagers attribute their salvation to a miracle—the intervention of their divine protector, San Acacio. Years later, after decades of amicable coexistence between Hispanic settlers and Indian residents, the Ute Indian chief, a main protagonist in the legend's narrative, was being treated for a serious illness by a Hispanic *curandera*, or healer, in the San Luis Valley highlands. On behalf of her people and out of persistent curiosity, the woman asked why the Indian and his band had stopped their attack so abruptly and fled. He replied that the Indians had seen a regiment of armed horsemen behind a fierce soldier emerge from the clouds above the village. The powerful magic of this vision terrified the Indians, and they fled at once. By providing the missing elements and solving a long-standing mystery, the chief actually became the legendary narrator in subsequent tales of "El Milagro de San Acacio." Thus, since his revelation, he is always recognized as the teller of the story.

As a "pass down thing," the popular legend of San Acacio belongs to a genre of stories that celebrate the triumph of Catholic faith over pagan dangers. It is also interesting that the narration is presented in two stages, the initial enigmatic account and the consequent, equally mysterious explanation of the vision recounted by one of the main characters caught in a rather poignant situation years later. The legend additionally explains and legitimizes family connections (everyone wants to claim descent from the grandfather) and offers a tale of bravery and exemplary spiritual devotion. These, of course, are traits valued by San Luis society that continue to be venerated through storytelling themes and colcha pictorial narratives. Referring to certain families establishing their lineage through the old man, Josie says:

> Many names have been told to me that this man . . . But, of course, every family wants to claim him. . . . I've heard the Candelarias kind of talk about him as if it had been in their family. In many versions I have heard the old man called Jacquez [pronounced *hock-ez*], which is very possible because the Jacquez [family] settled San Acacio. And Jacquez is not an Hispanic name [it is French] . . . here you see the blend of the French. There was a lot of blend of culture, and there is a lot of history of generation to generation, in that family. So, it's a possibility that his name could have been that. . . . Almost everybody was related, so it depends on who is writing the story of the legend.[48]

The acknowledgment of limited familial connections in a community such as San Luis also extends to a notion of an external world of finite pools of relatives. The first night I visited Josie and Gene Lobato in their home we discussed all the interesting blood ties that make up families while they showed me their own photograph albums and framed portraits of relatives hanging on the walls. When Gene mentioned his French and Scottish blood, I said that I, too, was of French and Scottish descent. He exuberantly responded, "We are *primos* (cousins)!" His reaction echoed the natural and unquestioning acceptance of interrelationships typical of small and bounded communities in which the majority of families are truly related.

In some instances the most minimal facts are instantly recognized as indicative of the strongest ties, underscored by spontaneous demonstrations of good will based on the assumption that the local model reaches beyond the city limits. But we should not misinterpret these displays or attitudes as naive. They obviously represent an extension of hospitality and an acceptance of likable strangers rather than a misguided view of genealogy or an ignorance of the vastness of possible human interconnections.

*El Milagro de San Acacio* is divided into three spheres of action or zones: the village, the Indian band clustering outside it, and the celestial cloud of Spanish soldiers or conquistadores accompanying San Acacio. The presence of Spanish soldiers, often cited as putative ancestors by San Luis residents, is Josie's visual acknowledgment of local historicizing processes. Internally, these artistic and narrative conceptions serve to authenticate specific versions of heritage, which favor a strong Spanish origin as differentiating San Luis people from their American Indian and Latino (i.e., Mexican-American) neighbors. The image of San Acacio also refers to European history for inspiration and is conceived as the Roman centurion who converted to Christianity. His embroidered appearance is based on an elegant Italian plaster figure that currently dominates the interior of the San Acacio chapel.

The villagers are huddled in the "eye of the storm," totally absorbed in delivering their heavenly petition and in their hopes for deliverance. Josie describes the action and setting:

> all kneeling down in a group with their rosaries. I don't know if you can see my rosaries. They're a little more difficult to see because they were so tiny ... but the man in the white is the old man. That is not a woman, that is an old man, and the little boy kneeling in front of him is what the legend talks about. Of course, there was only women and children and I even have a baby there. It's hard to see but it's in its little cradle.
>
> I needed to make the village look like they were enclosed in this little plaza, so the vision on this side and the Native Americans coming, running in to attack the village on this side, had to sort of border it.[49]

As in her other colchas, Josie portrayed as many localizing elements as necessary to illustrate the specific nature of the scenery around the village of San Acacio. Among these were the *horno* (oven), wagons, some domestic animals grazing in a treeless meadow, all found in the landscape today but still, according to Josie's demand for historical verification, unsatisfactorily documented in her sources.

> I just had to use my imagination. This is totally my imagination. Of course, I know San Acacio. It has rolling hills. . . . [The scene] is typical of the area about 1854, I'd say. I more or less just sort of gave the landscape as I thought it would be like, the sagebrush and the wild grass, a meadow . . . I only gave it a small amount of trees because there aren't too many trees in the area. So this is typically what I. . . . My imagination fired me on this. There's no bounds to imagination, I guess.[50]

Josie also added a few wild animals for scenic accents:

> Of course, I put in one or two wild animals. I meant to have this one down here look like a squirrel and it ended up looking like a little fox or maybe even a little coyote. And, of course, I have got an eagle up in the sky to break . . . but of course some of the things I do are to break [up] color. I do this as a natural thing. I don't think I think about what I am doing when I am working with it. If it doesn't look right to me, I go back and I take out yarn and I put in a different color. . . . In almost everything I do I always break up the sky with different [colors]—sometimes with gray, sometimes with . . . just depending on whether I'm doing something very serious or doing something real light. To me this [San Acacio] was more of a "light type" in comparison, say, to the Penitentes [composition]. The color coordination had to be different.[51]

Color choice obviously highlights the contrast between the almost cinematic light-filled scene of the miracle and the opaque darkness and emotional intensity of the preceding penitente piece. Not only color, but the entire conception of the work was lighter for Josie. This attitude extended to her actual artistic engagement with the San Acacio embroidery, which was fairly detached and intellectually curious, unlike the personal struggles she had with the actual portrayal of the penitente ceremony.

In *El Milagro* Josie has filled the frontal picture plane with the most important action, the Indians witnessing the vision of San Acacio and his soldiers. The settlers are placed in the background, which is consistent with their preoccupation in praying and their unawareness of the drama occurring close by. On the one hand, as in *La Entriega* and *Mis Crismes* we as viewers are privy to all the dramatic action; on the other hand, both our omniscience and the formal effects of perspective and framing recast us as actual witnesses of the confrontation between the Indians and the divine army.

The Indians' reaction to the startling and horrific mirage materializing in front of them is registered in the way the chief's horse has stopped in mid-stride. Josie explains her intentions in conveying this: "I put the leg of the black horse in a halting position. This is about the point where he [the chief] might have seen the vision . . . as they began to come close to the village."[52]

The ethereal, unworldly qualities of the cloud vision are distinguished from the forceful, grounded physicality of the Ute Indian raiding party by its spatial arrangement, with figures descending from the sky like a reversal of "Jacob's Ladder," and by its color separation from the rest of the composition as contained within the white cloud. The cloud shape links the earthly and celestial realms by following a slight diagonal from the left corner of the composition to the foreground. Josie visualized the cloud as a way of conveying San Acacio and his entourage to earth and as a means of giving these visionary elements a formal and symbolic cohesion.

> I imagined them on a cloud. I had to imagine them on a cloud. And I had to imagine the cloud coming down into the earth and what it would have looked like [laughs] if it came down and hit the earth . . . like mist. But I also imagined that perhaps some of them had not quite made it all the way to the ground and they were floating up in the air. There was just no other way I could think to make it look like a vision. To me, it seemed it had to look realistic even though it was a vision.[53]

Josie learned about the subtleties of shading and contrast when she worked with different hues and gradations of white in rendering the bride in *La Entriega*. The white horses and the white cloud enveloping San Acacio and the conquistadores presented the same sort of technical challenges. She found that doubling her yarn for outlining certain figures produced a dimensional effect and created interesting textural details. Another difficulty was to render the illusion of transparency and haze associated with clouds, mist, and fog. Unlike painting, in which the artist can use washes of color to achieve illusory impressions, embroidery is restricted to opaque yarn or threads. Degrees of shading are usually achieved through the melding of various colors. Josie describes some of her concepts and experimentations:

> According to legend they were all white horses. That was very difficult for me. I had to blend it in with a gray . . . and I had to take apart some of those and shadow them differently because they were coming out so, so . . . they were sort

of melting into each other and into the cloud. In order to break that I had to come up with some ideas as to what kind of colors to put in there that would set them out, would bring them out. Some of them are double stitched. For instance, if you would check my top ones, they would be double stitched. They have double yarn and that puffs them out. They are denser. That makes them puff and stand out.[54]

Her work with white and its supplementary palette inspired Josie to consult the museum's historical colcha once again to learn how to wield neutral or natural colors in *El Milagro* and in subsequent colchas. The discovery of the intentional use of neutral color by the historical colcha maker re-inspired Josie to view background as a vital and interesting aspect of colcha creation. She began to see possibilities in utilizing natural colors to unify different forms within discrete areas so that they "blend together." This diverges from what she had expressed earlier about wanting the horses to "pop out" of the enveloping cloud.

"I have gone to look at the 'Tree of Life' in the [museum] theater so many times. She—whoever did this piece—was so wonderful because they put such a natural background on this thing."[55] Josie may occasionally have felt isolated from actual people who shared her enthusiasm and passion for all facets of colcha embroidery. Her imagination, however, was well populated with presences from the past. In addition to the unknown colcha maker of the nineteenth-century piece at Fort Garland, Josie also speaks of communing with Tiva Trujillo and St. Acatius. Her bond with Tiva was particularly strong at the time she was creating *El Milagro* because Tiva had grown up in the village of Old San Acacio and had also depicted scenes from her childhood in colcha embroidery.

> I feel St. Acatius and Tiva watching me from up there. I don't know why I feel drawn to that lady so much. She's driving me up the wall. I see her hands. . . . It bothers me. Maybe it's just that I'm so involved with it—with the idea. I never met her. . . . I think I'm in touch with Tiva Trujillo when I do any work on this.[56]

Josie's affinity for Tiva may appear inexplicable, but they share some very strong connections vis-à-vis their approach to visualizing their lives in colcha embroidery. In choosing her subject matter, Tiva Trujillo was also compelled to re-experience her own life through its recreation in art form. In an interview in 1979 she stated, "It's nice to think of yourself as a child, you know. That's something to think about now that you're getting old. When you go to your childhood or to your past, you think about everything. That's why I like to draw [embroider]."[57]

Plate 1. An embroidered map of the San Luis Valley by Tiva Trujillo, 1979 (40″ x 29″). (Courtesy Colorado Historical Society; acc. no. 79.198)

Plate 2. The *Mis Crismes* wool embroidery, by Josephine Lobato, 1990 (19″ x 24″). (Private collection)

Plate 3. *Los Penitentes* wool embroidery by Josephine Lobato, 1991 (21″ x 26″). (Private collection)

Plate 4. The wool embroidery *El Milagro de San Acacio,* by Josephine Lobato, 1992 (21˝ x 26˝). (Private collection)

Plate 5. A nineteenth-century wool-on-wool colcha embroidery with a combination of geometric and floral design elements (86˝ x 54˝). (Courtesy Taylor Museum, Colorado Springs Fine Arts Center; acc. no. TM 3775)

Plate 6. A nineteenth-century wool-on-wool floral colcha embroidery (76″ x 37.5″). (Courtesy Colorado Historical Society; El Pueblo Museum Collection, Pueblo, Colorado; acc. no. E1943.1a)

Plate 7. A detail of the wool embroidery *Las Misiones,* by Josephine Lobato, 1993–1994 (21˝ x 26˝). (Private collection)

Plate 8. The wool embroidery *El Rancho Grande,* by Sostena Cleven, 1988 (12″ x 20″). (Private collection)

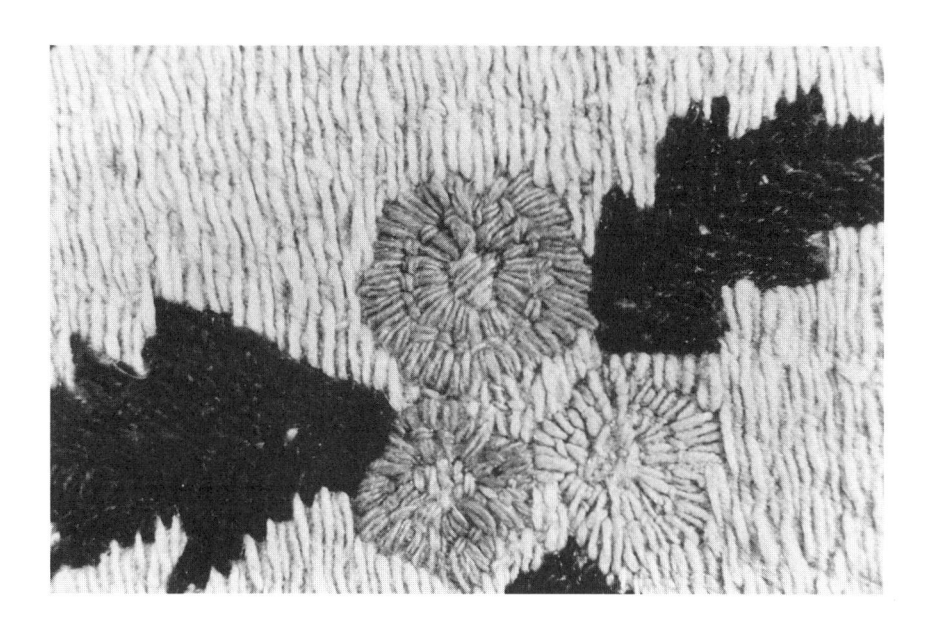

Figure 1. A floral detail from a nineteenth-century colcha embroidery showing the distinctive colcha couching stitch with its series of short, perpendicular anchoring stitches. (Courtesy Colorado Historical Society; El Pueblo Museum Collection, Pueblo, Colorado; acc. no. E1943.1a)

Figure 2. *La Entriega de los Novios,* a wool embroidery by Josephine Lobato, 1990 (21″ x 26″). (Private collection)

Figure 3. A nineteenth-century wool-on-wool colcha embroidery using a geometric design inspired by Rio Grande Saltillo-style weavings (68″ x 54″). (Courtesy Taylor Museum, Colorado Springs Fine Arts Center; acc. no. TM 3776)

Figure 4. The 1930s "Carson Colcha" created from recycled wool materials, attributed to Wayne Graves (78" x 44.5"). (Courtesy Millicent Rogers Museum Collection, Taos, New Mexico; acc. no. MRM-1978-6)

Figure 5. *Haciendo Ristras,* by Filomena Gonzales and A. Chavéz in the Villanueva style, 1981 (14″ x 22″). (Courtesy Millicent Rogers Museum Collection, Taos, New Mexico; acc. no. MRM-L-28-1988-39)

Figure 6. *Old San Acacio,* a wool embroidery by Julia Valdez, 1989 (12˝ x 20˝). (Sangre de Cristo Parish Collection, San Luis, Colorado)

Figure 7. *La Vega,* a wool embroidery by Evangeline Salazar, 1991 (16″ x 20″). (Private Collection)

Figure 8. *La Casa de Piedra,* a wool embroidery by Sally T. Chavéz, 1989 (26˝ x 35˝). (Private Collection)

Figure 9. *Magpie,* a wool embroidery by Pacífica La Combe, 1990 (12˝ x 9˝). (Private Collection)

Josie's reaction to learning about Tiva's embroidery inspired her to explore folkloric material. Although both artists feature the San Acacio village in their embroideries, Josie's representation focuses on the sacred legacy of the vision preserved through the dissemination of a local legend. Tiva's composition is more of a microstudy of village life in 1925 conceived as a patchwork of anecdotes, from hog butchering and doing the laundry to various tasks associated with agriculture and animal husbandry. The old adobe plaza figures prominently in both embroideries. Tiva has even stitched the chapel dedicated to San Acacio (the ultimate result of the vision) from which the village takes its name, with its adjoining graveyard marked by the figure of the crucified Christ surrounded by a cluster of crosses. Tiva's depiction could actually be construed as the secular and material consequence of the vision's aftermath. Her realization of the village as Eden or as a paradise becomes symbolic of the actual reward of the legendary and faithful Catholic settlers fervently praying in Josie's embroidered version of the story.

Not only is the conception of her village evocative of paradise (in her remembrances a truthful characterization); Tiva views her childhood idealistically as well: "If you draw a picture of your own past—and that's what I have been doing—every picture that I have drawn . . . it's my past. My life, you know, that's what it is. It's a true picture and a real picture. They were alive sometime . . . oh once upon a time."[58] Thus, in her embroidery Tiva combines personal memory and autobiographical bits and pieces with a view of social values and a treasured heritage: a small and self-sufficient community populated with industrious and cooperative villagers engaged in an idyllic scene where religion, education, and good times are prized. Josie's *El Milagro* presents an "origin" myth detailing the source of the ethical, moral, and familial underpinnings of San Acacio (and by extension San Luis Valley) society. Although Tiva's inspiration stems from her own individual memories while Josie consciously chose a colorful communal legend, the ideas embodied in their art illustrate the concept of cultural memory, which represents "the many shifting histories and shared memories that exist between a sanctioned narrative of history and personal memory."[59]

Tiva grounds her own individuality in her embroidery practice and her joy at portraying her childhood through art. Her idealistic version of village life, however, is more representative of collective remembrance and nostalgia for "better times" than of personal biography. Josie's intention is to chronicle a shared memory of a religious miracle, but the outcome affirms society's faith in God and is a picture of the materiality and source of significant bloodlines that personalize the shared ancestry of her local community.

The major themes in Josie's colchas are transition and change. Although unaware of the significance of the transitions occurring around her during childhood, her move away from the valley and then her return after a considerable time intensified her responsiveness to these changes. Josie collects personal and social memories from her community and charges them with her own will and being. Many of these are central to the perceived identity of the San Luis community, but their vitality stems from Josie's interpreting patterns of change through her own life experience.

> Of course it has changed today because everything changes, you know. It could be that for me the change came because I left. Maybe that's why I feel that change, because I wasn't here. And then when I came back it was different. To me it seemed like it wasn't quite like it was when I was growing up. But it never is. But this [colcha embroidery] pretty much reflects what I think there was at the time ... probably at the time when I was in the most important part of my life, which was my teenage years. The important thing of my life was what was happening in the church, because it was all connected with my schooling. There was just no disconnection between what was happening in this building [school] and what was happening in this building [church]. It was all together. It all just melted together.[60]

Josie's themes of cultural enactment, which are staged against backdrops of transition and change, parallel the mutability of present-day San Luis, which has adapted rather rapidly to a series of alterations under Father Pat Valdez. In an important sense, Josie's embroideries are an "art of rehearsal" in which the tensions and apprehension of cultural and social change are presented, addressed, and dramatized. As the theme of cultural transition persists locally, Josie's vision, underscoring the coexistence of transformation with traditional elements, is particularly relevant for contemporary San Luis society.

Generally, in Josie's pictorial narratives (and in other San Luis stitcheries as well) the use of memory is quite discerning, and occasionally the way it is wielded can be controversial. As the subject of an embroidered scene, memory often mediates between individualized recall and the prescriptive nature of social or "official" recollection. For example, the intended message of a piece of embroidery depends not only on whose memories are being recorded but on who is sanctioning their use as well. A specific memory repertoire (religious, ethnic or gendered, etc.) can be used symbolically to reinforce power and status of an individual or of special interest groups; or conversely, to underscore the absence of such power.

Not everyone in San Luis supports or identifies with Josie's personal visualizations as representative of shared collective memories. The theme of transition may be fascinating to Josie and aesthetically rich because of its hybridity and various manifestations. For other community members, however, it accentuates the incursion of external Anglo influence and heralds degrees of amalgamation that neutralized—or worse, dominated—the Hispanic culture of the valley.

Josie's visual narrations are marked by a loyalty to factual detail and accuracy (lightened by whimsical detail) that might obscure the point that the theme of transition also suggests "loss." To some this represents a fear of loss of community traditions or cultural identity. To others this very same loss is liberating in that it disconnects the present from the past and allows society to be reconstituted through selective remembrance. The tension between Josie and a few critics of her work reveals a disparity in attitude toward memory use. In some quarters this becomes an issue of cultural property and involves the repercussions of choice over which set of memories most accurately portrays the "official" or collective image San Luis wants to project to outsiders—i.e., which memories should dominate, and who selects them. These social dynamics further emphasize the intentionality of remembrance and its inverse, forgetfulness. During our association Josie usually regarded her recollections in a positive light, and consequently thought of her choice of theme and imagery as a reliable reconstruction of her childhood era. Josie's concepts depend on her individual positive recall, whereas different San Luis stitchers seemed happy to avoid these themes (hence forget them) because of their past associations with poverty accompanied by ethnic discrimination and traces of unease.

Josie's level of artistic intensity distinguishes her from other embroiderers in San Luis. Two years after the stitching workshop, Carmen Orrego-Salas still remembered this quality of commitment in her work and creative attitude. Señora Orrego-Salas alludes to this aspect of Josie's artistic drive in a letter addressed to the San Luis stitchers:

> Then I think how the benefit [of embroidering] is twofold. How persons who do something that is important to them also get rewarded with a voice—their own; how it keeps them company as they work and helps and encourages them to sort out the difficulties that all work entails. As Josie says, her solitary work became very revealing, it told her, how in the end her tapestry had become a rite of passage for her—how it talked through to her, and how it became necessary for her to keep at it until it was completed. So please continue creating—think

what a consolation it is while the work is being done and how it affects those who come in contact with it. It is a joy![61]

It is just this degree of intensity in Josie Lobato's approach to the artistic process and to the colcha art form itself that empowers her as an artist and a cultural interpreter. But her engagement with colcha is potentially much more encompassing than merely stitching scenes of commemoration. According to her, the force of artistic creativity transcends all aspects of remuneration or social and collective motivation: "I couldn't work on colcha without it meaning something to me. I don't do it for money. In fact, I may not be thinking what I am going to leave [as a legacy to her children]. I may be doing it . . . just because it's inside of me and I want to get it out.[62]

As Josie became more adept and more dedicated to art, colcha embroidery profoundly influenced her artistic and religious consciousness. In 1993, during what could have become a terrible family tragedy, Josie momentarily shifted from artist and cultural commentator to *santera* in the traditional sense of transmuting prayers into art—of creating an art work as votive offering. Her granddaughter suffered serious head injuries in a freak accident while riding on an off-road vehicle near Josie's home. During her vigil in the hospital waiting room, Josie prayed that if her granddaughter recovered she would dedicate her next embroidery to Santa Rita, her mother's patron saint.

Her granddaughter survived the accident, and while she convalesced, Josie began her embroidery as part of the celestial bargain she had struck. Like the historical icon makers, Josie regarded the creation of this embroidered *retablo* (a two-dimensional sacred effigy) as a very private act. Her choice of religious imagery is understandable given the circumstances, but generally this type of theme was eschewed by other stitchers and embroidery workshop leaders in economic redevelopment projects. The consensus was that its highly personal value and expressly Catholic focus interfered with its marketability. Another reservation was more technical. Most stitchers found the human figure daunting to work with due to their view of themselves as "non-artists" and their perceived lack of artistic skill. These issues will be referred to in later chapters discussing the ramifications of various embroidery revitalization efforts.

Tiva Trujillo's conviction that her embroidered narratives revealed the truth and reality of her past in the utopian time zone of "once upon a time" meshes with Josie's use of the past for inspiration and content, but deviates from Josie's focus on a liminal time frame positioned between zones of tradition and alteration. In her votive image of Santa Rita, however, Josie activates more than memory and artistic documentation. Her conception and personal response to her mother's patron saint have created another imagined partner in dialogue—an act that continues to amplify the spiritual elements so inherent in her colchas. Josie repeatedly states that she cannot embroider unless there is special meaning for her, which ultimately results in the total involvement so evident in her attitude toward colcha:

> For me to colcha stitch the way I am doing now, it has to have some special meaning. Because I have to squeeze it into my life and I have a very tight schedule. So, it has to mean something and it has to interest me in the sense of— It's almost like I am living through that piece. I can't even explain it. It's hard for me to explain my feelings. I don't know, it's almost like I am living through that piece . . . maybe Tiva felt like this.[63]

# 3

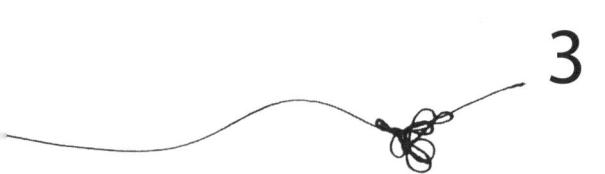

## change and tradition in historical colcha making

…it is a knitted or crocheted bedspread, used probably as the more familiar colcha was used by the Spanish colonial people. It came to us as a knitted colcha and as we have no information on this type of material, I am in the hope that you may be able to tell us something definite regarding it.

—M. A. Wilder

To understand the attraction and power of historical colcha embroideries, try to imagine Josie Lobato silently examining her inanimate guide and companion, the nineteenth-century colcha, in the semidarkness of the Fort Garland Museum Soldier's Theatre where it is on display. The solitary image of Josie bent over the coverlet eagerly looking for answers and revelations conjures up a scene from the past of a frontier woman sitting alone also totally lost in the creative moment while mentally reviewing the day's events. Through the kinetics of stitching (the arm's movement, the needle thrusting in and out), this phantom stitcher from the past converts her reveries into design patterns, which in turn are permanently embedded in the ground fabric of memory.

From the preceding chapter on Josie's work we recognize that colcha embroidery as an art object is a visual symbol—a cultural and aesthetic expression that exists apart from the written word. Every time a colcha is removed from storage and unrolled on tables in basements and back rooms of museums, the past becomes manifest in the present through the very act of scrutiny and analysis. History of manufacture, use, and interpretation merge into a richly complex tapestry of experience. Despite the absence of artifactual records, the colcha's communicative power eloquently evokes the contents, the styles, and even the circumstances of its many uses through the overlays of different time periods. Even today as a colonial relic, a traditional colcha embroidery bears the imprint of artistic decision and choice projected over vast temporal and geographical distances.

When I initially began to research colchas in the early nineties, the very term "colcha" was troublesome. Confusion and peculiar assessments of colcha embroidery's origins and authenticity were everywhere—in texts, in debates among museum curators, prevalent in attitudes of stitchers, and apparent in the popular imagination as well. In fact, I was surprised to find the same quandary and misinterpretation echoed sixty years earlier in a couple of letters dating to the 1930s, which I discovered in the Taylor Museum archives in Colorado Springs, Colorado.

> To Mr. H. Schweitzer from M. A. Wilder:
> December 23, 1936
> ... it is a knitted or crocheted bedspread, used probably as the more familiar colcha was used by the Spanish colonial people. It came to us as a knitted colcha and as we have no information on this type of material, I am in the hope that you may be able to tell us something definite regarding it. The materials are all native hand spun. The design being in large diamonds.... The specimen in no way resembles any *xerga* [spelling variation of *jerga*, a local twill-woven fabric

often used as rugs] that I have seen, so I am considering it rather as a variation of a colcha [see fig. 3].

Schweitzer's reply:

> December 26, 1936
> My Dear Mr. Wilder:
> I have your letter regarding a knitted or crocheted bed spread.
> So far as I can judge from your description it is something that does not have any particular place, or *belong to any particular type of Spanish product* [author's emphasis], so far as I know.
> I have seen several in my time that I think are the same and they might have been made by *any other* people than Spanish [author's emphasis].
> At any rate I am sorry to say that that is all I can say at this distance without seeing it.
> Very Truly Yours,
> H. Schweitzer

From my own frustrating research experience with the meager information on colchas in museum collections, I recognized the puzzle pondered by Wilder, the director of the Taylor Museum, and misinterpreted by Schweitzer, a well-known collector of Southwestern artifacts. With just a casual examination, colcha construction (dense wool embroidery on a woolen base) seems in its appearance to resemble weaving or tapestry, possibly knitting. When they are turned over, the impression is more likely to be that colchas are imitating weaving or tapestry techniques but are a unique genre. For this reason, a lack of familiarity with them can lead to mistaken assumptions, as witnessed in the correspondence between Wilder and Schweitzer. Aside from this, I was also intrigued by these letters because of the persistent mystery that accompanies colcha studies and the hidden dynamics—the cross-currents of doubt and certainty emanating from Wilder's and Schweitzer's exchange.[1]

During the long interval since these letters were written, colchas have been somewhat cursorily investigated—more rigorously in recent times, but not yet definitively. However, I tend to empathize with Wilder's caution and his more conservative opinion. From my perspective and with some professional hindsight, his speculative inquiry merits more credibility than Schweitzer's confident and adamant reply that, certainly, the mystery textile did not belong "*to any particular type of Spanish product.*" Of course, Schweitzer's opinion must be regarded leniently since he did not actually view the piece in question. In retrospect, however, Wilder's estimation, based on a modest or somewhat guarded appraisal of style and historicity, was more accurate than Schweitzer's. Wilder's erroneous allusion to knitting is outweighed by his correct attribution to the Spanish colonial style. That particular colcha (fig. 3) is now regarded as an exemplary nineteenth-century traditional wool-on-wool colcha embroidery found in Southwestern collections.

As a cultural expression couched within the artistic language of a colonial society adapting to a strange environment, colcha embroidery represents a historicizing process. Similarly, colcha as subject to cultural and geographical influences depends on artistic choice, adaptation, and available materials. Colcha is an accretion of layers of past and present meaning and intent. By their very existence, colcha embroideries are reliquaries—not objects of devotion, but containers of the relics of time, cultural survivals, past use, and former contexts. Concretely and abstractly, colcha is a multilayered textile or visual text akin to Robert St. George's description of language as an "open archaeological site of preexisting meanings historically rooted in multiple and often conflicting social relations which are then fitted into new conditioning contexts."[2]

Despite its deceptively quiescent state, a colcha artifact within a museum setting, to quote Mikhail Bakhtin, "is not a neutral medium . . . it is populated—overpopulated—with the intentions of others."[3] Embroideries as heirlooms are crowded with the voices of their creators, their owners, and others that used them. They signify the tracery of genealogy and relationship special to history, for "without markings, all ancestors become abstractions."[4] Despite our sensitivity to the silent overtones enveloping museum artifacts, both Josie Lobato and I had fairly specific agendas—intentions—when we approached historical colchas. She sought technical guidance and "company" through a process of contemplation and inquiry. I was looking for clues to direct my research investigations.

When working alone in museum storerooms, often the only recourse available to researchers attempting to unravel the mysteries of provenance and circumstance is to try to imagine or coexperience the original sequence of artistic decisions by closely examining every facet of visual evidence—from single stitches to overall designs. Most early nineteenth-century colchas are covered with individual stitches that skillfully convert the rhythms of minute gestures into expanses of patterned fields so dense they appear to be woven. Conditioned by degree of talent and virtuosity, each stitch reveals traces of an anonymous artist's touch. Occasionally, these needle tracks betray moments of awkwardness and the resultant loss of touch in negotiating the intricacies of more difficult patterns. Glimpses of defeat and frustration are rare, however, since most stitchers ripped out mistakes and hid these problem areas by embroidering over them. This is consistent with Josie Lobato's solutions to vexing problems. So many times Josie speaks of ending frustrating stitching sessions by ripping out the stitches and redoing them until they are satisfactory.

Inevitably, one also finds faintly visible carbon or charcoal marks on the ground fabric—ghostly relics from an embroiderer's initial design. Indicative of an artist's mind at work or the mapping of a selection process, these barely perceptible marks signal a deviation from the original artistic intent. Still intact, but forgotten and marginalized, faded lines from the past allow us to identify the nature and extent of change as a necessary determinant of creative decision making.

Similar insights result from noting anomalies within a traditional colcha's compositional format. Color differences or disparities in alignment and measurement of design elements occur frequently (fig. 3). Alterations in the repetition, substitution, or deletion of specific motifs are also apparent. Framed within the overall design, irregular factors often signal conscious aesthetic decisions privileging asymmetry over alternate arrangements of symmetry and balance. Tendencies toward a modicum of randomness rather than a predictable bilateral symmetry could also indicate cultural conditioning or preference—possibly even the presence of more than one stitcher involved in making these pieces. Nevertheless, if a piece was created by a single individual, perhaps that person was so absorbed in the act of stitching or intrigued by technical matters that the creation of a completely balanced and consistent composition was of secondary interest.

Observing Josie and her contemporaries in the San Luis Valley, it is apparent that once embarked on an embroidery, they experience a "point of no return." This is the moment where they relinquish objectivity and critical distance to yield to the dynamics of a forceful internal dialogue between themselves as embroiderers and the artistic demands of their piece. Perhaps some of the inconsistencies in the design of old colchas indicate that the nineteenth-century colcha makers were as ensnared in the actual creative process as are the contemporary stitchers in San Luis. Under these circumstances complete immersion in their embroidery served to offset the kind of conscientious conditioning in which design rudiments totally influence compositional standards or choices. These women tend to be more captivated by the excitement of creating and stitching embroideries than by adhering to the most careful layouts.

## Traditional Wool-on-wool Colcha Embroidery

As mentioned earlier, colcha embroidery is commonly described as "tapestry." In fact, Josie often uses the word "tapestry" as synonymous with embroidery in reference to colcha. However, tapestry's association with embroidered fabric is more descriptive in a colloquial sense (or as common vocabulary) than in terms of accurate technical usage. In the Taylor Museum in Colorado Springs there are a few colcha examples which by their *appearance* alone merit the label "tapestry." In these examples, known as wool-on-wool colcha embroideries, the balanced plain weave (warp and weft counts are equal) of the handspun woolen ground fabric, *sabanilla,* is so densely and completely overlaid with embroidery that it simulates a carpet-like appearance. This is achieved through the lush texture of stitchery and the formal complexity of composition.

Because of the narrow Spanish looms, most colchas consist of two widths of fabric joined down a center seam that is usually obscured by embroidery stitches, as is the ground fabric itself. Thus, in the density and completeness of their surface embroidery, these textiles visually resemble woven tapestries rather than stitched fabrics. Functionally, this additional layer of stitches also provided another thickness for warmth in the cold and intemperate climate of the New Mexico frontier.

Two wool-on-wool colcha embroideries from the Colorado Taylor collection exemplify these characteristics. They date from the same early period. Both were stitched with paired strands of yarn threaded through a single needle rather than the twisted or plied fibers found on later colchas. Because of the use of fine handspun churro wool, undyed or colored with natural dyes of indigo (alone or in combination with yellow to produce green), tan, and gold, these fabrics may predate the 1860s. Following that decade, two factors irrevocably changed textile production in New Mexico: the long-fleeced churro sheep were supplanted by the finer, short-staple, kinky, greasy Merino fleece; and the importation of commercially produced aniline and other synthetic dyes replaced the more durable natural dyes. By 1880 the arrival of the railroad also contributed to the shift from locally produced materials to cheaper commercial trade goods (including fabric and yarn). Availability of native products was compromised by the railroad as regional marketplaces were eliminated and local trade sites disappeared.

One of the Taylor textiles is a piece measuring more than two meters long by almost one and a half meters wide. It is completely covered by parallel bands of colcha-stitched embroidery composed of rows of interlocking sawtooth ridges separated by three distinct strips of floral imagery. At first glance the floral borders appear indistinguishable from the continuous serrated zigzags of the outer and central zones until one notices their subtle shadings and softened, slightly curved petal-like edges.

These evanescent floral motifs may have been inspired by Chinese silk embroidery patterns. Chinese shawls, *mantón de Manila,* with delicate stitchery capable of rendering the most subtle painterly effects in thread, had been very popular throughout the Spanish empire—so popular, in fact, that in the early eighteenth century they had become an integral part of native fashion in New Spain.[5]

Chinese textiles reached the New World via the Pacific galleon trade. During the colonial era, Mexico was the geographical conduit through which these trade fabrics passed on their journey from the Far East to Spain. They were originally exported from East Asia and routed through the Philippines (part of the Spanish dominion), to arrive at Acapulco on the west coast of Mexico. Then the trade caravans traveled overland to Vera Cruz, an eastern seaport, and were finally transported across the Atlantic. Between 1565 and 1815 the bulk of the Manila galleon export trade passed through Mexico on its way to Spain.

Despite their secular and decorative qualities, Chinese embroideries were listed as altar frontals in eighteenth- and nineteenth-century New Mexico church inventories and invoices.[6] Thus, the shawls' elevation to ecclesiastical furnishings coupled with their scarcity on the frontier zone (despite their ubiquity throughout the rest of the Spanish empire) argues for the New Mexico stitchers' inspired appropriation of Chinese designs and techniques. The adoption and transference of Asian motifs to colcha embroidery was predicated on artistic visibility and notions of appropriateness, preciousness, and genuine aesthetic delight.

The composition of the Taylor Museum wool-on-wool colcha, with its horizontal bands of alternating floral and geometric rows, is evocative of a rectangular Mexican altar frontal of similar design dating to around 1825. The motifs on both pieces are secular rather than religious, but Mexican frontals such as this one adorned altars on special occasions and are still found in Mexican churches today.[7] In New Mexico this type of embroidery and its colonial "cousin-in-style," the colcha, were valued as portable ecclesiastical items indispensable in transforming profane spaces into temporary sacred settings. As such, they were necessary accouterments for early peripatetic missionary-priests traveling along the religious circuits of the frontier.

Artistic and aesthetic training of young people traditionally occurred in Mexican convents and monasteries and was regulated by the Bishopric in Durango, Mexico. It has been suggested that religious orders on the frontier were also the source for artistic mediation and production.[8] Because colcha making is extremely involved in terms of time and labor, it is tempting to attribute the intricate craftsmanship associated with colcha production to nuns cloistered in colonial New Mexico.

In the Santa Fe, New Mexico, Museum of International Folk Art collection there is a nineteenth-century Mexican sampler composed of panels embroidered and stitched together by Mercedarian nuns, an order that originated in thirteenth-century Spain. The work was completed between 1867 and 1869 for a former lady-in-waiting, Irene Escandon, who was entering the convent upon retirement from service to the Empress Carlotta after Emperor Maximilian's assassination in Mexico in 1867. Customarily, elaborate gifts comprising a type of religious dowry were offered upon a noblewoman's entry into a nunnery.

Spanish colonial or northern Rio Grande wool-on-wool colchas are a class of luxury items that could have been included in such a religious inventory. Notwithstanding a brief mention of a convent in connection with the New Mexico mission of Santa Ana in a document probably dated to mid-eighteenth century, however, there is no explicit evidence of the presence of nuns on the frontier until a hundred years later. Around 1850 references to the Sisters of Charity and the Sisters of Loretto start to appear in Bishop Jean Lamy's correspondence.[9] Thus, the Bishop's letters document the arrival of these religious orders in New Mexico subsequent to independence from Mexico and just after the apogee of wool-on-wool colcha production.

The second wool-on-wool colcha embroidery (fig. 3), of dimensions similar to the first, complements it in terms of native handspun materials enhanced by a carefully coordinated color scheme of natural dyes. This particular colcha was the one previously described by M. A. Wilder in his letter as a "knitted or crocheted bedspread"—a false impression (in terms of technique) probably created by its soft pliable appearance, derived from the inherent loft and resilience of wool yarn. The design field is composed of a series of large diamonds centered between rows of serrations that form repetitive patterns of zigzags as they radiate outward. Like ripples these rows appear to slip over the outer edges thus creating visual rhythms that encompass the entire fabric and almost pulsate beyond its selvages.

Diamond shapes and their variants are associated with a group of serapes and blankets produced around Saltillo, Mexico. Every autumn during the colonial era, this was the site of one of the most active eighteenth-century trade fairs in the territory. It was a place of lucrative exchange where buyers from Texas and New Mexico traded various regional commodities for European and Asian textiles, as well as those from Mexico.[10] Synonymous with the Saltillo style, diamonds and serrated designs gradually migrated to New Mexico via the trade network, ultimately becoming formally linked to a specific class of Rio Grande Hispanic weaving.

The second Taylor colcha (fig. 3) appears to be an embroidered copy of—or perhaps it was inspired by—a Rio Grande Saltillo-style prototypical blanket. Its large-scale diamonds are prominently situated within a compositional format dominated by angular shapes rendered in subdued colors. Acknowledging the conventional notion held in the past by some art historians that styles progress towards greater sophistication, these simple repetitive motifs could be characteristic of a nascent elemental style and could indicate a development toward greater complexity and refinement.

More likely, this geometrically designed colcha reflects the opposite—a later stylistic stage still based on Rio Grande Saltillo motifs. Perhaps it represents a process of abstraction moving away from complexity and multiplicity to large-scale, simple forms? Accordingly, instead of the intricately modulated designs and subtle color gradations of the first colcha, the second represents a reduction in the number of design elements and a shift to an enlarged, less involved, compositional format. Since both of these colchas probably predate the 1860s, I would estimate the first colcha to have been executed between 1830 and 1840. The second one is slightly later, possibly around the middle of the century.

The mystery remains, however: why would an embroiderer painstakingly stitch a fabric to resemble closely a design pattern so strongly associated with weaving traditions when it could be created with greater ease, less frustration, and more accuracy on a loom? Was this artistic endeavor a demonstration of consummate skill and virtuosity? Perhaps it was simply the intention of a talented artisan adept in both weaving and embroidery to replicate the one in the other? Or might it have been motivated by an interest and curiosity kindled by the challenge implicit in the transference of aesthetic properties from one medium to another? It would appear that such a transference, a crossover between media, not only courts ambiguity and raises a number of questions, but could represent a form of visual code-switching that simultaneously highlights and subverts the innate qualities of each medium (weaving and embroidery).

The challenge of designs crossing over from weaving to embroidery is apparent in an exchange I had with a stitcher in the San Luis Valley. During an interview, Shirley Ortega, a weaver and colcha embroiderer from Alamosa, Colorado, told me that she intended to create a colcha inspired by weaving motifs. Ortega simply enjoys working with geometrical designs—whether she is weaving or embroidering.[11]

The woven foundation for traditional colchas has been described earlier as a precisely constructed, balanced plain weave (equal size and spacing of warp and weft), natural wool fabric called *sabanilla*. In a section on "post-loom decoration" in *The Anthropology of Cloth*, Jane Schneider discusses the evolution of design patterns as part of the process of liberation from "the grid-like geometry of warp and weft."[12] Because colcha embroidery's very existence depends on a supportive network of closely aligned horizontal and vertical elements, its mobility is essentially a blend of synthesis and independence. The colcha stitch weaves in and out of the ground fabric, usually congruent with the limitations imposed by the dominant rectilinear format of warp and weft. But these grid-honoring stitches are also capable of defying the basic geometrical matrix as they collectively transform series of right angles into floral patterns that organically curve and undulate, thus obscuring their angular base with curvilinear surface decoration.

The genre of contemporary pictorial narratives in San Luis, for instance, illustrates the most extreme and ultimately liberating stage of grid-defying stitches operating as post-loom decoration. In these pieces the stitches serve primarily to amplify the cadence of the story and are inherently entangled in the formal composition, thus overriding basic structural constraints such as grid lines, fabric width, and conspicuously visible center seams.

Again, referring to historical colchas, one disadvantage inherent in symmetrically determined designs of geometrical elements is that mistakes are more visible. Note that in the second Taylor Museum colcha (fig. 3) the alternating diamonds do not exactly replicate each other. In this instance, in order to mask or accommodate the error the stitcher created a series of graduated borders enclosing each central lozenge. Thus, by accentuating and coordinating the modulations of the separate nesting frames, the color and size disparities between the inner diamonds are made less noticeable. As mentioned earlier, these compositional inconsistencies may be the result of more than one hand at work, with two or more stitchers embroidering different sections.

Without primary documentation and personal testimony, concrete visual evidence of artistic accommodation and change provides our only insights into the creation of each of these textiles and offers a singular opportunity to evaluate the extent and force of the creative process. According to art historian Jules Prown, "the self-consciousness of artistic expression makes it less neutral as cultural evidence than . . . mundane artifacts."[13] Prown might classify colcha embroidery as a "mundane artifact," but the highly complex process of creative decision-making behind these pieces is reflected in the degree of their artistic expressiveness. Furthermore, as folklorist Henry Glassie points out, the creation of complex artifacts requires equally complex artistic decisions. The art object is the residual product of compound solutions to different design options.[14]

It is through our perceptions and analyses of art that we gain access to an understanding of the range of artistic possibility and the sense of a "particular mind in operation." By means of the empathetic analytical act, we acquire a "cultural understanding by imaginatively becoming the maker of the object being studied, the poet of the poem, the potter of the pot. Objects read as the tangible record of vanished consciousness . . . [allow] the readers to reproduce [them] by [repeating] all the decisions the original designer had to make in order to create [them]."[15]

## Colcha Entanglements

Such analyses of artistic processes based on viewers' perceptions appear to be less problematic than are recent attempts to create a definitive terminology for colcha making. In fact, curator Nora Fisher explicitly claims the term "colcha" is "emotionally charged," "beyond definition," and recommends using it primarily as a modifier and adjective: e.g., colcha stitch and colcha embroidery.[16] In common usage, however, the label colcha is often applied interchangeably to both stitch and textile. Nora Fisher's precursor in colcha scholarship, E. Boyd, distinguished between the Spanish word *colcha* and its practical application throughout the frontiers of New Spain: "The Spanish word *colcha* signifies a quilt or bedcover, but the New Mexican colcha is not a quilt in the sense of being a cover filled with inner material and tacked or quilted. . . . Such a quilt in New Mexico is called a *colchon* [usually a mattress]."[17]

The colcha stitch itself is a type of self-couching stitch that is anchored to the ground fabric by a smaller stitch running almost perpendicular to it. Consequently, when a series of these crossover stitches are repeated in rows or clusters, they produce an interesting secondary aesthetic effect, subsidiary to the dominant design. These sequences of consecutive anchoring stitches actually create an internal textural pattern distinct from the larger visual patterns of the total composition (see fig. 2).

Since the same stitch has been disseminated through time and space under a variety of names (Romanian couching, Oriental stitch, convent stitch, figure stitch, Deerfield stitch, Bokhara couching, the lazy stitch), its universality attests to its adaptability and to the numerous advantages associated with it. Among these are: efficiency, variable length of stitches depending on the type of thread or yarn used (cotton, silk, wool), its ability to cover large areas thus economizing on yarn, its ability to move in any direction, curving and undulating in concert with the aesthetic demands of certain patterns, plus the striking subtle shading and textural effects that are the hallmark of colcha embroidered tapestries (fig. 2).

The identification of the colcha stitch is often the key to establishing legitimacy or registering the "line of descent." This is true today when individuals like Josie Lobato, involved in contemporary revitalization projects, employ the colcha label as a kind of "colloquial" verification of its status within a chain of historical consequence. The classification is used as a determinant to confirm that an embroidery (and its subsequent progeny) is indeed a colcha. In some instances the appearance of the colcha stitch as an eloquent indicator of authenticity signifies a type of genetic correspondence among textiles of diverse origins, as in the possible relationships between northern Rio Grande colchas and Chinese silk embroideries or seventeenth- and eighteenth-century Iberian textiles from eastern Portugal,[18] which will be discussed later. The appearance, knowledge, and use of this particular stitch, then, provides evidence of a technical linkage between conceivable prototypes and various colonial or postcolonial colchas.

By extension, the complete *absence* of the colcha stitch in Spanish and Mexican embroideries also confounds scholarly expectations of artifactual connection between Rio Grande Southwestern colchas and what should be their immediate stylistic antecedents, textiles of Spain and Mexico. In addition to issues of contemporaneity, these expectations are probably predicated on beliefs in the far-reaching imposition of Spanish cultural hegemony or in the logical northern extension of Mexican artistic influence. The appearance of the colcha stitch on New Mexican textiles, however, signals the extent of autonomous artistic choice and the impact of diverse and migratory influences on frontier societies still "bafflingly alike and different from the parent culture."[19]

During the colonial era, colcha tapestries symbolized tangible symbolic lifelines to Spanish culture. Items such as embroidered colchas, which appear as luxuries offsetting the harshness of life on the distant boundaries of the empire,

> are endowed with special significance as *cultural necessities*, that is objects which appear superficial but nonetheless carry great symbolic weight. Such objects are clues to the artist's or owner's opinion of what is valuable, beautiful and worthy of protection or sacrifice. In New Mexico, such "necessities" are guideposts to those elements of Spanish, Catholic culture which had to be maintained in order to assure the *colonists'* emotional connection with the civilization from which they had come.[20]

Thus in the mindset of the early frontier days, art objects from Spain or central Mexico (those specifically associated with European influence) were revered as emblems of status and considered of great value in maintaining some aura of an extension or outreach of elegant Spanish society. Colonial colchas were an indigenous artistic response that symbolically alluded to European culture through a native style and local materials. Thus their appearance, use, and function register the impact of transition from a parent culture to another—fueled by the desire to validate the bond. Colchas as relics of regeneration (a new life in a new place with a semblance of the old) echo Josie Lobato's embroideries in theme and in the way her work helped her adjust to feelings of dislocation. Josie creates her pieces to represent the themes and consequences of transition while virtually clinging to the creative process as a lifeline to the community she left years before. Similarly, the historical colchas may have served as emotional or psychological buffers against the frontier experience of strangeness and isolation, loss of connection to the homeland, and displacement. These textiles of exile, then, are sites of predicament and promise. For, in the words of Simone Weil, "To be rooted is perhaps the most important and least recognized need of the human soul."[21]

In their efforts to replicate materially certain aspects of life in Europe, settlers continued their importation of Spanish luxury items throughout the colonial era. This trade was still insufficient to provide the volume of goods demanded by the settlers on the northern borders. This lack of availability probably contributed to the accrued preciousness of the imported Chinese shawls, resulting in their subsequent appearance as treasured items decorating colonial altars in New Mexico and Colorado.

In addition to commercial avenues, personal collections of valuable possessions including luxury items from dowries or trousseaus were another means by which prototypical art works, especially textiles, arrived in colonial territory. Some cherished remnants of a dowry traveling to New Mexico from the Old World could have originated in textile workshops on the Iberian peninsula. In Portugal, even today, there is a genre of workshop embroideries still popularly referred to as *colchas*.

Although the Spanish word *colcha* means coverlet, bedspread, or quilt, its use as a label for these Indo-Portuguese embroideries is conjoined with the presence of a couching stitch similar to the colcha stitch of New Spain.[22] Despite E. Boyd's claim that "no Spanish or Mexican antecedents were found for Rio Grande Hispanic colcha embroidery," Portuguese textiles resembling New Mexican embroideries in design and technique were created on the Spanish-Portuguese border throughout the colonial era, especially from the sixteenth through the eighteenth century. Furthermore, for part of that time Portugal was politically dominated by Spain.

Consequently, with reference to origin, I prefer to allude to a general Iberian influence. My preference implies a process of cultural transmission not necessarily emanating directly from Spain, but traveling through Spanish channels. These channels could be domestic or commercial; for instance, trading networks or migrations of New World colonists transporting a few of these textiles as part of their own domestic cargoes.[23]

I stress the phenomenon of the domestic carrier because no Portuguese embroidery has been found in New Mexico or Colorado museum collections.[24] If these pieces appeared on the frontier, it was probably a sporadic occurrence, most definitely a private one. Evidently, they were passed on within families rather than into public collections. But if only a handful of these textiles (or memories of them) reached the Spanish empire's remote boundaries, their presence could suffice to stimulate some degree of creative adaptation of native materials to European prototypes, and in this way invigorate the few artistic traditions already in place.

The Indo-Portuguese textiles were created by Indian artisans or Portuguese embroiderers living either in Portugal or in her seaports, from Goa to Malacca. Within Portugal, the Castelo Branco area near Spain has been the most active site of embroidery workshops, from the seventeenth century until their recent twentieth-century metamorphosis into a network of viable cottage industries.

These polychromatic coverlets are embroidered over their entire surface in designs comprising fields of intricately arranged motifs. Some are classically derived depictions of rinceaux or curvilinear vines, exotic birds, floral elements, and trees of life. Other embroideries include heraldic symbols such as addorsed stags and double-headed eagles with heart-shaped breasts. The latter are often associated with Hapsburg medallions and are also found on Mexican embroideries and Rio Grande Hispanic colchas. In addition, inanimate objects such as urns and undulating ribbons abound, enlivening and unifying various pictorial elements into a cohesive composition.

Interpretations of colcha origins based on a stylistic correspondence between motifs and design patterns attribute the source of the predominantly floral compositions of Rio Grande pieces to East Indian chintzes (known as *pintados* in Portugal and as *indianas* or *indianillas* in New Mexico). Indian trade fabrics were noted for their fluid handpainted designs of paradise motifs representing the tree of life, butterflies, flowers, and tropical birds, either free-floating or clinging to the tendrils and curling leaves of meandering vines or rinceaux.

These patterns are often associated with antique classical and Near Eastern design motifs, and reached India via the spread of Islam. They were then recirculated and disseminated to Europe through various trade networks, including the Indo-Portuguese textile manufacturing workshops, particularly those located on the Iberian peninsula. Stylistic variants of these motifs were already in place in Spanish and Portuguese art as a result of the ancient Roman presence and vestiges of the Muslim occupation originating with the eighth-century arrival of the Arabs. Thus, direct contacts with Arabic culture provided another channel for the influx of Near Eastern art forms into the Iberian peninsula. This produced the hybrid Hispano-Mauresque or *mudejar* style, initially associated with Spain and eventually transmitted to her colonies. Spanish-Moorish tradition also became the distinctive sign of New Mexican culture.

Trade fabrics manufactured in India flowed into both Portugal and the New World. Thus, Indian chintzes may have influenced both spheres.[25] The "chicken-or-the-egg" nature of this argument is not as important as the recognition of the complexities of cultural transmission, interconnection, and cross-fertilization with regard to artistic influence, receptivity, and source.

The Colorado Historical Society owns a pair of wool-on-wool colcha bedspreads, approximately two meters in length by one-and-a-quarter meters. They date to the second half of the nineteenth century. One is located at El Pueblo Museum in Pueblo, Colorado. The other is Josie Lobato's "guide" in the Fort Garland collection in the San Luis Valley. Both are made of handspun, naturally dyed wool embroidered on *sabanilla*. The red embroidery yarn, however, is probably synthetically dyed wool unraveled from a trade blanket or yard goods. Red was a special color and doubly precious because of scarcity, hence its recycled origin.

The expansive designs of curvilinear floral motifs interspersed with enlarged paisley-like leaves on both colchas are reminiscent of the stylistic repertoire associated with Indian chintz fabrics and Portuguese Castelo Branco embroidered coverlets. With the exception of the large red zigzag twisting down the center of the Fort Garland example, the dominant iconography of paradisiacal imagery (branches from the tree of life surrounded by fertile vines bearing buds and flowers) symbolizes immortality and fecundity. These floral icons provided a vitally important symbolic program for an agrarian frontier society, which not only valued but depended upon procreation in terms of descendants and prolific crops. In turn, this imagery also represented and underscored stylistic links to Iberian and Asian prototypes.

The design elements on these northern Rio Grande colchas, however, lack the degree of refinement, density, complexity, and intricate ornamentation characterizing prototypical textiles from Europe and India. Of course, the limitations of working only in wool rather than silk thread, modified by a restricted palette of natural colors, would have resulted in larger, simpler design shapes characterized by less detail with more space separating figural arrangements.

**Colchas as Cultural Lifelines**

From 1750 to approximately 1850, the emergence of Rio Grande colcha embroidery as a "naturalized" art form not only depended on the remote location of its New World birthplace coupled with waning Spanish-Mexican influence, but was also the result of an internal, native artistic stimulation and cultural reciprocity. Colchas as emblems of a regional culture evolved out of a type of localized artistic interdependence that arose from the basic ordeal of frontier experience. Consequently, in style and materials colonial colchas represent the intersection of external and internal artistic forces ultimately shaped by the frontier stitcher's resourcefulness and ingenuity.

On the Fort Garland colcha the angular geometric figures meandering amidst a field of softly curvilinear shapes (vestiges of European influence) could represent a stylistic referent to a regional variant of an abstract Saltillo-style design element popular in local contemporary Rio Grande Hispanic weaving. The presence of this solitary lightning-like geometrical figure probably indicates mutual influence, inspiration, and exchange among frontier weavers and embroiderers. As such, it also signifies an element within a vocabulary of mutable and adaptive stylistic components generating the ongoing and self-perpetuating "internal artistic dialogue" of the upper Rio Grande Valley of northern New Mexico.

Colonial colchas ultimately eclipsed their European antecedents as luxury items. The type of wool-on-wool colchas described above became material symbols of wealth and status. They were especially coveted by the affluent class of New Mexico society, largely composed of European Spaniards or *criollos* (native born) from Mexico City. Occasionally, marketable colchas were listed in inventories of goods passing along the well-traveled southern trade route into Mexico, the Santa Fe–Chihuahua Trail.

In a lawsuit involving the estate of one of these *ricos,* Joseph de Reano II, a "quilt decorated with colcha embroidery" was listed among the inventory being contested by his widow.[26] The date of the invoice is 1756, which is the earliest documented mention of a colonial colcha.[27] The *Will of Juan Antonio Suaso,* dated April 26, 1818, details the distribution of everything from corrals and hayracks to a chocolate pot, bedding, and "one colcha."[28]

As status objects, elaborately carved colonial bedsteads dominated domestic and social space. They were used for honored guests, bridal couples, receiving visitors during a mother's lying-in, and to support a corpse while the wake was celebrated prior to the funeral mass. One can imagine that colchas, with their luxurious appearance and prolific imagery relating to paradise, fecundity, and the afterlife, would be appropriate furnishings for these beds. Furthermore, many of these same images, particularly intertwined buds and blooming flowers, were also symbolic of the Virgin's fertility and maternity. Their presence on bedcovers reflected the spirit of folk or familial Catholicism so evident in the attitude behind domestic display which permeated all levels of spiritual practice in this region.

Many of the colchas under investigation here were patched with scraps of *jerga* or, as in the case of wool-on-cotton colchas, pieces of twill or khaki military cloth.[29] Sometimes this work is so subtle that it is barely noticeable. In other instances the patching techniques are crude, the result of haste and expediency. Nevertheless, mending reinforces the idea of the singular quality and preciousness of these textiles. It underscores their endurance and conservation through time and effort. Patches are also indicative of the concept of the "past manifest in the present." They represent the idea of a dialogue continuing over time between creator, repairer, and user through the reconstruction as it was carried out and as it is imagined through the latter-day beholder's artistic and perceptual experience.

Given the presence of colchas in the households of the *ricos* and the fact that they were highly time-consuming and labor-intensive to create, we can also assume that women of this class, with the help of their American Indian servants (*criadas*), generally embroidered during leisure moments. Possibly, some of the inconsistencies noted in colcha compositions (e.g., unbalanced designs, asymmetrical elements, the visible differences in technique and skill level, etc.) might be attributed to children occasionally joining in the stitching. In contrast to the *ricos*, other working women involved in a ceaseless round of daily chores without servants and with spare time only in the evening hours apparently embroidered only intermittently.

Another constraint on production time was the limited amount of daylight hours or natural light available in which to stitch. Glazed windows were a late development, and dim lamplight was unsatisfactory for detailed work such as embroidery. Stitchers in Villanueva, New Mexico, mentioned the difficulty of embroidering at night even in modern times. During interviews with stitchers as recently as 1975, Isidora Madrid de Flores laughingly recalled embroidering late one night only to discover in the morning that she had stitched green feet on a white dove because of inadequate lighting.[30]

## Wool-on-cotton Colcha Embroidery

In the second half of the nineteenth century, political and economic factors altered the style and appearance of Rio Grande colchas. The wool-on-wool pieces created largely from hand-worked materials were replaced by pieces of factory cloth embroidered with commercial wool yarn. However, the complex interplay of hand embroidery and commercially produced materials did not inevitably result in the degeneration of artistic expressiveness, as might be assumed. Instead, these materials, wool-on-cotton, inspired an embroidery style different from the wool-on-wool colchas. The new style was characterized by free-floating, predominantly curvilinear designs juxtaposed against bare expanses of tightly-woven cotton ground fabric.[31]

Stylistically, this was the ultimate step in liberating colcha design motifs from the interlocking grid-lines of the supporting woven base. Technically, this step was necessary. The shift to freestanding designs created from brightly colored commercial embroidery yarn resulted from a combination of factors. Delicate handspun fibers would have frayed and split when used on tightly woven twill manufactured cloth. In addition, it was virtually impossible to use commercially plied yarn to fully cover these densely woven ground fabrics. Their compact, solid weave was like armor compared to the loose open structure and pliability of hand-woven sabanilla. The mere physical act of continually punching the needle in and out of these tough twill fabrics until completely covered with stitches would have been frustrating, as well as tiring and difficult.

Stylistic and technical changes were also catalyzed by other events. After Mexican independence in 1821, Spain withdrew from the New World, ending her political hegemony and relinquishing her monopolistic trade practices.[32] At the same time the opening of the Santa Fe Trail from the East as an avenue of commerce and link to Anglo-American cultural influence heralded more change. Finally, by 1850, following the signing of the Treaty of Guadalupe-Hidalgo in 1848, Mexico ceded the northern territories to the United States, thus politically, economically, and culturally emancipating New Mexico from any vestige of Spanish dominion.

An altar cloth from the Taylor Museum dating to the second half of the nineteenth century is a typical wool-on-cotton colcha. Its imagery is based on a constellation of floral motifs and starlike shapes limited to an almost monochromatic color scheme of blue accented with shades of yellow. The general orientation of its design is dependent on its function as an adornment for a rectangular altar. The top panel is outlined by an intermittent border of flowers and stems, which surrounds a pair of birds facing outward. Floating leaflike forms interspersed with stars enliven the sides, which would normally cover the altar front.

Evidently, there was a reciprocal influence between the designs embroidered on altar cloths and those painted on *retablos*—altarpieces or flat boards decorated with sacred imagery.[33] For example, both genres, rendered in a similar flat style, appear to share distinctive floral motifs; e.g., a particular type of tricolored rosette common to altar screens and colchas.

The compositions of wool-on-cotton colchas typify an international style composed of various combinations of vestigial European floral elements accompanied by urns and ribbons, Asian tropical imagery (birds and plants), single and composite designs inspired by native flora and fauna (butterflies, buffalo, deer, wild roses), and motifs from Anglo-American crewel work. This last source, associated with New England craftsmanship, entered the Southwest via trade goods brought over the Santa Fe Trail after 1821. Crewel work's compatibility with wool-on-cotton colchas shares a strong stylistic correspondence based on freestyle designs that were executed in colorful wool yarn upon neutral cotton backgrounds. Moreover, cotton colcha designs incorporated other stitches like the stem and chain as well as the traditional colcha couching stitch. Greater elaboration in stitching vocabulary could have resulted from exposure to the more diverse techniques identified with Anglo-American crewel work.

At its inception, Hispanic culture in the Southwest was initially associated with colonizing forces. Its artistic expressiveness, as in the case of wool-on-wool colchas, was an aesthetic melange of European cultural remains transformed through adaptive, accommodative, and innovative processes into an indigenous art form. Art as representative of frontier cultural attitudes symbolized continuity with the dominant parent culture in terms of hegemonic connection and identification, discontinuity in the incorporation of native materials and influence, and emergence as an entity apart from European influence.

As Spanish authority weakened and ultimately withdrew, New Mexico frontier life became the crucible from which distinctive Southwestern Hispanic cultural forces emerged. Through the practice of internal borrowing and local artistic stimulation a specific native style coalesced, as exemplified by the wool-on-wool colchas. The primary florescence of the colcha style as a product of differentiation and internal development coincided with a period of respite from foreign domination, an interregnum (1820s to 1850s).[34] These often artistically fertile, but temporary, circumstances have been characterized as an "interlude of release" between regimes.[35] Accordingly, these inward-looking periods foster conditions quite favorable for strengthening and promoting a localized or inner artistic dialogue.

Referring to discourse, Mikhail Bakhtin similarly identified the tenor of intervals such as these artistically creative periods as shifts from an "authoritative discourse that is preeminent, powerful . . . the singular voice of political and moral authority" to an "internally persuasive discourse born in a zone of contact." The emergent social or cultural entity "trying to speak in an expressive, formal voice" tends to mute the authoritative voice. In the interim between one such singular voice and the next a particular cultural group appears, "marked by a different kind of awareness and identity."[36]

During the early nineteenth century wool-on-wool colchas were created on the New Mexican frontier within the "zone of contact" between Spanish colonial authority and Southwestern Hispano subordination. Colchas were one of the artistic vehicles that materially registered or manifested a type of ethnic consciousness for Hispanos living in New Mexico. These textiles were differentiated from European models through technical skills and stylistic choices conditioned by the availability and use of certain native materials. In this way, the interpretation of the emergence and development of traditional Rio Grande colchas is analogous to Bakhtin's literary paradigm distinguishing a fertile creative zone between the "authoritative voice" (Spain or Mexico) and the "internally persuasive" voice (localizing factors). As a status symbol and emblem of ethnicity, the wool-on-wool colcha represents the burgeoning autonomy of Hispanic culture in the southwestern United States, one of the means by which Spanish artistic hegemony was progressively subverted during the colonial era.

Wool-on-cotton colchas evolved from their all-wool antecedents. Although linked stylistically, the wool-on-cotton subgroup is the product of creative modification by means of a convergence of strategic, commercially produced materials obtained through an outreach of the Anglo marketplace, the Santa Fe Trail. Despite the temptation to view these colchas as emblematic of a kind of Anglo-American mercantile colonization of Hispanic culture achieved through economic domination, wool-on-cotton embroidered textiles continued to retain the integrity of the Hispanic aesthetic system as outlined above.

By the end of the nineteenth century, however, even the wool-on-cotton subgroup of traditional colchas had been supplanted by the commercialization of other types of less unique or individualistic needlework, such as crochet, quiltmaking, and prestamped embroidery patterns. This move signaled a general fragmentation of artistic cohesion that paralleled the influence of other externalizing factors on Hispanic frontier culture in New Mexico primarily due to Anglo immigration and large-scale trade and land development—all instrumental agents of change. These forces weakened the internal dialogue underpinning the florescence of the nineteenth-century New Mexican art style of which traditional Rio Grande Hispanic colchas were exemplary.

Colchas are articles of imagination as much as they are artifacts of history. They were originally created by Spanish colonial exiles out of a deep need to identify with the parent culture both materially and symbolically. Colcha symbolized a cultural necessity largely engendered by distance from the European homeland and by a greater sense of loss and displacement. The role of colcha as a cultural indicator reveals the gradual weakening of Spanish colonial ties offset by the critical need for continual artistic innovation and adaptation to alleviate the overwhelming isolation of living on the frontier zone. The colcha aesthetic character, therefore, is more a consequence of hybridization than the result of a direct link to specific prototypes issuing from Spanish territory.

Technical correspondences relate colcha stitchery to Chinese shawls and Indo-Portuguese textiles. Iconographically, these fabrics along with Spanish and Mexican ecclesiastical and domestic embroideries suggest a kind of stylistic kinship with colonial colcha embroidery based on the dissemination of vestiges of Euro-Asian design forms. None are worked entirely in wool, nor are any totally and distinctively covered by couching stitches—with the exception of the Portuguese silk coverlets.

There is an interesting correspondence between Josie Lobato's embroideries and those of colonial colcha makers. Both initially responded to external inspiration. However, through a process of localization of materials and iconography, the frontier embroideries ultimately became artistically conditioned by an "internal artistic dialogue," thereby assuming an autonomous cultural identity in the face of Spanish political and aesthetic dominance.

Similarly, Josie created her first embroidery, *Old Fort Garland,* in response to the externally promoted localized and marketable version of colcha. By the time she started her next embroidery, *Mis Crismes,* she had already appropriated the colcha medium in terms of her own creative expressiveness, which she interpreted through a specific lexicon of personal and cultural imagery. Josie's contemporary colchas and the historical Hispanic embroideries were originally shaped by outside influences that were ultimately inverted by an internal aesthetic system itself determined by native or personalizing forces.

Colcha embroideries are unique and aesthetically rich textiles resulting from an era when frontier sensibility sought a visual expressiveness conditioned by cultural memory and inspired by the poetics of independence—a time of waning European influence and increasing local artistic development. Colchas are an extraordinary materialization of colonial artifacts without specific traceable or identifiable links to Spain, the colonial parent society. Despite this contradiction, colcha embroidery, with its symbolic referents to European precedents and its striking visual appearance, over time became the yardstick to determine Hispanic cultural legitimacy throughout the twentieth century whenever revitalization of Hispano folk art occurred.

With reference to the verities of artistic transmission, the collective "forgetting" of colcha's origin and purpose also caused some twentieth-century traders and stitchers to regard these pieces as authentic Spanish embroideries created hundreds of years before on the Iberian Peninsula. During an interview in 1991, stitcher Frances Graves from Carson, New Mexico, reiterated several times that the nineteenth-century colchas she repaired in the 1930s "were supposed to come from Spain," and later, "they claim the originals came from Spain."[37] Thus, her interpretation imaginatively leapfrogged over the notion of colonial progeny to authenticate the parent culture itself.

Reconsidering the attitude toward the "Spanish enigma" in the correspondence cited earlier between Wilder and Schweitzer, colcha scholarship is most productive when it examines cultural forces embedded in all aspects of artistic creation and choice. These include the relationship between the necessary desire for legitimacy and the reality of authentication, cultural inversion, inspired ingenuity, the collective practices of remembrance and forgetting, and above all, the degrees of perpetuating tradition subtly conditioned by change.

# 4

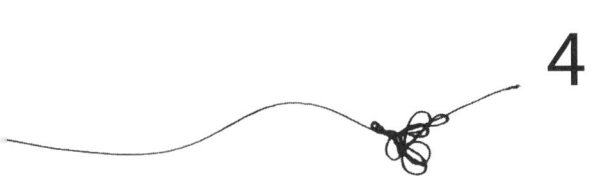

## embroidery revivals

You know it was fun. It was like a blessing. It's amazing how God helps you, those that help themselves. And we have this [tapestry] to show that it's the truth—and we did it.

—Isidora Madrid de Flores

In 1777 Father Morfí criticized the act of tithing to New Mexico churches in the name of the Bishop of Durango, who presided over the religious state of the colony from his bishopric in Mexico. Father Morfí argued that revenues from tithing provided generous profits for the Spanish nobility that collected them without directly benefiting those who were taxed. Instead of supporting the colonial oligarchy, Father Morfí recommended that tithe collection be allocated locally to encourage regional industries in weaving, carpentry, and hat making. He felt these crafts combined with a diversified marketing system would help offset New Mexico's economic malaise.[1]

With minor variations, this same theme has persisted intermittently in New Mexico and southern Colorado for more than two hundred years—i.e., economic recovery through art or skilled crafts training accompanied by the marketing of handwork and cultural artifacts. Generally, benefactors like Father Morfí are enlightened outsiders dedicated to improving village life through schemes that rest on the continuance of native traditions and the presumption that villagers are talented craftspeople naturally adept at handwork (clever, self-sufficient tradition-keepers). Throughout the twentieth century, entrepreneurs and craft workshop facilitators also assumed that village artists were cognizant and proud of their cultural identity and its attendant value system, while Hispanos countered by measuring the merits of different craft programs against their own needs. Assumptions made by a few on behalf of the often voiceless were supported, tested, rejected, or ignored in countless ways typical of centuries of interactions between patrons and artists.

Always susceptible to individual purpose and changing contexts, tradition is one of those mutable concepts that is constant or elastic depending on who is wielding it at the moment. Without this word cited on the agenda of revitalization or reform programs, it is impossible even to invoke the notion of revival. This chapter is concerned with twentieth-century activities surrounding colcha embroidery revitalization, which could more accurately be considered "vitalization" since frequently the form in which it was being revived had not existed previously within those particular contexts. The idea of what constituted traditional Hispanic needlework was much contested by those who maintained that they were cultivating extant Spanish styles and by stitchers who were caught up in the pleasures of handwork and were equally enthralled with creating tea towels or pictorial narratives. Artist-teachers such as Carmen Orrego-Salas, who conducted many embroidery workshops in the San Luis Valley, emphasized the creative act over the weight of tradition and cautioned stitchers to avoid the "ruts in mere replication." Orrego-Salas considered lively innovations based on tradition marketable as well: "You can kill a tradition by continuing it [blindly]. Why not start something else that can infuse the embroidery with life and help economically? If they are good, they can be sold."[2]

Whether tradition is revered or altered, revitalization movements are powerful ways in which the past emerges in the present. As mentioned in our discussion of traditional colchas, on various occasions when the old pieces are examined and appreciated, elements in the past are actuated through the "very act of scrutiny and analysis." Individual entrepreneurs and embroidery workshop leaders expressed their understanding of this phenomenon differently. Although they implicitly acknowledged traces of the past embedded within the present, they emphasized and promoted their concept of the power of past history as a rationale for contemporary revitalization efforts. For example, training in the techniques and marketing of handcrafts such as spinning, weaving, embroidery, and pottery where these have historical associations can invigorate and extend the possibilities of the present as one of the outcomes of revival projects. According to Hermann Bausinger, the "past is not an excuse to turn one's back on the present, but rather a source of revitalisation and refreshment."[3]

The traditional Rio Grande colcha was symbolically linked to Spanish culture as its progenitor. It was also created out of the New Mexico frontier experience as a concrete aesthetic response to the colonial cultural and economic environment. Although a hiatus intervened between colcha as a domestically created nineteenth-century art object and its appearance within the public arena of twentieth-century revival movements, colcha embroidery's "substantive content" (those reverential elements linked to social identity) helped establish its viability and importance as an ethnic icon. For entrepreneurs and artists alike, colcha symbolically embodied notions of Spanish heritage, the aesthetic system of the Southwestern frontier, and the exoticism of a distinct ethnic enclave surviving within the dominant Anglo-American society.

Once an understanding of tradition has been recognized as a benchmark in the revitalizing process, then the reintroduction of an art form is predicated on its plasticity and capacity to accommodate adjustment. In such cases the extent to which a craft can be successfully transformed into a timely artistic expression depends on its capacity to be "retrospectively reformed by human beings living in the present."[4] Artifacts tend to be altered through the very act of revival. It is the nature and degree of that alteration, conditioned by the impact of external and internal cultural agents, that really concerns us.

The following sections discuss the different revitalization efforts that arose in New Mexico and southern Colorado during the early years of the twentieth century. Their existence was the result of a series of aesthetic interventions through private and government programs whose social consequences and historical effects ultimately influenced the San Luis Valley projects of the 1970s and 1980s. Informing and motivating these movements was a set of philanthropic concepts influenced by outsiders' concern for cultural preservation, their encouragement of ethnic artists, and the promulgation of Anglo value judgments through "enlightened" social mediation. Underpinning all these tenets was a firm belief in the economic viability of Hispanic arts.

The previous chapter indicated that embroidery skills in general persisted into the twentieth century, but in most instances the specific art form of the colonial colcha did not. Therefore, basing their conceptions of colcha embroidery on extant colonial pieces, the revival efforts of such organizations as the Spanish Colonial Arts Society in the 1920s and the subsequent state and federal projects of the 1930s were rather conservative and limited. With the exception of the Carson colcha group (an internally generated movement), it was not until the second half of the twentieth century that the colcha medium was radically changed into the pictorial narrative format. During the early period that preceded this transformation, colcha was basically a faithful reconstruction of traditional embroidered textile composition and techniques. Consequently, because of the careful imitative processes associated with these revivals, at times it is difficult to distinguish between revitalized colcha styles from this period and some historical examples (particularly wool-on-cotton specimens).

## Spanish Colonial Arts Society

The founding of the Spanish Colonial Arts Society in 1925, followed by the establishment of its commercial arm, the Colonial Arts Shop, and then by the latter's replacement by the Native Market in 1934—all represent a marketplace theater in which various levels of commercial and artistic endeavors were enacted. Mary Austin and Frank Applegate, two members of a group of artists, writers, and patrons originally attracted to Santa Fe, New Mexico, in the early twentieth century, were the prime instigators of the Hispanic craft revival. Austin's contribution has been described by the New Mexico writer Roland Dickey as fueled by the "fire of an old fashioned Methodist revival."[5] Due to the combination of aesthetics and benevolence, a kind of evangelical tone often attached itself to these craft revival movements. Actually, the mere use of the term "revival" implies shades of religious ardor stemming from thoughts of reawakening, conversion, and redemption (salvation through hard work).

Some of Mary Austin's zeal surfaced as a form of separatism emphasizing the cultural difference and destiny of the Hispanic artisan: "Why ask them to become average installment plan Americans, socially and intellectually inferior to standardized Anglo labor, when they can be highly individualized artist-craftsmen?" Assessing the critical role of the Spanish Colonial Arts Society as cultural agent, reformer, and omniscient parent, Austin concluded, "It is for us to make the most sympathetic, happiest, and so effective, use of them [the Hispanic artists]."[6]

Another Spanish Colonial Arts Society member, Leonora Curtin Paloheimo, also sought to combine marketing, craft demonstrations, and a reverence for tradition in the Native Market. This enterprise was subsidized by Miss Curtin and replaced the shop of the Spanish Colonial Arts Society. It existed from 1934 to 1940. During an interview, Leonora Curtin remembered how the idea of a comprehensive craft revival first aroused her interest. Even her words have an evangelical ring to them: "My enthusiasm rose quickly as the numerous possibilities unfolded, and ever mindful of the advantages in self respect that earning power offers over charitable or government aid, I made bold to speak out; I talked craft revival, teaching, marketing and every aspect to all who would listen."[7]

Although she employed a specific set of aesthetic criteria to monitor authenticity in terms of certain styles restricted to natural native materials and techniques, Leonora Curtin also encouraged the adaptation of colonial designs to fit modern demands. Consequently, colcha embroidery created in a traditional manner was modified to decorate pillows, upholstery, table furnishings, and draperies, just as it had during the colonial era. A few of these uses were slightly innovative, but the basic alliance of domestic ornamentation and utilitarian functions tended to replicate colcha's historical role in colonial interior decoration.

However, the Society's interests, implicit in the entrepreneurial opinions of the Native Market, continued to allow only a limited range of artistic invention. Any alterations were ultimately subject to the external conservatism of the marketplace. In her description of the Portal Case involving the issue of authenticity in relation to contemporary Native American jewelry, Deirdre Evans-Pritchard argues that the dictatorial role assumed by the marketplace in monitoring tradition for commercial purposes supersedes the function usually assigned to the historic culture-bearer as an agent of conservation.[8] Analogously, the Native Market of the 1930s, through selective practices of aesthetic arbitration, eschewed embroideries that were not constructed of natural handmade materials nor restricted to a carefully coordinated palette of native dyes. Innovation and change were not considered. It was as if both technically and stylistically colchas and their creators were cast in amber. They had to remain static to remain authentic.

But this was not to be the final analysis. Because of its fluid, plastic nature, post-loom decoration such as embroidery is more susceptible to individualistic impulse and free invention than many other types of textile creation. Since colcha compositional design was not entirely subject to its function, the revival textiles embody the beginnings of the liberation of colcha embroidery from a primarily utilitarian sphere into the realm of decorative art. This development marks a transition that will eventually characterize colcha revitalization in the 1970s and 1980s. The early efforts of the Spanish Colonial Arts Society and the Native Market to monitor authentic artistic expression in terms of contemporary taste led to the valuing of colcha as more than a domestic item. Its popular enshrinement as an emblem of Spanish heritage and legitimacy was finally complete when colcha was framed and openly hung on walls, as in Villanueva, New Mexico, in 1976 and more recently in San Luis, Colorado.

In 1965 the Spanish Market was revived by E. Boyd, historian and scholar, under the aegis of the Spanish Colonial Arts Society, which she had reinstated in 1952. It is still held in Santa Fe every summer. Promoters and jurors continue to judge authenticity and to impose limitations in its name. In 1991 when I interviewed Shirley Ortega, a Colorado embroiderer from Alamosa, located near the center of the San Luis Valley, she expressed her irritation at some of the reactionary policies determining the acceptance or rejection of colcha artists vis-à-vis the Spanish Market. She commented on restrictions pertaining to (traditional) color choice but was particularly unhappy with the idea that New Mexico was considered "Spanish" territory while Colorado was not. Historically, the San Luis Valley, through which the headwaters of the Rio Grande river flow, constituted the northern boundaries of the New Mexico frontier zone (dating back to Juan de Oñate's 1598 proclamation in the name of Philip II of Spain). Furthermore, most Hispanos living in southern Colorado are descendants or relatives of New Mexico families. Thus, Shirley Ortega is remonstrating that the use of a state boundary to demarcate the extent of Spanish heritage in an area in which residents are so heavily interrelated seems rather arbitrary and artificial.[9]

Shirley Ortega's reaction delves even deeper into the power relationship between the marketplace and the artist. By not being recognized or being left out of the arena of legitimacy, her work, along with that of other artists who share her predicament, is met with a kind of silence that tends to erase the existence of contemporary colcha embroiderers who do not fit within established parameters. Ironically, their creative vitality is sapped or its purposefulness eroded by reverberations still emanating from well-intentioned craft projects established years before to benefit their Hispanic artistic forebears. These projects, then, assume a complex position of power brokerage when artistic expressiveness is governed by the potential marketability of an art work in proportion to its putative authenticity.

## Local and Government Revitalization Projects

During the 1920s and 1930s there were several craft revival programs. With motives similar to Leonora Curtin's belief in the restorative power of earning a living through craft production and sales, the federal and state governments sponsored relief projects in Hispanic villages to combat poverty and attrition. They hoped to supplement waning agricultural activities with self-sustaining arts and crafts cottage industries to offset the effects of the 1930s Depression. The National Youth Administration, the Works Progress Administration, the Agricultural Extension, and the Smith-Hughes Vocational Training agencies provided funds and personnel for crafts education, training, and marketing in the villages of southern Colorado (particularly Las Animas, Costilla, and Archuleta counties), and in the twenty-four New Mexico communities located mostly in the northern Hispanic regions of the state.[10]

In 1933 the New Mexico State Department of Vocational Education (SDVE) also established a network of training schools in Spanish colonial arts throughout northern New Mexico. The director of this enterprise, Brice Sewell, recalling certain antimodernist sentiments, privileged nostalgia for hand crafts over industrial machine-made products. He advocated an agenda similar to that of the Spanish Colonial Arts Society concerning the marketability of handmade cultural objects: "students must be thoroughly grounded in the knowledge of the best examples of the past, particularly the Spanish Colonial, and the finished product must be superior in beauty and durability to the machine-made product."[11] The vocational programs not only agreed with the Society's ideological stance but also provided skilled artisans and inventory for the Native Market and other retail outlets.

Series of SDVE instruction manuals, Trade and Industrial Bulletins (Bluebooks), were mimeographed and distributed to craft teachers and their students in vocational schools. The contents of one bulletin in this series specifically relate to colcha embroidery. The hand-drawn designs and commentary were based on extant colchas from the collections of Carmen Espinosa and Leonora Curtin. As editor of these bulletins, Carmen Espinosa carefully researched historical backgrounds, explained technology, and drew diagrams inspired by compositions and designs from traditional textiles. In the colcha manual the composite drawings and instruction patterns composed of combinations of tri-lobed leaves, zoomorphic creatures, meandering vines, and floral strips clearly derive from the imagery of traditional colonial colchas, especially the wool-on-cotton style.

Carmen Espinosa's diagram of the embroidery stitch used in colcha making is technically correct. However, her term "colcha knot stitch" is a misnomer (see fig. 1). This was the result of a common misconception at the time of the 1930s craft revivals, that the execution of the colcha stitch entailed creating knots—an impression derived from appearance rather than from the actual construction.

There were other constructive influences during this period. Carmen Espinosa's retrieval of authentic designs, and Nellie Dunton's book *Spanish Colonial Ornament* dating from the same period, also inspired contemporary stitching groups like El Arte Antiguo. The founding of this sewing circle was not the consequence of external forces intervening on behalf of economic necessity but was internally motivated. El Arte Antiguo was started by Hispanic women living in the Española area and continues with some of the original members today. From its inception the group's meetings have been characterized by fellowship and love of sewing. As an informal rite and acknowledgment of competence based on skill, commitment, and accomplishment, the original twelve members were required to embroider bedspreads of identical designs. In a newspaper article dating from 1987, Aggie Serna lamented that it took her four years to complete her bedspread: "You don't make one of these in a day."[12]

Much of their contemporary work, however, has been created from commercial materials according to their own tastes, usually brightly colored interpretations of traditional motifs. Because El Arte Antiguo was internally motivated and generally inner-directed, its members had greater freedom in reinterpreting colonial colchas and in ignoring marketplace restrictions than members of other concurrent federally or state funded needlework revival groups.

For a while El Arte Antiguo exhibited and sold their embroideries at the revived Spanish Market. They conformed to the rules by making the requisite concession to natural materials and dyes. Nevertheless, they were reluctant to sell works that held personal meanings and attachments, so some members resorted to a type of retailer's subterfuge in order to keep their colchas. "We don't have much to sell—we don't want to sell what we have left," said Serna in the same news article. Once at the Market she decided to overprice her embroideries to discourage customers. She priced one piece at "a stiff one hundred dollars, not expecting it to sell. But sell it did."[13]

With the exception of women from such an egalitarian indigenous movement as El Arte Antiguo, Hispanos like Carmen Espinosa (who was also connected with El Arte Antiguo) and Nina Otero-Warren frequently played major catalytic roles in the more mainstream, Anglo-dominated cultural revivals of the 1930s. Within that context they acted as intermediaries between Anglo patrons of the arts and Hispanic artisans. Their role is generally interpreted by scholars today in terms of representing class distinctions rather than ethnicity, a stance that informs the work of Deutsch and Forrest. Sarah Deutsch claims that Hispanic upper-class women, motivated by a tradition of *noblesse oblige,* shared with their Anglo counterparts a condescending attitude toward villagers not of the elite class. Furthermore, as outsiders, both Anglo and Hispanic patrons used the arts to "render the villages closer to the romantic vision they wanted the Hispanic culture to fulfill."[14]

The themes of cultural mediation and romanticism are echoed in Suzanne Forrest's analysis of the relationship between Hispanic villager and patron:

> Upper class Hispanos, while not entirely exempt from prejudicial treatment by Anglo Americans, maintained such a strong feeling of class status that they did not identify with lower class villagers. Instead, acting and thinking like the patrons of an earlier day, they, like Nina Otero-Warren, saw themselves as power and culture brokers, mediating between the villagers and Anglo reformers, whose romantic aims and goals they accepted as their own.[15]

In his study of cultural revitalization in southern Appalachia, David Whisnant identified the dynamics of hierarchy intertwined with issues of class and society as "cultural politics." Whisnant believed that in order to understand any culturally enclaved area within a larger pluralistic but essentially assimilationist social system, one must inevitably talk about the politics of culture.[16] Although concerns with ethnicity are missing from Whisnant's analysis, the overarching theme of cultural politics has the right ring when applied to the sequential craft revivals of the Hispanic Southwest from the 1930s through the 1980s.

Within the context of revitalization, we can regard colcha making as an arena in which an intricate set of relationships between elite individuals identified with a dominant society and members of subordinate village communities exercise active and passive power. Regardless of class, most Hispanic women could appreciate the artistic nature and decorative possibilities of embroidery in terms of both familiarity and practice. But how did village women regard educated upper-class Hispanic women acting in league with Anglo entrepreneurs as the legitimate interpreters or guardians of local culture? Within the parameters of village experience, how attractive was the Hispanic *patrona*'s promotion of an agenda extolling redemption (self-respect via economic opportunity) through handwork? Furthermore, how meaningful to the average villager was the particular alignment of colcha aesthetics with symbolically correct cultural associations, i.e., the mapping of authentic elements onto visual expression (as promulgated by these same craft promoters)?

Due to its relative autonomy, El Arte Antiguo was able to bypass these issues most of the time. However, villages targeted for economic development by external agencies had to contend with this agenda on many levels, from the artistic/aesthetic to the social/cultural. Personal responses to these questions were embedded in people's heads and hearts and have disappeared with the passage of time and the absence of their voices. But similar inner feelings may be reflected in the actions and attitudes of women still involved in colcha revitalization programs. In the summer of 1991 I went to Villanueva, New Mexico, because I suspected that such a place, where revitalizing efforts in the mid-1970s centered upon the communal creation of an impressive embroidered tapestry for the local church, might provide some information relating to issues of ethnicity and class and "ownership" of traditional with respect to change.

Aspects of the Villanueva project are similar to the 1930s government programs, but due to village solidarity and a strong group identity, it has more in common with El Arte Antiguo and the San Luis Ladies Sewing Circle in Colorado than with the earlier state enterprises. However, the complex internal issues relating to villagers and *patronas*, especially with regard to the role of Carmen Orrego-Salas (who worked with most of the later revival projects from the 1970s on), will be extensively examined when I explore the San Luis Ladies Sewing Circle in later chapters.

## The Carson Colcha Revival

Before I describe some of the findings from my field research in Villanueva, it is important to make a slight detour in time and space to examine the colcha movement that was originally identified with the community of Carson, New Mexico during the 1930s. This group of colcha makers predates El Arte Antiguo as well as Villanueva. Furthermore, a study of Carson colchas indicates just how variable the circumstances, technology, thematic material, and motives of colcha production can be. This locally bounded enterprise was an interesting mix of Anglo Mormon and Hispanic involvement that developed and continued outside the mainstream cultural revival programs sponsored by the government or associated with the Catholic Church. The Carson venture was such a successful local vitalization of the craft that many of the wool-on-wool colchas created during that era were mistaken for colonial textiles by contemporary collectors and marketing agents. They can still elicit confusion when they surface in museums with no documentation of provenance or history of collection.

In a confidential report to the Taylor Museum in Colorado dated November 1951, Harry H. Garnett, collector and writer, details the evolution and strategies employed in the creation and marketing of the Carson colchas. A journalist by trade and a rather colorful character, Garnett was responsible for acquiring many outstanding pieces for the Taylor Museum's Southwestern collection. Garnett begins his report by tactfully referring to these colchas as "reproductions." But further on in his manuscript, when he describes how colchas were stitched with yarn unraveled from ragged Rio Grande blankets on patches of old *sabanilla*, he simply calls them "fakes." Among a few curators and collectors this term still retains currency, although it hardly does justice to the range of circumstances of creation and marketing and the variety of embroideries produced.[17]

Originally, Carson colcha manufacture was a salvage operation spearheaded by Elmer Shupe, a blanket trader and son of Mormon Judge W. K. Shupe, who founded the northern New Mexico community of Carson in 1909. Elmer Shupe started to collect old Rio Grande weavings and colchas during the early years of the twentieth century. For some time, the area around Alamosa in southern Colorado was a major site of his collecting operations as well as his place of residence. At the beginning of his trading career, Shupe moved throughout the region on his bicycle, gathering antique textiles. Stories still circulate telling of his arrival in small villages like Capulin, Colorado, armed with persuasive arguments that convinced people to exchange their old and "worn" colcha bedcovers for the more up-to-date bedspreads he offered in trade. These tales always end with the image of Shupe pedaling off down another dusty back road in search of more textiles and treasures.

According to Garnett, much later in the 1930s, when rare traditional colchas were selling for five hundred to eight hundred dollars and few could be found, Elmer Shupe and his brother-in-law, John Graves, amassed as much sabanilla or fragments of it as they could find. These were then pieced together to form the backing for the embroidered patterns later identified and categorized as "Carson colchas." In fact, evidence of this piecing technique on older colchas today signals their origin as Carson colchas and distinguishes them from other sets of revival embroideries. Consistent with their resourceful and expedient application of reused materials, Carson residents also stitched their colcha designs with handspun and naturally dyed wool yarn unraveled from frayed woven blankets or colchas that were beyond repair. Many of these old textiles were ideal for recycling because they were so worn that they had lost their value as trade objects. Mixing narrative with opinion, Garnett reported, "Shupe told me that the colchas cost him eighty-five dollars to make. They were so near perfect that only an expert could tell they were reproductions."[18]

During an interview conducted in 1991, Frances Varos Graves, one of the original Carson embroiderers and Shupe's sister-in-law, mentioned that the real catalyst for the Carson "revival" was the speculative leap that she made one day from repairing an old colcha to being inspired to copy it. Her husband, Richard Claude Graves, had collected an antique geometric-style colcha composed of a series of small checkered blocks. He found it in the nearby town of Ojo Caliente and brought it home for Frances to mend. Its poor condition only stimulated their interest further, "so, we took that apart until we finally found out how to do it."[19]

Frances also believed that the old colchas that she and her sisters mended were originally from Spain—"they claim the originals came from Spain," she stressed over and over again in her interview.[20] Combining an interpretation of Frances's honest belief in the historical authenticity of these textiles with inferences in H. H. Garnett's statements about Shupe's intentions to create genuine embroideries that could "pass" as originals, one perceives an interesting core of sincerity and commitment (on the part of the stitchers) overlaid with a marketing strategy predicated on triggering the same type of beliefs espoused by Frances Graves but targeting future buyers. Until recently textile connoisseurs have been just as confused, and just as opinionated, about colcha origins and provenance. This was certainly demonstrated in the correspondence between Wilder and Schweitzer also detailed in chapter 3. It is unclear whether Elmer Shupe initially recognized these embroideries as colonial frontier efforts or thought they originated in Spain. The acknowledged point of origin in this case does not really matter, since Shupe's main objective was to create something "old," antique, and marketable in the first place.

It is evident that the Carson group's consolidation was based on an intricate web of kinship relations resulting from a series of marriages between the Hispanic Varos sisters and the Mormon Graves brothers. Frances Graves referred to almost any male member of the Carson group as "my brother-in-law". The set of relationships is as follows: Elmer Shupe married Winnie Graves, whose brothers Richard Claude and Frank married the two sisters, Frances and Sophie Varos, respectively.

Their sister Agnes Varos Fernandez also embroidered, but she died young, leaving her daughter, Mary or Maria, who spent part of her childhood with Frances Graves and learned to do colcha embroidery from her aunts. Mary Fernandez ultimately married Buddy Graves, the son of another Graves brother, John, thus heralding a subsequent maritally entwined generation. John Graves was mentioned earlier as initiating the colcha "recovery" project with his brother-in-law, Elmer Shupe. Therefore, the kinship interlace binding these families together through intermarriage and industry further reinforces their relationship via mutual involvement in the creation, evolution, and maintenance of the Carson colcha legacy.

Given the predominance of geometric patterns over floral motifs in the designs of early traditional colchas, the piece Richard Claude Graves recovered in Ojo Caliente, which became a kind of heuristic model for Frances, probably dated to the second quarter of the nineteenth century. It was a bicolor (indigo and natural) wool-on-wool–style colcha completely covered with parallel rows of simple unadorned colcha stitching. In their reconstruction techniques Frances Graves and other Carson stitchers faithfully copied this method of stitching. Consequently, instead of the curving and undulating stitches that follow the formal dictates of the pattern as in various Spanish colonial examples, Carson colchas are characterized by the presence of solid lines of unidirectional stitches all moving in one direction, either vertically or horizontally, throughout the composition. The result of these patterns is, of course, quite "grid-determined," characterized by even and regular rhythms, unlike examples of more lively organic designs of post-loom decoration pushed to the outer limits of imaginative application.

The replicative style of the colcha couching stitch that Frances and others revived is as distinctive individually as it is collectively. Universally known as the "lazy stitch" because it covers more space in less time, many of these stitches can span several inches in length. Their linearity is also heightened and accentuated by a succession of anchoring tie-down stitches crossing over the single extended thread at fairly regular intervals.

During the period in which I was often traveling to New Mexico, I was also working rather closely with Josie Lobato just on the other side of the Colorado border. Some of the findings from my research with Frances and her niece, Maria Fernandez Graves, excited Josie's curiosity—especially the way these women used extended rows of couching stitches as effective space fillers. This particular method of stitching actually inspired Josie to experiment with the use of the "lazy stitch" in order to cover more area in the background of her penitente piece than was possible with clusters of the shorter colcha stitches. Like Maria and Frances, Josie also called it the "lazy stitch" and mentioned that one of the Anglo volunteers at the Fort Garland Museum referred to this stitch by the same name. All these individuals qualified this label by immediately associating it with Native American stitchery derived from an original connection to beadwork, employed for the same purpose—to fill in large areas quickly by anchoring multiple rows of beads to the base fabric. Clearly, "stitch" modified by "lazy" is intended to denote expedience—faster and more efficient with less effort.

It was mentioned before how foundation fabrics were pieced together from scraps of old wool sabanilla, which in turn became an identifiable characteristic of Carson colchas. Unlike textiles repaired by patching, the distinct separateness of these fragments is obscured by the dense embroidery that covers their surface. Thus, they appear integrated into the foundation fabric's matrix and not appended to it. In this manner maintenance skills used for mending and repair became techniques that transformed older recycled materials into fresh new textiles. Aside from the set of discernible traits by which we identify the Carson colcha style today (e.g., stitching mode, fringed borders, large size, etc.), early Carson embroideries not only simulated antique colchas but were also promoted as such and, as inferred, were often mistaken for traditional pieces.

Instead of an iconography confined to purely Spanish colonial representational imagery including floral and zoomorphic motifs, the Carson artists introduced simply rendered pictorial themes inspired by their perception of tourists' and collectors' expectations of the Southwest: herds of buffalo, wild horses, wagon trains, and Indian chiefs on horseback. A few colchas even featured scenes inspired by the mysterious practices associated with the lay Catholic Brotherhood, popularly known as the Penitentes (see chapter 2).

Sophie Graves, Frances Graves's sister, created a colcha during the 1930s in which she embroidered a wagon train under siege encircled by mounted Indians. This colcha is now in the Millicent Rogers Museum collection in Taos, New Mexico. Despite the dramatic action they portray, such scenes as this one are infused with a certain static quality determined by the constraints of medium, composition, and style. Perhaps these rather stationary pictorial arrangements, decorative yet somewhat realistic, basically remained tied to the underlying grid format with respect to design orientation and spatial placement.

For many years, collectors persisted in identifying the Carson textiles as antique Spanish colonial artifacts. Early interpreters of the colcha embroidery genre were still susceptible to the lure of "traditionality" and legitimacy as realized and promoted by Elmer Shupe and his clan of embroidering relatives comprising artists, needle workers, and traders. As late as the 1960s an anonymous article appeared in the *Denver Post* in which these pictorial colchas by the Graves family were still described as colonial pieces: "Many of the flowers and leaf designs are of Spanish and Moorish origin, but the early [implying nineteenth-century] colcha-makers were also pictorial journalists. In their needlework they told of Penitente marches and attacks on wagon trains and pictured the buffalo and deer of the area. But, the saints were probably their favorite subjects."[21]

Frances Varos Graves maintained that she was inspired to create Western scenes because her husband, Richard Claude, was a "cowpuncher." Both she and her sister Sophie had also grown up listening to their grandfather, Jose Manuel Varos, tell stories of buffalo hunts and other exploits on the New Mexico frontier. Her favorite images, however, were saints, which were borrowed from painted *retablos* (paintings) and traditional *bultos* (three-dimensional images). Although Frances was raised a Catholic, she "didn't like it." Neither her move to Carson nor her subsequent marriage into a Mormon family had an acknowledged impact on her religious orientation. She claims that she has no religious affiliation.[22] Frances Graves's niece, embroiderer Maria Fernandez Graves, is equally casual about her religious observances. Yet she is just as enamored of saints' images, the *santos,* which inspire much of her work as well.[23] Perhaps the affection Frances and Maria feel for their saints simulates or is close to the emotional bond (as opposed to spiritual ties) between the traditional *santeros* (image makers) and their artistic creations.

> I didn't become a Mormon. When I was young I went to the Catholic Church . . . but I didn't like it. I couldn't understand their priest . . . so, I'm still that way. I was the one who started doing religious imagery . . . because the old colchas never had anything like that. It was only flowers and [checkerboard], something like that. But there were no images. But I think the santos are really beautiful, you know. So, I started making some . . . then everybody wanted those.[24]

It is commonly thought that the strong Mormon presence behind the Carson Revival permitted the depiction of santos and religious scenes such as penitente activities. The notion is that as non-Catholics, Mormons tended to be unaffected by Catholic feelings of sacredness or what might conversely be construed as sacrilegious motifs. Moreover, it is conjectured that because of their literal disengagement from Catholic interdictions and taboos, Mormons, as "outsiders" in the religious community, could probably depict clandestine penitente subjects on their embroideries without fear of censure or reprisal.

It is interesting to compare Josie Lobato's own ambivalence and frustration regarding the penitente theme with the attitude of the Carson colcha makers of the 1930s. Her sense of dislocation resulted from a kind of personal and artistic blockage she experienced while trying to aesthetically appropriate her husband's memories of penitente practices. It was as if there were too much emotional distance between Josie and her subject. The Mormon artists, however, had intentions other than artistic veracity for its own sake. The Anglo men who designed the Carson penitente pieces tended to create these colchas to appeal to external (collectors' and tourists') notions of the sensational aspects of the mysterious rites of the Brotherhood. It is assumed that by virtue of their own position as cultural outsiders living in Catholic Hispanic territory, Mormon artists were able to make these colchas with religious and emotional detachment.

The idea of a certain degree of impartiality as an asset or as necessary for depicting particular subjects also extends to Frances Graves's personal indifference toward institutionalized religion, which she expressed during our discussion on santos iconography in the interview cited above. Frances's creative expression or attitude actually inverts the consequences of neutrality as experienced by the male artists in her family. Although she eschews religiosity in practice, Frances differs from her male relatives in that she really enjoys working with images of saints. The type of objectivity practiced by Mormon artists drawing penitente scenes is definitely not part of Frances's approach to these subjects, which she loves regardless of their religious connotations.

Apparently, in their time colchas with penitente themes must have been convincing to people other than collectors and tourists. Writing on New Mexico village arts in 1949, Roland Dickey, like other critics of his era, mistakenly described many Carson pieces as authentic products of Hispanos working in a traditional context. As a result, his interpretation of their religious nature also differed from the more recent views or theories of using secularized motifs in the manner described above. Unlike the prevalent notion that only non-Catholics could create sacred imagery for secular purposes—an act which, according to some, verged on blasphemy—Dickey believed that these colcha embroideries were specifically designed for church use. His assumption was based on their iconography, since "religious elements were frequent."[25]

In the confidential report quoted earlier, H. H. Garnett implied that the choice of penitente themes by Carson artists was based on opportunism stimulated by competitive market forces. Garnett wrote that Elmer Shupe's business partner, John "Shorty" Shumate, was encouraged by Shupe's success, but wanted to create a different type of colcha, so "he put the Graves clan to work making penitente colchas. These colchas were embroidered with the figures of the penitentes whipping and carrying crosses."[26] In Garnett's opinion this development was bad for business and connoisseurship. He wrote, "Shumate killed the sale of fake colchas by making penitente colchas. Anyone who is familiar with the penitentes, knows that they would never make a bulto or colcha showing the brothers whipping or carrying crosses. The late Dr. H. P. Mera of Santa Fe was going to do a booklet on Colchas [sic], but as he told me, he found so many fakes he gave it up."[27]

In their narrative power and imagery, Carson pictorial colchas, including the genre "penitente colchas," were intended to impart as much visual drama and novelty as possible for commercial purposes (i.e., salability). One Carson colcha in the collection of the Museum of International Folk Art resembles a "sacred" text dense with iconic motifs associated with patriotism, religious mysteries, and Native American belief systems—all embedded in an array of pan-Southwestern themes.

The red and blue color scheme and stylized eagles are Anglo-American emblems extracted from a collection of Americana. The penitente themes, the Holy Week image of the Crucifixion repeated on all sides, plus the intertwined diamondbacked serpents arranged around a central Saltillo-style diamond rendered as a "god's-eye," intensify the symbolic program of this piece. This collection of disparate elements appears to be designed as a calculated concession to a collective notion of tourist taste. Moreover, it was assumed that the marketability and commoditization of colchas embroidered with visible references to the reclusive Penitente Brotherhood was certain to titillate outsiders' beliefs concerning these mysteries and, in turn, to promote a sale.

A different colcha from the same era with a slightly more cohesive symbolic program also pertains to Penitente Brotherhood rites during Holy Week. In 1933 Mary Cabot Wheelwright, collector and philanthropist, arranged for the Spanish Colonial Arts Society to purchase this colcha from Wayne Graves, another brother-in-law of Frances Varos Graves. In a note concluding the transaction, the writer Mary Austin, on behalf of the Spanish Colonial Arts Society, wrote that the check was for "a penitente Colcha [sic] Mary Wheelwright *dug up*" (emphasis in original). A descriptive newspaper clipping accompanied these records: "The [colcha's] body is white wool with a border of points of brown wool enclosing small crosses; inside of this is another border of the variety of cactus known as cholly. In the middle space is a carefully worked-out design of a Penitente crucifixion. The *Cristo* is on the cross surrounded by a whipping procession with *cantador* [singer] and *resador* [reciter] and Penitentes whipping themselves with bloody flagils. At one side is a presentation of a *morada* in brown and over it a moon and a star."[28]

"Cholly" (cactus or cholla figures) comprising one of the interior borders are actually *tenebrarios*, which are triangular candelabra used for the Tinieblas ceremonies enacted in the moradas at the culmination of Holy Week. It is interesting that the narrative referents in the news clipping are to plants (cactus) common to the New Mexico landscape rather than to sacred items recognized from a knowledge of the interior furnishings of a Brotherhood morada. To be able to identify these forms as candelabra entails a familiarity with penitente practice and religious accouterments gained from observing or participating in rites inside morada chapels. This calls into question whether or not Carson artists had access to private penitente ceremonies and could characterize certain sacred items like the candelabra associated with Las Tinieblas as representative of special Holy Week services.

Another possible means by which this "local" knowledge might have been acquired was seeing or handling objects like these that were traded through Elmer Shupe's commercial network to various collectors and museums. During the 1930s some moradas actively sold or traded sculptures and artifacts to restore severely depleted revenues or to upgrade their collections to a level considered more in line with contemporary mainstream Catholic fashions in terms of sacred furnishings—

i.e., European-produced plaster holy figures and so forth. Among his papers in the Taylor Museum Archives are accounts of H. H. Garnett's role in acquiring penitente objects for regional collections in this manner through trade or modest remuneration.

Other pictorial colchas depicting penitente iconography were probably based on witnessing activities occurring in the area around the moradas. Processions of Brothers moving through the hillsides, particularly on Good Friday, were probably more common during the 1930s than today. Thus, there were greater opportunities (possibly serendipitous for those curiosity seekers) of encountering and observing some of the ceremonies occurring outside Brotherhood chapels within public view. Perhaps these processions had much the same affect on startled travelers and livestock as the San Luis pilgrimage walk that I participated in every Good Friday not far away in the Colorado highlands, which drew throngs of people to the crossroads and sent herds of animals scattering to the far end of the pastures.

Both Cleofas Jaramillo and Lorenzo de Cordoba (Lorin W. Brown) wrote about penitente activities in the 1930s in New Mexico. They also described the happenstance of meeting penitente groups flagellating themselves as they progressed along back roads in the foothills.[29] The Carson populace would also have been aware of when these events took place. They might have had friends, possibly Hispanic relatives, among the Brotherhood, since membership was much more widespread then than it is today. These opportunities of participant observation presumably provided them with visual information they could then transmute into colcha iconography.

Although the preceding account merely mentions that Mary Wheelwright obtained the "Penitente" colcha from Wayne Graves, it is generally recognized today that Graves was also the creator of the piece. At this point it is necessary to discuss Graves's work very briefly, because it exemplifies some of the stylistic considerations and the enigma surrounding Carson colcha scholarship relevant to issues of traditionality and authenticity. The discussion will also be important in subsequent analyses of San Luis colcha making.

I believe that two colchas in the Taylor Museum collection were designed and drawn by Wayne Graves. When I was working with the collection in the early 1990s, Taylor Museum acquisition records still documented one of these embroideries as a late nineteenth-century piece.[30] Nevertheless, this colcha matches all the criteria associated with the Carson colcha style. It is entirely colcha-stitched from recycled, carefully color-coordinated native yarns on patched sabanilla. These woven fragments obviously formed the support for the embroidered field and were not added later as the result of repair work. The red accents within the composition were created from commercial yarn recovered by unraveling trade blankets or colcha fragments.

The colcha's large-scale pattern of twisted morning glory vines, a type of classical rinceaux, is symmetrically arranged on a neutral background. The presence of a meandering ivy border is typical of Carson colchas, which characteristically employ some kind of repetitive framing device, whether undulating vines or pyramidal color blocks. The edges of Wayne Graves's work were usually hemmed, in contrast to other Carson pieces, which were ordinarily surrounded by colorful fringe made of complementary colors that accentuated the customary geometrical or curvilinear borders.

In 1974 Graves's colcha was featured in a traveling exhibit mounted by the Boston Museum of Fine Arts. According to the dates listed in the exhibition catalogue, *The Spanish Southwest,* it was supposedly created sometime between 1860 and 1870. This estimation was supported by the writer, Roland Dickey, in the commentary accompanying a photograph of the colcha, in which he credited its rather innovative artistic format to the correct source of influence, but the wrong century: "While embroidered with the traditional New Mexican long couched stitch, this colcha is more sophisticated in design and color than earlier examples, indicating the influence of eastern settlers."[31]

In retrospect, elements Dickey attributed to nineteenth-century Anglo influence from the East were actually the result of the twentieth-century Carson Anglo Mormon synthesis of Hispanic traditional stylistic techniques with their innate European-derived aesthetic taste. Since the Carson group was also at the center of an active textile trading network, it is probable that the European cast of the Carson colchas was the product of an eclectic mix that was the outcome of exposure to Spanish colonial colchas, embroidered fabrics from New England, and Anglo materials found in local Mormon households.

It is interesting to note that in an undated photographic advertisement for their collection, the Taylor Museum also used Wayne Graves's ivy colcha as a backdrop for a portable *nicho* (niche) that enshrined a *bulto*, a statue, of Job. The inclusion of Graves's colcha as a prop in this promotional photograph signals its putative authenticity as a Spanish colonial artifact.[32]

Another work attributed to Wayne Graves that is relevant to our discussion hangs in the Millicent Rogers Museum in Taos, New Mexico (fig. 4). Created before Graves's death in 1935, it is made from recycled native and naturally produced materials. The accession records, which had not been updated when I was researching this piece, indicate "old Navajo textiles," probably due to its monochrome, earthy color tones and geometric style. This colcha is a careful study in the subtle manipulations of tan and brown. It is framed on top and bottom by a series of dark brown scalloped meanders reminiscent of ornate lambrequin arches associated with Hispano-Mauresque architecture. These are shadowed by symmetrical rows of graduated arches receding into the background. The overall configuration is punctuated at regular intervals with lines of carefully positioned flowers along its lateral axes.

Wayne Graves's success at representing traditionally identifiable motifs is illustrated by the following incident. During my slide presentation at a workshop held in the San Luis Valley on the history and techniques of colcha embroidery, when audience members saw a slide of Graves's colcha they remarked how much it reminded them of decorations on Spanish tiles, or more accurately, those found in New Mexico. Tile decoration and technique is mostly Hispano-Mauresque in origin; it was transmitted to the colonies during the Spanish occupation and has since been identified as an essential feature of Southwestern style.[33]

Wayne Graves's design arrangement is also suggestive of the rippling diamonds and serrated borders of the colonial geometrical-style colcha from the Taylor Museum discussed in chapter 3 (fig. 3). While the composition of the traditional colonial colcha is slightly asymmetrical and lapses sporadically into irregularity, it is visibly enlivened by an essentially organic sense of formal interdependency and mutuality. The Graves piece, however, with its strictly delineated design elements, is characterized by precise placement and meticulous planning without anomalous patterns or variable compositional array. In general the tenor of Graves's work is deliberately conditioned by an overriding sense of Anglo-American taste and sensibility; hence, Roland Dickey's observation in the 1974 Boston Museum of Fine Arts exhibition catalogue that "this colcha is more sophisticated in design and color than earlier examples."[34]

The idea of sophistication also extends to an appreciation of the colcha's iconography and formal design scheme. By utilizing Hispano-Mauresque *mudejar* designs, Wayne Graves purposefully drew upon Spanish colonial stylistic vocabulary, with its symbolic allusions to Iberian heritage and historic Spanish dominance. Graves's conscious iconographic program also reveals an awareness of the significant roots of the colonial New Mexico cultural system, the same Hispano-Mauresque tradition historian Marc Simmons called "the framework within which the distinctive matrix of New Mexican culture evolved."[35]

Wayne Graves's work typified the original Carson colcha style, but the Carson movement transcended the limitations of a revival style to become a flourishing subgenre within the colcha category. After the 1930s and 1940s revitalization period, Sophie and Frances Graves (along with their Anglo sisters-in-law) continued to stitch from recycled materials garnered from their blanket and weaving repair businesses. The bright accents in their work from the 1960s and 1970s derive from their incorporation of synthetic yarns, particularly acrylic, into contemporary colcha making. But the use of synthetics was ultimately moderated by buyers' preference for natural materials and the requirements of the newly revived 1960s Spanish Market, which adhered to much the same criteria for determining authenticity as the original Market of the 1930s.

Because of its rarity, patched sabanilla was eventually replaced by commercial monk's cloth, an open weave material that is easy to embroider and readily available in fabric stores. The Carson embroidery technique remained the same, long stitches anchored to the foundation fabric with short ones. The reverse side of a Western style colcha by Frances's niece, Maria Fernandez Graves, shows the proliferation of tiny stitches scattered on the back. The reverse pattern reveals a fairly clear image of the figure featured on the right side. Even today the "correct" technique for finishing colcha backs is hotly contested by embroidery practitioners in New Mexico and Colorado. The manner in which backs are stitched then becomes a measure of "authenticity" as interpreted in terms of the colcha legacy from frontier times, and is also indicative of some of the principles established as part of a group's ethnoaesthetic system. On the one hand some stitchers believe they are carrying on a tradition by using a version of the colcha stitch that is "economical with little thread on the reverse side."[36] This is particularly true of San Luis members of the Ladies Sewing Circle, and is of course a salient characteristic of the Carson colcha style. Josie Lobato, on the other hand, believes that the reverse side of a colcha should be as dense and thick as its front. She notes that the appearance of the traditional colcha in the Fort Garland Museum, which is her "consultant" in matters of authenticity, corroborates her view.

Another generation of embroiderers associated with the nucleus of the original Carson group is represented by María Fernandez Graves. María Graves learned to mend blankets and to embroider from her aunts. At the age of eleven or twelve, María officially became an active member of the stitching clan when Frances Graves successfully traded one of María's bird-and-flower colchas at a store in Ojo Caliente. Today María Graves alternates between using new materials and recycling materials in the Carson tradition, transforming into embroideries yarn unraveled from old sweaters she finds at garage sales in the Taos area.

Following in the footsteps of her aunts, María Fernandez Graves began to participate in the annual Spanish Market in Santa Fe. María tries not to use anything but natural yarns and fabric in her pieces, and has conceded to the marketplace emphasis on Hispanic heritage by using the Spanish version of her given name,

Mary. Her most popular embroideries are solitary saints' images initially inspired by Frances Graves's enthusiasm for these figures. Although María Graves usually works in a smaller scale (15″ x 18″) than her elderly relatives (typically 48″ x 60″), a number of her colchas also include different themes adopted from their older embroidered compositions—particularly the unconventional and distinctive imagery of multicolored bear paws framing the central santo portrait. Unlike traditional santeros' (wood carvers') strong devotion to the images they create, the Graves women enjoy working with religious imagery but are not vitally connected to it on a spiritual level. Like the 1930s Carson prototypes, contemporary pictorial saints are still created for the marketplace rather than from some devout inner necessity on the part of the artist.

The question of the authenticity of Carson colchas as replicas of Spanish frontier textiles, then, is complex and problematic. When the Carson pieces are removed from a context limited by comparative judgments based on their relationship to colonial embroideries and are examined instead as a subgenre of colcha embroidery, they seem to correspond to the anthropologist Nelson Graburn's notion of a "reintegrated" art form. However, the Carson situation was more complicated. In "reintegrated arts" as Graburn conceived them, villagers appropriate materials and ideas from industrial societies and recombine them with their own traditional elements to create a synthesis that signals a new expressive art form, a "fertile new form."[37]

The Carson situation in the 1930s, on the other hand, was a complex intermingling of Anglo Mormon entrepreneurial guidance with Hispanic and Anglo artistic collaboration. Carson colcha making was conditioned by commercialism and modeled by a conscious sense of historicity and choice of picturesque imagery. Elmer Shupe, his partners, and his brothers-in-law promoted an art form geared for tourists and collectors that drew upon the symbolic resources of at least two indigenous groups—Hispanics and Native Americans. Their intent was to reduce these neotraditional images or contrived assemblages of ethnic emblems to uncomplicated forms with immediate visual impact and considerable semantic access. In this manner Carson colchas operated as a type of tourist or collector's art characterized earlier by Paula Ben-Amos as a simplified visual system whose meaning is accessible to the greatest number of people (see chapter 2).

As Frances Graves said, "Everyone in Carson worked on those colchas!"[38] The Carson enterprise leaves an afterimage of a mixed community (including Anglo embroiderers), integrated by familial and kin relationships as well as living arrangements, engaged in craftsmanship (mending, designing, stitching), all superimposed on a landscape affected by degrees of isolation and the circumstances of the 1930s

Depression. However, Carson colchas transcended the temporal constraints of a [re]vitalization movement to become the foundation of a bona fide independent artistic trend, or at least a viable colcha subgroup. The aesthetic results of this movement not only hang on museum walls but also endure through the pride, skill, and enthusiasm immanent in the work of the surviving Graves women.

**Villanueva Tapestry**

Villanueva was a different type of colcha enterprise. This northern New Mexico community, briefly alluded to earlier, was the scene of an exemplary stitching project created during the later colcha revival period of the mid-1970s. It was just one of several communities targeted for embroidery workshops sponsored and promoted by the Museum of International Folk Art in Santa Fe. The energy that fueled this enterprise came from the united efforts of the Museum's director, Yvonne Lange, and artist-stitcher Carmen Benavente de Orrego-Salas, a native of Chile.

Printed advertisements posted around northern New Mexico in Abiquiu, Pecos, Villanueva, Mora, Rainsville, and Guadalupita recruited women for stitching workshops by promoting the concept of embroidery as pictorial narrative and stressing the use of everyday experience as a source of creative design. The overall intent behind this campaign was to enrich and stimulate village crafts through workshop activities, and thereby (hopefully) to benefit these communities economically. Circulars, written in both Spanish and English, began with a welcome to all, then related Carmen Orrego-Salas's background as instructor and muse, and finally outlined the goals of the program.

> Bienvenida a todas las mujeres de Nuevo Mexico....
> Nacida en Chile, America del Sur, Carmen Orrego Salas conducira las clases de bordados con enfasis en disenos creativos relacionados con la vida diaria de los participantes. El proposito de estas clases es el de enriquecer y estimular las [*sic*] artes en los pueblos.

> Welcome to all women of Northern [*sic*] New Mexico....
> A native of Chile, South America, Carmen Orrego-Salas will be conducting embroidery workshops with emphasis on creative design as it relates to the daily lives of the participants. The purpose of the workshops is to enrich and stimulate crafts in the villages.[39]

Carmen Orrego-Salas's efforts in embroidery revitalization movements began in 1971 when she traveled briefly from her residence in Indiana to the Chilean village of Ninhue near her birthplace. There Señora Orrego-Salas started a successful workshop based on crewel embroidery techniques she had learned by herself in the early 1960s. Her enthusiasm and her belief that "authentic art must come from one's heart and life" have endeared her to workshop participants ever since. Most of the women attracted to these classes were already needle workers, so Carmen Orrego-Salas's customary role was to freshen and refine technical skills and augment stitching vocabulary.[40]

She introduced various stitches associated with crewel work, but afterward noted that during her experience in the Hispanic Southwest, several of these acquired local names: "the back stitch and the stem are . . . called plain, common or regular; the Palestrina becomes Palestino; the Romanian, which in New Mexico and Colorado took in the past the name of Colcha now is referred to as Spanish. Finally Turkey work, at least with one Villanueva stitcher has become Turkey walk."[41] For most Villanueva stitchers the Palestrina stitch became a symbol of virtuosity and commonality. They included it in every panel of the communal church tapestry as an emblem of connection and as a hallmark signature for the project. According to the transcripts of interviews done by the Museum of International Folk Art, one stitcher thought that the localization of Palestrina, "Palestino," signified that the stitch came from Palestine, thus establishing a conceptual link to the Holy Land, furthering a bid for legitimizing its sacredness, and emphasizing its appropriateness for an ecclesiastical tapestry.[42]

During the mid-seventies, Villanueva's visibility as the site of a prodigious embroidery project was established with the creation of the Villanueva Tapestry. The emphasis and scope of the project distinguished this community from the other colcha revitalization projects in New Mexico. Although the term "tapestry" is used, it is descriptive and not technical. The concept for this collective enterprise was conceived in 1974 by the parish priest, Father Louis Hassenfuss, and was supported by Carmen Orrego-Salas as a bicentennial project. Their idea was to have the Villanueva stitching group (the eleven core members grew to thirty-six by the end of the project) create a tapestry that would encompass the history, folkways, and religious life of their community. Although the impetus for this endeavor was a byproduct of bicentennial fever reaching westward from the east coast of the United States, the tapestry is a unique pictorial narrative of Spanish exploration and occupation of a particular site in the Southwest from 1625 to 1976. It contains no allusions or commemorative events associated with British colonial United States or Revolutionary War history.

When stitcher Isidora Madrid de Flores initially heard the plan and helped measure the church interior where the tapestry would finally hang, she recounted, "I said 'we'll do it.' [But] I didn't sleep for two nights, because I thought—my goodness, two hundred and sixty-five feet! ... and, I figured why did I say 'yes?' But you know, it just seems like a miracle, that it was just wholeheartedly that we did it."[43]

The Villanueva Tapestry is a monument to cooperation and enduring fellowship. According to Señora Madrid de Flores, "nobody knew about art," but the network for a successful collaborative enterprise was already in place. "We were a small village [everyone knew each other]; all Spanish, all Catholics and mostly everybody is related." The group was composed of different generations with varying interests: "There were grandmas and grandchildren and people who had never opened a book."[44]

In addition to using the regional mobile library, the participants were so enthusiastic and curious about their themes that they traveled to libraries in other towns to gather information. Often the grandchildren helped the elders with their drawings as well: "My deer got about two feet long and the horns were. ... So, I got my grandson and he helped me and he did real good and I did some of it. As you can see one of my rabbits has only one eye, the other one you can see [has] a lot of things out of proportion."[45]

Carmen Orrego-Salas very carefully fostered self-confidence in the stitchers, and instilled a belief in their own creativity despite their personal despair or self-consciousness concerning their rudimentary skills as "artists." In the workshop context, her initial emphasis is usually to encourage stitchers to draw inspiration from their own experience. This was not always easy to communicate, nor was it readily accepted. In fact, during a telephone conversation when she thought I was being too protective of San Luis stitchers, Carmen described the kind of self-discipline she advocated and felt was essential in order to be a more effective mentor to stitchers and a better monitor of artistic standards. "We need to be brutal . . . to encourage and stress individual expressiveness by saying, 'It is you (the work is you, the piece is you) because you are unique.'" She later qualified this by reiterating, "You have to be brutal with a lot of sense of humor."[46] As an art historian schooled in the shadow of the unique artist-genius, I understood Carmen Orrego-Salas's stance. But in the village context where people have been living and acting communally forever, where generally people have been marginalized in the Anglo world for their Hispanic heritage, it is difficult for well-intentioned outsiders to foster individuality and uniqueness and be openly appreciated for these efforts.

Despite this difference in interpretation, Carmen Orrego-Salas's methods are obviously effective. By counseling women to examine their own life histories for artistic themes, she ultimately gets stitchers not only to trust familiarity and experience personally as inspirational sources but to learn that such themes are of interest to others as well. This shift in consciousness and pride does not occur overnight. But Orrego-Salas believes it to be an inevitable byproduct of these workshops.

> Why start with tapestry? Here before their eyes is a mirror of themselves. They become proud of themselves. That does not mean to continue to create tapestries forever. Even practical things [tea towels, placemats, etc.] can be created. [These things are part of] their original engagement with this medium—their traditional entrance. . . . Of course, this development [confidence and belief in originality] takes time—five, six, seven years—constantly working on one's own, growing accustomed to each individual voice. This is an excuse to bring in freshness (which is a requirement to sustain vitality in any movement), not to pollute [these efforts] with sentimentality from the past. Why not make beautiful things today? [The women need] to become what they are and be conscious of who they are. They must [rely] on the confidence and humility to be themselves.[47]

Since the Villanueva Tapestry was not conceived as an economic project, embroiderers were free to explore the aspects of stitchery that appealed to them (once hesitancies were overcome), as long as their discoveries were confined to an experiential field of interest and dovetailed with the project's goals. Consistent with the opinion expressed above, to Orrego-Salas the most important element was the integrity of the embroidered piece—not the compromises made for the sake of sophistication or virtuosity. Señora Orrego-Salas sums up her attitude in these words written more than a decade before we spoke in 1990:

> There are sections where . . . the coarseness and lack of precision serve a different purpose as in the treatment of certain landscape details which gain in dramatic power. There is an economy of means to convey the pictorial message, totally in keeping with its *primitive character*. This is a refreshing attitude because there is no virtuosity per se in the search for effect but an integrity of purpose which is simple and direct and true to the spirit of love that inspired these women to create this gift for their community.[48] [emphasis in original]

Other than her use of the term "primitive character," which has a negative connotation today, Orrego-Salas's assessment accurately highlights the tapestry as a powerful piece of cooperative handwork created out of dedication and purpose.

The Villanueva Tapestry excited interest far and wide, and the group received donations from supporters outside of New Mexico. The enormous amount of background fabric made of homespun cotton was donated by stitching specialist and writer Jacqueline Enthoven of Santa Barbara, California. The embroidery's style is similar to the earlier traditional wool-on-cotton colchas where the plain background contrasts with slightly three-dimensional embroidered designs. In this instance Villanueva stitchers used commercial Persian wool yarn rather than native handspun yarn.

The tapestry is composed of a series of forty-one individually embroidered cotton panels just under two feet wide, which when sewn together from end to end extend two hundred and sixty-five feet. Fifteen years after her nightmares about completing something so immense, Isidora Madrid de Flores proudly told me it was longer than the eleventh-century Bayeux Tapestry embroidered after the Battle of Hastings. "We beat this one by thirty feet!" The stitchers did not realize they were beating a historical record when they finished the Villanueva embroidery. It was only after comparisons with the Bayeux Tapestry were made in the press and in subsequent publicity that the women added this awareness of art history to their narratives, now told with pride and a sense of a contest not entered, but won.[49]

The embroidery wraps around the interior of Villanueva's Our Lady of Guadalupe Church and even ascends to the choir loft. The first embroidered panel represents *Tierra Bendita*, the blessed earth, a depiction evocative of Eden as a pristine wilderness before humans arrived. The intervening forty panels represent a range of history, daily events, and sacred activities: plastering the church, fiestas, weddings and Saint's Days, rituals of the Penitente Brotherhood (created by Isidora Madrid de Flores's thirteen-year-old granddaughter), Coronado's arrival, the creation of the local state park, and Archbishop Robert Sanchez's investiture in 1974.

The tapestry culminates in a view of "The Coming of Our Lady of Guadalupe." The action of this scene, with its focus on the arrival of the Virgin's image from Mexico, denotes the beginning of Villanueva's spiritual life. Marking the end of the continuous embroidered narrative, *Nuestra Señora de Guadalupe* functions as a thematic framing device. Since this scene represents the religious conquest (Catholicism over indigenous beliefs), it parallels the earlier portrayal of the arrival of the Spanish conquistadores in the area (military domination of indigenous people).

As a symbol of intercession and redemption through which Heaven-on-Earth, *Tierra Bendita*, is attained, the icon of Our Lady of Guadalupe also corresponds to that paradisiacal opening scene. In this manner the climactic representation of the Virgin refers the viewer back to the tapestry's beginning, thus metaphorically perpetuating the eternal cycle expressed in the liturgical formula, "World without end."

Scattered throughout the scenes are bilingual *dichos* (proverbs) Carmen Orrego-Salas encouraged the women to include as expressions of the remembered wisdom of families and friends. One of the most frequently quoted sentiments is, "In olden days men didn't buy appliances, they married them." Isidora Madrid de Flores laughs when she repeats this one, but also interprets it seriously, revealing the unstated truth behind the joke so characteristic of this verbal genre: "Everybody gets a kick out of that one. It's true. There were no appliances to buy in the first place but the ladies would help with everything. I remember my mother churning butter that she made at home—not big batches just a little to use.... There were so many things that we used to do." At the beginning of the tapestry Señora Madrid de Flores stitched a favorite dicho of her mother's generation: "El cojo le hecha la culpa al empedrado" (the limping man blames the rock), which shifts from the idea of self-sufficiency without mechanical aids to comment on the human tendency to avoid responsibility for one's actions.[50]

Borders on the top and bottom of each panel further unify the tapestry. These spaces are the repository for caches of assorted free-floating imagery, symbols or titles, plus some of the dichos, and key words relating to the scenic contents sandwiched in between their margins. Carmen Orrego-Salas gave embroiderers a free rein in their choices. Most of the women were also grateful for her technical advice—especially when they were in a quandary. Remembering how Carmen dealt with those uneasy moments, Isidora recalls:

> When we made a mistake.... Like I made a chicken, a bird, rather, and he was ... let's see ... on the other side of the fence. The fence was in between. And I didn't know what to do. Take it off? Or do it over? I didn't know.... And she [Carmen] said, "You can see his legs. Put the legs underneath." And there was another lady who did the Rosary [recitation]. It was in the woods. And she says, "I made the Rosary and it doesn't look good in the woods." And she [Carmen] says, "You can't take it off because you pray the Rosary wherever you are."[51]

From her vast experience as an artist utilizing the unexpected, Orrego-Salas deftly handled mistakes by exploiting them. But what is also interesting is her instant switch from technical insight to an explicitly Catholic attitude toward the praying of the Rosary—an insightful act on her part that suddenly eases the stitcher's chagrin at her mistake and unites the two women (and all who remembered this moment) in a sympathetic understanding of religious observance. Furthermore, Isidora Madrid de Flores's commentary acknowledges a shared belief that sacred action imbues the space around it with religious spirit and that spiritual power resides in its abstract form, the artwork, as well.

After its completion the visible success of the tapestry inspired some founding members of the Villanueva Tapestry Corporation to create and market small individual panels of domestic scenes in the same wool-on-cotton pictorial narrative style. These were also stitched with commercial Persian wool in the meticulous technique characteristic of the tapestry. This technique utilizes a similar repertoire of stitches inspired by crewel work. Two examples from the Villanueva revival in the Millicent Rogers Museum collection were embroidered in 1981 by Rosabel Gallegos, then president of the Villanueva Tapestry Corporation, and Filomena Gonzales, who was also an original member of the group.

*Mi Fogoncito* (my fireplace) by Rosabel Gallegos depicts a cozy household interior with her traditional adobe fireplace as the central focus. Gallegos's technique is impeccable. Despite the small scale of the embroidery, she utilized many of the more popular stitches associated with the colcha-as-crewel work revival led by Carmen Orrego-Salas: chain stitch, Turkey clip, feather, running, lazy daisy, stem, outline, and blanket. By cutting off a portion of the floor and slightly tilting it, Gallegos uses the perspective of the piece to give the illusion that one is sitting in the room—just as the stitcher probably sat and stitched in front of the fire. The serene mood suggests an enjoyment of the solitary moments embroiderers have stolen from household chores and other necessary duties over the centuries.

Filomena Gonzales collaborated with Arnold Chavez to create *Haciendo Ristras* (making chili garlands, fig. 5). Continuing the practice of the Villanueva Tapestry creators, both names are stitched into the composition to indicate stitcher (Gonzales) and the person who drew the design (Chavez). Also reminiscent of Isidora Madrid de Flores's combination of natural patterns and symbolic forms in her earlier tapestry panels, Gonzales and Chavez substituted the New Mexico state symbol (the solar circle with four directional rays radiating from it) for the actual image of the sun. Although certain key elements (chilies, pastoral activities, the state emblem) are requisite for localizing the scene, they also relate to outsiders' expectations of picturesque New Mexico and serve as tourist icons.

Carmen Orrego-Salas feels quite strongly "that future stitchery projects should be built around people meeting because they enjoy stitching together. Any other reason is doomed to failure."[52] God and self-reliance also go together in these endeavors, according to Isidora Madrid de Flores; she describes what it is like to be part of a stitching group:

> You know it was fun. It was like a blessing. Like when you get together, you figure you enjoy ... I don't do nothing but talk. I enjoy meeting with the ladies. And there's ladies that I had never known and I go. . . . I make lunch for my husband and I take off ... and it's amazing how God helps you, those that help themselves. It's the truth. And we have this [the tapestry] to show that it's the truth—and we did it.[53]

The Villanueva Tapestry and the individual artistic efforts it spawned actually represent a different categorical set of textiles from colonial and revival pieces of the 1930s. In addition to a more varied stitching vocabulary, the most profound difference is the primacy of the subject matter and the conception of the embroidery as a narrative art form to be framed and displayed on walls. According to Carmen Orrego-Salas, "stitchery is a way to paint with wool."[54] This attitude indicates a shift from utilitarian decoration to a conscious artistic expressiveness intended (as part of workshop agendas) to convey explicit multiple culturally aesthetic messages. Not only does the pictorial narrative format provide a visual commentary about idealized village life; it also concretizes abstract values associated with external notions of Hispanic cultural identity such as simple and harmonious rural lifestyles, cooperation and solidarity, environmental awareness, and satisfaction in handwork.

When Carmen Orrego-Salas spoke of Hispanos originally being adept at embroidering domestic items like tea towels, she indicated that the development of contemporary colcha workshops was predicated on the premise that the majority of people in Hispanic villages targeted for economic revitalization excelled in several types of handwork. Throughout my research I frequently encountered women from this area who were as enthusiastic about crocheting and quilting as they were about colcha embroidery, sometimes more so. My experience does seem to match outsiders' belief in the legacy of the individual Hispanic stitcher's ability to embroider "from birth." But whether this is typical of rural communities associated with a certain generation, and not necessarily due to skills *determined* by ethnicity is another matter. Nevertheless, this external attitude of native needle working talent plus the choice of the pictorial narrative format as a canvas for stitchers' life stories were coupled with the entrepreneurs' romantic and antimodernist notion of an innate Hispanic aesthetic sensitivity to an ambiance of local color defined by outsiders as "traditional life and custom."[55]

Consequently, Hispanos were considered to be artists simply by virtue of being raised in a particular culturally rich atmosphere and being constantly surrounded by it. Never mind that the populace of these picturesque hamlets might interpret local color to signify poverty and depression, accompanied by geographical and cultural isolation. Overriding this possibility, the promoters of these workshops (museum personnel, cultural specialists, entrepreneurs) believed that the stamp of legitimacy resting on the fortunate combination of "birthright," inherited skill, and ethnic residence would insure the embroidery projects' success and productivity.

Oscillations between external revitalizing forces and inner cultural responses reverberate throughout this chapter. It is tempting to dismiss outsiders' influence on village culture as a one-way street governed by exploitation and control. Instead of this limited view, I envision a more inclusive picture of mutual interaction between cultures, one that entails constant adjustments and adaptations. Periodic revitalizations of colcha making actually represent a "delicate stylistic and functional balance struck at particular historical moment[s] between two cultures in contact."[56] This fine balance is doubtless achieved through mutuality, reciprocity, and other mediating influences, all interactively engaged. Reflecting on the complexity of this type of interrelationship, Barbara Kirshenblatt-Gimblett notes that the "alliance between institutions of 'dominant cultural production' and communities whose endangered heritage we strive to protect is a tricky one."[57] It is interesting that the phrase "we strive to protect" echoes some of the intentions behind the earlier "salvage" operations of the Spanish Colonial Arts Society espoused by individuals like Mary Austin and Mary Cabot Wheelwright.

In northern New Mexico, colcha was revived and marketed as an emblem of Hispanic ethnicity. In the case of colcha, where dominant art-world values were introduced into what was a craft-oriented form or into the embedding folk-oriented community, the outcomes were seldom one-sided. The effort at economic development of hand crafts attempted to renew community resources and also to kindle pride and plant seeds of self-sufficiency. On the entrepreneurial side, despite good intentions, we catch glimpses of paternalistic, often condescending attitudes among outside orchestrators of craft revivals toward the nature of village life and the quality of the art work. Despite her aesthetic sensibilities and strong feelings for the cultural landscape, Mary Austin in conjunction with the Spanish Colonial Arts Society could not refrain from writing, "make the most sympathetic, happiest, and so effective use of them [Hispanos]."[58]

Outside entrepreneurs, however, did not always have the final word in monitoring taste and aesthetics. Over the years stitchers discovered individual ways to quietly subvert some of the dictates of the Anglo-American marketplace. Sometimes they used synthetic fibers that appealed to their color sense and were easy to find and to keep clean (e.g., Carson colchas of the 1960s and 1970s). To assuage their own creative urges, embroiderers often chose less ethnically identified, more generic subjects and themes that satisfied particular tastes and personal whims. Some of these favorites were decorative scenes with embroidered owls or mushrooms. As Isidora Madrid de Flores revealed in a conversation with her friend Stella Madrid,

> Like I tell Stella (she makes pillowcases, she makes dolls, she makes all kinds of embroidery) . . . anything done by hand, it's worth more than stuff that you buy from the store. Because you do it with your own hands, your own talent. . . . The meaning, the value, is what you have done with your own hands. And I figure, I did it and I made it. Even if you are making mistakes, you have that pride. . . .[59]

But Carmen Orrego-Salas also believed in a more inclusive notion of creativity, where "practical things like tea towels can be created." In Orrego-Salas and Isidora Madrid de Flores, then, we see two women from divergent backgrounds in accord over the dynamics of the creative process as the touchstone for the meaning embedded in artistic action. Although Carmen Orrego-Salas advocates and sponsors elaborate embroidery projects, she recognizes (like Isidora Madrid de Flores and Josie Lobato) the intrinsic value of creative action. The outcome can be glorious or commonplace (tapestry or tea towel), but it is the stitcher's hand, the artist's touch, in that process that enlivens and is significant. Tiva Trujillo also expressed the importance of this when she said, "That's why I love to draw. I love to draw my own tangles ... embroider my own tangles. This has been something real nice for me to work on, you know. It's hard, but it's nice. It's proud."[60]

At the beginning of this chapter it was noted that art forms reintroduced by governmental institutions or marketing agents not only invigorated village economies but also renewed other—perhaps dormant—traditional arts as well as establishing a matrix for reemergent artistic skills. Colcha stitcher Victoria Mascareñas from Ribera, New Mexico, told me that she learned colcha embroidery as a child while sitting in Leonora Curtin's Native Market every afternoon waiting for her father, master weaver David Salazar, to finish work.[61]

In a rather fitting sense of interconnection, Señora Mascareñas's expedient yet beneficial apprenticeship and her subsequent artistic career arose from an informal contact with the commercial institution created by Miss Curtin when she "talked craft revival, teaching, marketing and every aspect to all who would listen." Thus, the presence of the Anglo-American marketplace inadvertently provided the opportunity for Victoria Mascareñas's exposure to colcha stitchery. As a fledgling artist, Mascareñas learned embroidery skills casually through curiosity and observation rather than as a student enrolled in a planned vocational training program. Today Señora Mascareñas, who is considered a tradition bearer of this genre, not only continues the practice of colcha embroidery as an avocation but also demonstrates her skills seasonally at El Rancho de Las Golondrinas, a living history museum and the former Santa Fe ranch of Leonora Curtin Paloheimo. Victoria Mascareñas's experience exemplifies the mutual interdependence of external commercial enterprise and the perpetuation of personal and cultural expressiveness, with benefits for both sides.

Especially in the 1930s, the predominant entrepreneurial role of culture broker in the Hispanic Southwest typically embodied romantic and conservative views. In a fairly recent analysis of "folklorismus," folklorist Venetia Newall describes concepts similar to the antimodernist notions of Austin and the Spanish Colonial Arts Society. One hypothesis mentioned in Newall's article is that folk art can originate as aesthetic compensation for loss of economic power, which is then replaced by the recovery of inner values. The resultant revival of these values, which are tangibly realized in the art object, functions as a protest against urbanization and industrialization.[62]

Although these statements were intended to characterize recent European folk cultural reenactments, they illuminate some of the issues implicit in the New Mexico arts and crafts revival as well. Considerations such as these also raise some questions that must trouble colcha needle workers. For example, in the minds of the village artisans, how are aesthetic compensation and economic solvency to be compared? When the rest of the world is benefiting from technology and industrialization, are inner values and a simple "romantic" lifestyle satisfactory? Who is evaluating the relative merits of both, and whose agenda is it?

Responding to some of these concerns, the Villanueva Tapestry brings in moderate revenues as a tourist attraction during the summer. Villanueva is located in a rather remote but beautiful setting overlooking the Pecos River valley. It takes an effort to get there. Obviously, tapestry viewing cannot support a community; yet individuals like Isidora Madrid de Flores are not isolated. She has children active in Santa Fe society and has traveled to Europe. Like any other small community in the United States, there are people in Villanueva and other Hispanic villages with lively imaginations, who are curious about travel and other cultures and who get involved in civic projects. There are others who are economically disadvantaged and do not have much freedom of choice.

Carson colchas are still made, but the original movement was inner-directed, not the result of outside agencies. El Arte Antiguo is similar to the Carson artists in terms of self-sufficiency, and as a group continues to stitch. Villanueva women create embroideries individually for church fundraisers, but have never worked collaboratively since the tapestry was completed. Although these efforts wax and wane, they are more or less steady and consistent.

The idea of grafting a rather monolithic artistic revival from the outside onto a village society with all its variables needs to be considered carefully. Apparently the more successful projects are consonant with present lifestyles, come closest to providing the means for self-sufficiency, and exercise the greatest latitude in terms of expectations and goals on behalf of all participants.

In her comments, Carmen Orrego-Salas keeps returning to one theme: the idea that vibrant and spirited embroidery grows out of self-identity, "a mirror of themselves," which engenders pride. "[The women need] to become what they are and be conscious of who they are. They must [rely] on the confidence and humility to be themselves."[63] Perhaps Carmen Orrego-Salas is really expressing the true meaning of "birthright" here. It does not spring from ethnicity or local color but is responsive to opportunity and circumstance. The reality of privilege for some and not for others is still inherent in comments like these that refer to "confidence" and "humility" aimed at people to whom these traits may seem unattainable or not desirable. But the belief in the potential of creativity as a subtly reflective process that revolves around skill as a mainstay while it builds self-confidence in many who have never had access to such opportunities before is honorable. The role of the creative act as connected to societal values and self-esteem is implicit in operative local aesthetic systems as well. This emerges from Isidora Madrid de Flores's observations on the significant power derived from creating objects by hand: "The meaning is what you have done with your own hands. And I figure, I did it and I made it. Even if you are making mistakes . . . you have that pride."[64]

# 5

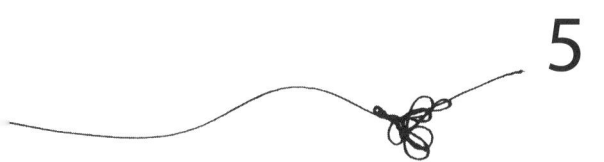

## the ladies sewing circle of san luis

Cantemos 'l alba,
ya viene el día
daremos gracias,
¡Ave María!

Let's sing to the dawn
The day is breaking;
We shall give thanks,
Hail Mary!
— Traditional song, reproduced in Ruben Cobos,
*Dictionary of New Mexico and Southern Colorado Spanish*

Julia Valdez remembers an older male relative rising at dawn to sing this song, '*l alba,* to the morning star. When she first heard these plaintive strains through the walls of her room as a child, Julia recalls, "her skin prickled."[1] After he finished singing the old man went back to sleep. The tone of the day had been set. He could resume his sleep and awaken to an order already in place.

Individual devotional acts integrated into daily rhythms affirm that religious practice has been and remains one of the main organizing principles for life in San Luis. As was noted earlier, Catholicism wedded to ethnicity forms the bare bones of the cultural landscape in Costilla County. Thus, the structure of the Catholic parish historically supports, balances, and frequently absorbs the counterweight of secularizing forces.

### Religion, Memory, and Marketing

The iconography of two pictorial colcha embroideries in particular reveals the centrality of the Catholic church for Hispanic people of this area. *Old San Acacio* (fig. 6) portrays Julia Valdez's memory of the village near San Luis that was her home for the first seven years of her life. The image of the church of San Acacio dominates the scene and is represented as several times larger than any other building in the landscape. By exaggerating the scale of the chapel, Julia emphasizes its symbolic role as the focal point for this small community. The clerical portraits of priest and nun moving through the foreground on the way to church are equally out of proportion and magnified. These figures draw the viewer's attention toward the sanctuary, just as the people they represent must have actually drawn parishioners to worship in the past. Decades have passed, but the names of Sister Joan of Arc and Father Mortarell are remembered and continue to figure prominently in the recollections of San Luis residents and in the religious history of this area.

Reminiscing about her childhood, Julia Valdez believes that "people were very religious years ago—much more than now. During Holy Week they would go to church every day."[2] Her allusion to modern church practices lacking the ardent religiosity of the past might more accurately portray the situation in San Luis prior to Father Pat Valdez's arrival in 1985. But shortly after Father Pat had taken up residency as head of the Sangre de Cristo Parish (which includes a small number of outlying mission churches), church attendance increased and public religious enactments or demonstrations also became more commonplace. It is largely due to Father Pat's personal dynamism and his efforts that the Sangre de Cristo Church and its satellites, such as the San Acacio church, have reclaimed their position at the heart of these communities. Julia also cites Tiva Trujillo's 1980 San Acacio embroidery, *Old San Acacio in 1925,* as inspiring her to create a version of her early childhood there. Tiva's embroidery and Julia's memories recall an idyllic pre-Depression period of extended families living in a close-knit community. However, Julia's memories are truncated by her family's departure in the mid-1930s for California, a move based on hope for better jobs in a place that became the lodestar for many leaving their homeland for the West.

> I'd like to do a view of what I remember when I was a little girl. See, we didn't live too long over there [San Acacio]. Maybe I was seven, eight years old when we moved away from there. But I still remember. I remember what it looked like. I think that's real interesting, to do things like that instead of flowers and stuff like that because . . . you express and you remember. I remember my grandparents' house, and my great grandmother's house, and our house, and my aunt's, and it was just like a little village there. It's so nice. . . . Tiva says [hers is] 1925, see that was the year I was born. So she remembers that time. I don't remember that at all. [Laughs] Maybe 1938—no, 1936, is the time that I remember.[3]

Another contemporary colcha embroidery that commemorates and synthesizes the holy with the secular, *El Convento* is based on Daisy Ortega's memory of her childhood in San Luis. In Señora Ortega's embroidery the figures and the convent building are more realistically proportioned than in Julia Valdez's representation of the San Acacio church and its revered caretakers. In *El Convento* Father Mortarell leaves Sister Mary Ursula on the porch in front of the convent of the Sisters of Mercy while Daisy Ortega and her sister, Emma Espinoza, play hopscotch alongside it. Señora Ortega remembers that she and her seven siblings were constantly at the convent or in the priest's rectory, where they were showered with affection and sweets. In her words, these recollections "always brought happy memories [of the] Sisters of Mercy. We were little pests, I suppose, but the sisters were really good to us . . . we were always there. They would give us candies, cookies; they were really good to us."[4]

Today the church remains an integral part of Daisy Ortega's adult life. In addition to singing in the choir, on Catholic Holy Days she and her husband, Prax, often climb the Mesa to the Grotto beyond the Shrine where she sings *Ave María* alone in front of the image of the Virgin. Daisy's Catholic faith has sustained her through a number of family tragedies. In her own words, "God is good to us. He gives us strength to cope with everything. When everything is going so nice or we're so happy, I always pray, whether it's [because of] happiness or [not]."[5]

In their colcha embroideries, two other stitchers, Esther Romero and Mary Martínez, also draw on similar vintage memories of Father Mortarell. Both women depict the weekly ministrations of the curate on his rounds among the distant mission churches. In almost identical versions of the same scene the priest approaches his classic 1920s sedan, which is parked in front of the San Pedro village church of St. Peter and St. Paul, one of the outlying mission churches linked to San Luis's Sangre de Cristo Church. The theme of mobile village cleric acknowledges Father Mortarell's style of vehicular ministry as an essential supportive element within the infrastructure of the satellite church network. During his tenure, Father Pat has also reactivated the mission church circuit and can be glimpsed on weekdays speeding from one village church to the next on his way to hold Mass.

Interestingly, all of these commemorative colchas were created in the late 1980s as products of stitchery workshops conceived as part of Father Pat's economic development plan for San Luis. These stitched compositions could be interpreted as nostalgic pictorializations of an earlier era of religious and civic harmony graced with the beneficent presence of Father Mortarell. Nevertheless, as artistic creations from the present, they are also symbolically linked to Father Pat's recent role in the restoration of the Sangre de Cristo Church and the renewal of San Luis's vitality in general. Conceptually, through colcha iconography Father Pat and the historical figure of Father Mortarell are connected across time in the creative imagination of these four stitchers as pastoral representatives of religious and communal solidarity.

In her colcha *Las Misiones,* Josie Lobato used this same sort of play between the present and the past to underscore religious continuity and the centrality of Catholic priests in San Luis society:

> The church at San Luis is the largest because it's *home.* That's where the priest resides and that's where the religion is. It sort of goes out from there in all directions.... It has to ... show that the religion was everything, was the center. This is Father Mortarell . . . [he] was very very very influential in getting all these mission churches up, [or] at least maintained. It could have been his [predecessors] may have been responsible for the building of a lot of the churches.... But, Father Mortarell was influential in the development and growth and maintenance of all the little mission churches as they were then and still are today.
> 
> I feel that each one of these priests has entrusted each to the next. So there really is a connection between all of them. [Father Mortarell] is a very strong memory.... He was the priest for thirty years before he died. When he came here, this was home. And this is where he's buried, right in the churchyard. For many people he was the symbol of the faith. He was a very strong, a very domi-

neering kind of figure, and yet he was very gentle and very loving and very firm. But he was very influential in a lot of lives. I am sure he was.

So, I think, a lot of people's lives were influenced by what he did and said. And, of course, the Catholic Church at that period of time was very strong. And I have always felt anyway that in Costilla County any rite of passage was . . . everything was centered around the church. The church was there for everything in your life. I look at it like a cycle—the cycle of birth all the way to the cycle of death. It was like the church was in the middle and . . . everybody's life revolved [around it].[6]

Señoras Valdez, Romero, and Martínez gave their embroideries to Father Pat soon after their completion. They now hang in the old convent building, El Convento, which was renovated and converted into a bed and breakfast inn. Daisy Ortega's embroidery is also on loan to Father Pat, and appropriately hangs in an upstairs room of its namesake (the old convent). In a grand design of reciprocal action, these gifts that match memory to cultural construction through artistry acknowledge Father Pat's gift of spirituality and rejuvenation to the San Luis community. In turn, Father Pat exhibits these colchas on the hostelry walls of El Convento to be seen by visitors and guests as cultural artifacts in which extant communal ideals and values are represented through this imagery stitched from the past.

The stitching act, coincident with transmitting certain kinds of visual information, becomes a form of memorializing in itself. As Julia Valdez says, "You express and you remember." Memory, then, is a dynamic process that produces images conceived and visualized in terms of how these women fashion and edit their recollections in alignment with their conceptions of San Luis society and its values. Colcha embroidery is the medium that actively shapes images of social and cultural practice out of the twin processes of recall and creativity. Colchas are objects of memory created by individuals from collective memories that further provoke the practice of remembering for San Luis viewers—also based on memories commonly acknowledged and sanctioned by the majority. Colcha artists selectively choosing themes of "idyllic" religious times are making choices inspired by their current perception of a religious and social renascence in San Luis that evokes an earlier period they have over time come to remember as Arcadian and devout. Thus, the pursuit of memory is a fluid process which, as Gregory Bateson proposed, "promotes and maintains cultural formation in all its fullness."[7]

From the strategic position of his parish, Father Pat stands Janus-faced, looking forward and backward. Facing inward at the economic recovery and regeneration of San Luis, he is loved by his parishioners as El Padrecito, the "little father" (an epithet that derives not so much from his size as from his boyish character). Looking outward, Father Pat maintains connections to the Catholic hierarchy far beyond the Sangre de Cristo mountains bordering the San Luis Valley. Within parish boundaries, he mobilizes his congregation into communal action—renovation, shrine construction, civic and art-related projects.

Once in a while, under the pressure of so much change within the community, the pulpit functions as an *ex officio* arbitrator. Among his ministerial duties, Father Pat is reputed to have appropriated Mass time to mediate and publicly resolve hostilities flaring up along the occasional battle lines that inevitably arise within long-term interrelationship and constant proximity—conditions endemic to small, semi-isolated communities such as San Luis. Despite the impression of cohesion and accord that prevails in San Luis, dissent occasionally surfaces in reaction to both internal and external circumstances. A few weeks after the Shrine Dedication in May 1990, regional newspapers like the *Valley Courier* and the *Pueblo Chieftain* reported a riot in San Luis. It was actually a local confrontation between a hostile, diverse bar crowd and the sheriff. Both newspapers noted, however, that some of the angry revelers capitalized on the publicity to express their disenchantment with the development of the San Luis shrine and to vent their hostility toward visitors. Following Dedication Weekend, stories circulated locally that bar patrons were placing bets as to which Station of the Cross would be vandalized first.[8]

Ladies Sewing Circle members adored Father Pat, and their positive feelings toward him were validated by a steady flow of attention from the outside. Beyond San Luis, Father Pat was recognized in *Newsweek* as "1989 Volunteer of the Year." He has been called "one of Colorado's heroes." In 1990 he received the Governor's Prize for Excellence in the Arts; then in 1991 he received the Colorado University Board of Regents' Distinguished Service Award. Behind their loyalty to him, people in San Luis were always aware that Father Pat's residency and eventual departure were mediated by the Bishopric on the other side of the mountains. When I discussed what life in San Luis would be like without him, the women were concerned that the town "might suffer again," but they remained fairly philosophical about it. They cited their feelings that the revival of their community and its renewed spirit were well entrenched and would be able to withstand Father Pat's departure. Evangeline Salazar, one of the founders of the Sewing Circle, hoped that "perhaps the town could learn lessons from the past and stand on its own two feet."[9] A few years later, however, when the Diocese ordered Father Pat to leave the San Luis Valley for Colorado Springs, parishioners actively resisted this mandate by circulating petitions to keep him from leaving. As a result his pastorate was extended another two years, with a proviso that the community regard this time as a transitional period and begin to organize and reorient for a new, possibly different type of pastoral regime.

Trust and affection for Father Pat reaches back to his early success in encouraging and sustaining the revitalization of San Luis based on his belief in economic viability as inextricably linked to cultural expressiveness. This recalls Carmen Orrego-Salas's advice that fiscal recovery programs such as these cannot be "superimposed" on communities, but must be organically implanted into the fiber of the society. Father Pat's methods of uncovering the creative vibrancy of San Luis were also similar to Carmen's advocacy of recognition for and utilization of local handwork practices.

Back in 1985, when he was visiting neighborhoods to solicit help for his parish, Father Pat was impressed by the variety of homemade items decorating San Luis homes. However, beyond the initial stage of praise and compliment, he discovered that people were reticent to discuss or publicly display their arts and crafts. Recalling Father Pat's profound impression of these creative skills, the parishioners' reaction, and the ultimate marketing strategy that evolved out of this, Charles Manzanares of the local Economic Development Council in San Luis remembers, "Father Pat [was] able to boost people's morale by telling them, 'Look, what you've been doing all along has been great. It's something that shouldn't be kept a secret anymore. It's something that should be brought to light . . . more people should be aware of this. It's something that you could actually . . . [make] money at, if you want to.'"[10] During those early days, according to Charles, much of the Council's support was also in the form of encouragement, in order to raise self-esteem and confidence among regional craftspeople:

> a lot of folks that knew [how to do] arts and crafts in the area, they just did it as a hobby. They didn't want to show it. A lot of folks had stuff in their back rooms, "I just do this to entertain myself and I don't like to show it. I don't like to sell it." They'd give something away to friends. It's breaking into that secrecy, I think, [that] has been one of the things we've been trying to do . . . [to] show people, "Look, this is something to be proud of. This is something you should show . . . and make money off of it."[11]

Secrecy, or rather privacy, and gift-giving are elements that profoundly affect dialogues between external entrepreneurs and community artists. At the core of this almost territorial polemic between insiders and outsiders are the issues of ownership and power, or control over creativity and its artistic product. Among Hispanos gift-giving is a culturally expressive action that represents the pride of craftsmanship, generosity towards friends and relatives, and the perpetuation of ethnic practice. It implies reciprocity in relationships, binds the giver and the receiver, and stands as a continually visible symbol of emotional attachment. Personal involvement in the creation of a gift enhances these values even more.

When the action of bestowal interferes with professional commitment to an economic recovery program in terms of sales and the accumulation of inventory, it becomes problematic for marketing agents. On the other hand, reducing opportunities for the personal expression of generosity and affection also creates emotional difficulties for the artists involved. The tension between the commercialization of colcha (for economic reasons) and embroidery as a hobby (given as gifts) underlies the ambiguity inherent in the history and present role of the San Luis Ladies Sewing Circle, as they called themselves. This extends to what the group's purpose is and how it is conceived differently by its members and by those outside its orbit. Is the Sewing Circle an economic recovery project producing inventory for sale? Or is it, as Carmen Orrego-Salas believed such groups should be at the outset, organized around the pure enjoyment of stitching together, because "any other reason is doomed to failure"?

## The Evolution of the Ladies Sewing Circle

The ambiguous position of the Ladies Sewing Circle vis-à-vis the "marketing versus hobby" question really stems from its origin as a community-based, publicly funded project. In 1987, at the same time that local arts and crafts were being targeted by the Economic Development Council to energize financial recovery through reviving regional cultural traditions, Father Pat was approached by Paula Duggan and Carmen Orrego-Salas to consider San Luis as a site for a new colcha embroidery workshop. In the summer of 1975, Carmen Orrego-Salas had conducted weeklong embroidery workshops in San Luis, Capulin, and Center under the auspices of the Virginia Neal Blue Resource Center (VNB), a Denver job-training organization for women. Although separated by more than a decade, both the VNB and the Costilla County Economic Development Council were similarly motivated: they sought to promote home-based craft enterprises in order to improve economic conditions for Hispanic families and to build self-esteem and self-confidence through earned income.

In 1982 Paula Duggan had curated an exhibit of colcha embroideries from the San Luis Valley at the Center for Arts and Humanities in Arvada, Colorado, a Denver suburb. Many of these pieces came from Virginia Neal Blue workshops and were part of the colcha crewel work legacy traceable to initial contacts with Carmen

Orrego-Salas's instruction during the 1970s. Tiva Trujillo had died in September 1980, but her work was included in the exhibit. Her images of life in the valley, featured in the catalogue for the Arvada Center exhibit, *Las Artistas del Valle de San Luis,* were among those that inspired San Luis stitchers like Julia Valdez and, seven years later, Josie Lobato.

In the interval since the Arvada exhibition, Paula Duggan had moved from Denver to Washington, D.C., where she worked at the American Enterprise Institute for Public Policy Research. Apparently, the intermittent and discontinuous pattern of what she refers to as colcha "revivals" of the late 1970s troubled her. Thus, in 1988, accompanied by Carmen Orrego-Salas, Duggan returned to the San Luis Valley with the hope (echoed by Father Pat Valdez) that this most recent in a series of colcha craft implants would endure and flourish as a viable cottage industry in San Luis.

As the nexus for the religious community, the Sangre de Cristo parish was the obvious recruiting agent for the 1988 colcha workshop. Although the premise for this enterprise was economic need, the group's nucleus comprised mainly middle-class homemakers or retired women from the parish in their sixties and seventies, several of whom had been associated with Carmen Orrego-Salas's mid-seventies workshops. Only two women could qualify as low-income. Most women were connected with those San Luis families whose historical roots extended back to the end of the colonial era. Furthermore, as in many small communities, many members were interrelated through kinship and marriage.

Other people in the community who would have liked to see more diversity in membership have criticized workshops from both the 1970s and the 1980s for including restrictive age brackets (predominantly older women), for lacking social and economic diversity and integration (mostly middle-class), and for maintaining a type of social exclusiveness in the face of genuine financial need. One critic voiced her regret over the unfulfilled potential of the mid-seventies and the 1988 workshops:

> [the workshops were] definitely stratified with the more established families [dominating], not women who would be using this [skill] as their sole source of income . . . or for a new alternative. They could have gotten many women who were tied down with young kids, who could have worked in their homes and done this as a micro-enterprise. Because many of these women were related to each other . . . you ended up having a really cliquish situation that excluded having a real interchange. Many of these women already had sewing skills, so there was this pecking order of who was better. . . . I just never went back.[12]

Actually, the group that met with Orrego-Salas in January 1988 was more heterogeneous than past colcha workshops had been. There were veterans from the 1970s—Daisy Ortega, Ursulita Lobato, Esther Romero, Sostena Cleven, and Joyce Romero. Other accomplished stitchers, like Julia Valdez and Mary Martínez, had worked in the Virginia Neal Blue program, but had not learned techniques from Carmen Orrego-Salas. Teresa Vigil, Josephine Lobato, Edicia Manzanares, Julia Vigil, and Eva Sánchez were parishioners like most of the other women, but this was their first workshop. This was also the occasion on which Josie Lobato was first exposed to colcha embroidery. It has already been described how her future as a colcha artist was launched when she attended merely as an observer for the Colorado Historical Society.

Sally Chavez and Evangeline Salazar were active in the church and also directed or managed programs at the Senior Center, where the stitching sessions were held. Thus, although uninvited, they became class members by virtue of propinquity and interest. These women became so enthusiastically involved with colcha that the following year they received grants to conduct their own embroidery workshops, which were held in the same place. Sally Chavez remembers:

> It [the workshop] was held at the Center. Because we [Sally and Evangeline] were at the Center, Father called and said, "You should go." We had just gotten out of ... we were newly retired. We had always wanted to do something different other than teaching. If it had been held elsewhere, we wouldn't have been accepted. I felt like we were on our own grounds—in our territory.[13]

Sostena Cleven was the only person attending the workshop who was not a Catholic. She refers to herself as a Christian and is an active member of the local congregation of Jehovah's Witnesses. Sostena is also the sole embroiderer of saints' images, and is apparently not daunted by drawing the human figure—unlike some of the other women in the stitching group. One of Cleven's embroidered representations of the Virgin of Guadalupe is in Father Pat's collection. He is quick to point out that Sostena is able to create these embroidered *retablos* with a sense of disengagement and detachment because she is not Catholic, implying that parish stitchers might have greater difficulty than non-Catholics in rendering an image to which they are emotionally and spiritually attached. To some very pious women the act of stitching sacred imagery may seem slightly sacrilegious. Variations on this theme have been discussed before in relation to Carson colcha artists—specifically, Frances and Maria Graves's enjoyment of saints' iconography, and Josie's religious pact enacted during her granddaughter's serious accident, which resulted in her embroidered votive figure of Santa Rita.

Sostena Cleven explains her attitude toward saints' images, which she refers to as "idols": "I don't care to kneel down to the idols and pray to them. I don't care to have them. I ask God [instead of images], because I know He is the one who is hearing me. [Idols] don't hear me. That's the only thing I have changed from being Catholic to Christian. Religious images to me [as a stitcher] are only like a nice picture."[14]

In contrast, however, the worshipful stance of artist devoutly engaged with subject matter is by definition the crux of the relationship between the Hispano *santero* or woodcarver and the religious image. Perhaps the Catholic embroiderers of San Luis's Sangre de Cristo parish must compartmentalize devotion and artistry in order to avoid anxiety when challenging, or even threatening, formal artistic problems arise (like rendering the figure). This can be especially true of those more complex demands that engender a sense of technical inadequacy. Whatever the reasons, the majority of San Luis stitchers prefer nonfigural compositions.

Despite this hesitancy, Father Pat's long-range plans include the construction of a portable altarpiece with nine or ten detachable embroidered panels. He hopes the parish women will create scenes of themselves with their favorite saints. These panels would represent "acts of devotion," and must be "tied into the Catholic understanding [of] what saints are."[15] His concept for this project evokes the spiritual relationship between santero(a) and art form (art as a votive offering). Possibly, by appealing to their religiosity, Father Pat may (in good faith) coerce the stitchers to overcome their inhibitions concerning their artistic ability, which they regard as inferior and incapable of reliably portraying the human figure, in order to make a church artifact as an act of sincere faith: "Stitching their favorite saint as an act of devotion or ex-votive offering to the saint, they'd be willing to jump on the bandwagon. [This altarpiece offers a chance] to any person who wants to tell their story—their own story with them in it."[16]

The point has been made that stitchery workshops in southern Colorado promoted by outside agencies were predicated on the legacy of handwork practice rather than the historical reality of a continuous tradition of colcha making or extant colcha embroideries in homes or family collections. Carmen Orrego-Salas mentioned that among members of her mid-seventies workshops "no one knew about colcha embroidery prior to the workshops. They were also unaware of the colchas in the nearby Fort Garland collection."[17]

Sally Chavez was the only person I met during my time in San Luis who had any childhood memories of what she assumed to be a colcha embroidery in her family home. She remembered one bed cover with a floral design in a two-tone combination of olive green and cream. It was used only for guests on special occasions, much like the historical colchas described earlier. Unlike traditional wool-embroidered colchas, Sally thinks it was stitched with commercial embroidery floss because it was smooth and shiny. As a child, she was attracted by its sheen and enjoyed stroking it.[18]

Consequently, the connotations of "rebirth" implicit in craft-oriented revival movements, or even the concept of revitalization, are not accurate with respect to the history of San Luis colcha needlework conventions. If a firm line of cultural and artistic transmission is required for authentication, then the "birth" period prior to rebirth would be the brief interval from the introduction of the pictorial narrative colcha format by Carmen Orrego-Salas in the 1970s VNB workshops to her reappearance in the winter of 1988. Thus, revival connotes the second wave of an artistically, temporally, and regionally distinct form of pictorial colcha embroidery. This form emerged under Señora Orrego-Salas's tutelage during her initial sessions with San Luis Valley women in the mid-seventies, but does not extend any further back in time.

The situation in San Luis is remotely analogous to the concept of "vitalization" as applied to the Carson colchas created from the conjunction of economic viability with cultural eclecticism. Since there were no local or historical antecedents for the pictorial colcha format as interpreted by Carmen Orrego-Salas, the mode of vitalization rather than "re-vitalization" generated the first VNB workshops in the San Luis Valley. Any subsequently related art movements or economic recovery projects were variants of these original workshop initiatives. Thus, in order to track the ebb and flow of the cultural currents in the second generation of San Luis colcha workshops, it is necessary to understand the evolution of the Ladies Sewing Circle as it developed out of the 1988 stitching sessions with Carmen Orrego-Salas.

Carmen has always been welcome in San Luis. Despite her brief stays, she is remembered affectionately and is the subject of a litany of highly descriptive tales that circulate among the stitchers. These accounts feature her beauty, refinement, and especially her expressive hands. Listening between the lines, one is aware of an incremental sense of omission in the narration. Hidden within these stories is the tacit recognition by the narrators of the gulf that separates them from Señora Orrego-Salas in social class, worldly experience, education, and intellectual sophistication.

Although they speak the same language, the San Luis stitchers and Carmen Orrego-Salas as a member of the extended academic community of Indiana University do not share the same world view. In planning and conceiving colcha workshops the designers and promoters no doubt blended all "ethnics" of Spanish and Latin American descent into a single group designated "Hispanic."[19] For this reason the planners of these workshops probably assumed that a common language would ease some of the difficulties of relationship and rapport.

However, the assumption of unity based on language does not erase socioeconomic and cultural differences. Despite her affection for Carmen Orrego-Salas, one stitcher still complains that the Chilean Señora did not speak "correct" Spanish. Of course, this comment emphasizes an implied hierarchy of Spanish dialects as accepted by San Luis women (naturally biased in their own favor); but it also functions as a leveling mechanism to reduce the quasi-mythic stature of Carmen Orrego-Salas in the minds of the stitchers.

Furthermore, the idea of *pure* Spanish is linked to the corresponding locally held Eurocentric notion of a historic San Luis connection to colonial Spain free of *mestizo* influence (traces of mixed blood). Concomitantly, around the time of Orrego-Salas's 1988 visit, San Luis was an emergent community just getting its bearings after years of economic, social, and spiritual impoverishment. It was a fragile but crucial moment of self-definition for San Luis society. During that period it would have been particularly important to embrace and to present a distinctive image of ethnic pride and solidarity on the part of the community in the face of a cosmopolitan representative from the outside like Carmen Orrego-Salas.

In a bilingual environment such as San Luis, with its history of outsiders' prejudice against Spanish usage, the reassertion of a belief in Spanish hegemony through language is a potent symbol of transformation. The act of criticizing Carmen Orrego-Salas's Spanish indicates a subtle realignment from externally imposed criteria of sameness to a locally inspired exhibition of difference through the maintenance of language and the privilege of speaking it correctly.

The pride of heritage and cohesiveness found in San Luis today is not universal throughout the valley. When Carmen retraced her history of conducting workshops, she mentioned that the group meeting in Capulin, farther up the valley past Alamosa, specifically requested that she *not* speak Spanish because the majority preferred English as the dominant language. This was in 1975. Compared to San Luis in the late 1980s, the Capulin enterprise (which did not last long) dates to a time when identification with Hispanic culture still carried a negative connotation—especially for older women in their sixties and seventies. There was also the problem that the Capulin group itself was made up of women from different communities around Alamosa who had little in common.[20]

Despite undercurrents of rivalry and challenge, Señora Orrego-Salas's San Luis workshop had important and useful effects in that, among other things, it spawned the creation of the Ladies Sewing Circle and inspired Josie Lobato to become a colcha artist. Since most of the women who attended were fairly adept at needlework, Orrego-Salas concentrated on encouraging them to trust their own creative abilities and to draw on their imagination to portray biographical scenes, memories or *recuerdos*, landscapes of cultural interest, and imagery inspired by religious themes, folktales, legends, dreams, or fantasies.

Orrego-Salas's agenda was more artistically oriented and probably more sympathetic to individual conditions within the San Luis community than that built around the romantic mythologizing of ethnic enclaves by other outside entrepreneurs. Nevertheless, her program partially incorporated some earlier antimodernist notions predicated on nostalgia for the "vanishing" folkloric image. This was especially apparent when she advocated a picturesque idiom embodying formal and symbolic elements of artistic and ethnic purity.

Basically, Carmen Orrego-Salas believed that the original intention of the embroidery workshop was "[to] bring out the identities of the people of the valley. It was the healthiest thing for them—and the vibrancy of their art." In order to realize this goal, she instructed the women in a variety of crewel stitches using wool yarn on muslin. Carmen's role as instructor was to refine stitching techniques of already accomplished embroiderers and to revive the skills of other stitchers who had not used needle and thread since childhood. She pointed out that most women had embroidered previously with cotton floss on linens such as tea towels or pillow cases, "but not with wool or in this kind of format [pictorial]."[21]

Carmen frequently refers to these textiles as "tapestries." Colorado and New Mexico stitchers use the localized term "colcha." Some stylistic and technical similarities between historic nineteenth-century colcha embroideries and the late twentieth-century versions taught in Orrego-Salas's San Luis workshops are: the ground fabric is totally covered with dense wool yarn, a few floral compositions, and some use of the colcha stitch. Differences that exist are: contemporary pictorial narrative format; colchas treated as embroidered paintings in function and scale (they are intended to be framed and hung on walls, whereas their nineteenth-century predecessors were meant to be bed covers, curtains, or altar cloths); complicated, varied stitching vocabularies of specialized and decorative stitches; and commercial wool yarn on muslin.[22] The Villanueva pieces closely approximate San Luis work, but pictorial Carson colchas created in the 1930s are really a subset of these two types of colcha (the historical or traditional and the narrative format).

When the San Luis stitchers were searching for a name to symbolize the group's accomplishment in mastering a complex stitching vocabulary of twenty-nine stitches, Carmen Orrego-Salas proposed that they call themselves "Taller 29" (Workshop or Studio 29). Most of the San Luis women resisted this suggestion because the word was uncommon in Southwestern Spanish and could easily be confused with the English "taller," referring to height. Thus, it was rejected as a potentially meaningless, confusing, or nonsensical label. This is another example of language diversity or controversy at the center of a continuing adjustment and readjustment of dominance and subordination relative to social position and the privileges of education and urbanity—the final denominator being the right of acceptance or refusal.

Despite her emphasis on technique, in every workshop she facilitates Orrego-Salas continues to be sensitive to the "artistic voice" of the art work's inner spirit, and warns against the seduction of technical virtuosity over the creative vitality of the embroidery. Carmen alludes to this problem in terms of artistic transmission vis-à-vis teaching when she says, "I discourage students from teaching so soon after completion of training because they have a tendency to emphasize the technical aspects—the technique.... [T]he spirit of the piece is sacrificed." But she feels this difficulty can be circumvented because "this medium [colcha stitchery] has great potential if people design their own pieces and use stitches common to all kinds of embroidery. Stitches are then put to service expressing life.... They have expressed something fresh and important."[23]

From her vantage point as a recognized fiber artist in the fine art world of galleries and public exhibitions, Carmen Orrego-Salas's attitude (which is compatible with those of entrepreneurs, marketing agents, and art professionals) emphasizes originality and individual artistic expression. It contrasts with the very essence of the corporate, interdependent nature of the socioeconomic system of San Luis. The corporate village model has been in place since this area was a frontier zone, which in some respects it still is. Furthermore, to encourage individual action through unique artistic self-expression in a situation historically determined by social conformity could simply intensify stitchers' insecurity and trigger the low self-esteem they may feel as citizens of one of the most economically deprived counties in Colorado. In addition, it might create tension among women who tend toward self-consciousness and are rather apprehensive about exposing personal artistic talent or creativity to the scrutiny of others.

Although Orrego-Salas employs much of the vocabulary and stance of the art market, which promotes the idea of uniqueness and the one-of-a-kind art object, she is also sensitive and sympathetic to the dilemma of this group whose members are familiar with prejudice and vulnerability. She recognizes the "insecurity people feel who have not had a formal art education. They will always feel inadequate and defer to someone whom they consider to be an 'artist.'" During our telephone conversation two years after the workshop ended, Carmen was particularly aggrieved to learn that the San Luis stitchers in the Sewing Circle had engaged someone to draw their designs for them. Thus, her previous insight is compromised somewhat by the tone or tenor of this later observation: "[By empowering a putative artist-figure instead of themselves] the stitchers are essentially missing out on a profound spiritual education: one of accepting who you are; where you are; and, the time in which you are."[24]

There are several reasons why Carmen's beliefs might have disturbing overtones for some San Luis embroiderers. In addition to encouraging a mode of individually distinctive behavior that runs counter to the interdependent and conformist structure of San Luis village society, statements from well-intentioned outsiders frequently overlook the fact that an acceptance of "who or where you are" requires heroic effort on the part of local artisans to view poverty and continual discrimination as a wellspring of creativity.

Furthermore, the concept of a "profound spiritual education" predicated on a process of self-awareness through creating art might appear confusing and slightly incomprehensible to a people steeped in generations of Hispanic Catholic mysticism. Most parishioner/stitchers would consider this achievement a goal of religious practice and not art.

Finally, entrepreneurs, marketing agents, and art instructors have another existence apart from their association with San Luis. They can come and go. But embroiderers must continue to live together, regulating their daily behavior through a tolerance shaped by a common history of "lifelong mutual familiarities."[25] Peer pressure is frequently at work in local group interactions, whether among stitchers or parishioners, and it can tend to discourage the exceptional performer—especially in the arts. Under these circumstances the majority of San Luis stitchers would not feel at ease nor be inclined to pursue the full potential of individual expressive action.

The communal model of social enterprise prevails in the configuration of stitching groups. Despite occasions of judgmental behavior or the presence of critical attitudes, camaraderie and fellowship are vital to its existence. As noted earlier, Carmen believes that "future stitching projects should be built around people meeting because they enjoy stitching together. Any other reason is doomed to failure."[26] While this last is probably an exaggeration, it does illustrate Orrego-Salas's impressions in organizing and working with a large number of groups. It may also be the personal stamp she left on many of them.

## Fellowship and Stitching

The momentum generated by Carmen Orrego-Salas's workshop inspired Evangeline Salazar and Sally Chavez to apply for Folk Arts Master/Apprentice grants funded by the Colorado Council for the Arts. Their application was successful, and the stitching sessions were held the following year, one at the beginning and one at the end of 1989. Each grant project entailed one master with a group of apprentices—an unusual structure because most master/apprenticeship teams funded by the Council for the Arts are arranged one-on-one. However, it was recognized that plurality was an important factor in developing a viable commercially oriented embroidery program with potential for becoming an effective community-based economic resource.

Another uncommon feature of these particular grants, one that went unrecognized by the funding agency, was the presence of two veteran stitchers among the apprentices. In Sally Chavez's group, Julia Valdez had prior experience stitching and facilitating colcha embroidery groups for the Virginia Neal Blue Resource Center in San Luis during the 1970s. Esther Romero was listed among Evangeline Salazar's apprentices, but she had also worked for VNB and had attended Carmen Orrego-Salas's 1970s colcha embroidery workshops. Thus, neither Julia Valdez nor Esther Romero were novices, so technically they could not be apprentices.

Although Chavez and Salazar had just recently acquired their new specialized colcha embroidery skills under Carmen Orrego-Salas's guidance, their professional background as teachers combined with experience in school administration gave them the confidence and initiative to seek funding for the continuation of the stitching projects. Furthermore, during their tenure on the local school faculty, both women had taught most of the younger population of San Luis and also knew their parents. Consequently, despite their retirement, the community tacitly acknowledged their continuing influence. These are just some of the reasons why Julia Valdez and Esther Romero may have been content to be classified as apprentices. Probably their main interest was continuing to embroider and being with other women.

One motivation for Evangeline and Sally in organizing the Ladies Sewing Circle was to reestablish informal ties with others in the community. After years of being consumed by responsibilities at school, with little leisure time for socialization, they were anticipating opportunities for fraternizing and stitching: "Maybe those ladies saw us as teachers. We still were not the 'friend-friend' thing. We were just fresh out of school! They were afraid, I think, that we would be critical. And, I don't think we were. We just went in there [with] a positive attitude. We just had a lot of fun.... I think we were really trying to be accepted."[27]

Evangeline Salazar also administered the Senior Center where the 1988 workshop occurred. Sally Chavez assisted during special programs for seniors. The Senior Center happened also to be the location for the subsequent apprentice sessions. Thus, with these two women as organizers and embroidery instructors, the hierarchical arrangement of the colcha embroidery master/apprenticeships was the natural outcome of the exercise of authority associated with their former professional positions in San Luis society.

The Ladies Sewing Circle is the final manifestation of this series of stitching workshops, and the most enduring. It retains many of the people involved in the Master/Apprentice groups and continues to meet every Wednesday in the Senior Center. On my first visit in February 1990, the core of the group consisted of: Sally T. Chavez, Evangeline Salazar, Daisy Ortega, Julia Valdez, Edicia Manzanares, Eva Sánchez, Paula Cunningham (the only Anglo), Frances Martínez, Cordy Valdez, Pacífica La Combe, Louisa Valdez, Mary Olivas, Esther Romero, and Tina Santistevan.

After a few meetings Evangeline suggested I work on an embroidery sampler, with each woman teaching me her favorite stitch. She thought these "private" sessions would help me regain my fluency in Spanish and also give me an opportunity to interview stitchers individually. Daisy Ortega was my first instructor, and appropriately taught me her signature stitch, the "daisy stitch". Other women taught me French knots, satin stitch, turkey clip—an entire range of decorative stitchery, which enlarged my understanding of embroidery's kinetic and aesthetic pleasures and frustrations. More importantly, it helped me to meld into the group more as another person involved in stitching and less as a participant observer mindful of fieldwork goals. It also gave me something creative to do with my hands while everyone else worked with theirs. So, for two hours every Wednesday talk swirled around that room in the guise of a kind of contrapuntal or polyphonic exchange accentuated by small, repetitive embroidery gestures. Conversations blended and crossed over the unspoken but pressing private thoughts and worries concerning families and futures—all the while sharpening skills and insights.

By continuing to be absorbed in stitching on my rudimentary sampler and without actually resisting, I did manage to avoid drawing a design for a pictorial narrative. I was concerned that signs of my art school background might affect the women's joy in their own efforts and reactivate degrees of self-consciousness that had been evident when I first arrived. I did not care to add another layer of influence to a situation where my presence was strongly felt merely by my being an outsider. A year later, however, when Josie insisted that I embroider a pictorial narrative during her workshop, "Josefina's Cocina" (Josephine's Kitchen, where we sat around the table amidst cooking paraphernalia and aromas), I designed and drew a piece inspired by my life in the Rocky Mountains. Josie seemed to appreciate my ability without being discouraged by it. Nevertheless, the exercise of trying to choose a suitable subject to draw and then embroider while also experiencing the kind of vulnerability one feels in probing one's past in front of others increased my awareness of how challenging this process can be for all San Luis stitchers—despite my previous training and considerable skill.

The Ladies Sewing Circle was a sociable group whose conversations ran the gamut from gossip to counseling each other. There were always discussions about food, mostly aimed at what people were planning to serve that evening. One memorable exchange revolved around different attitudes and reactions to tortilla making. Paula Cunningham began by describing the shape of her tortillas as resembling "every state in the union, nothing round." Evangeline countered by admitting that her ex-husband's demands for tortillas made her so anxious and nervous "that she can't make them to this day." She went on to mention that her friend Mary Olivas calls commercial tortillas "No te levantas, Honey" (Don't get up, Honey), because women can just go off and purchase them at the store without having to rise at dawn to make them in the customary manner. This evoked laughter and knowing glances, thus directing a bit of sarcasm at a symbol of ethnicity, expectations of household management, and gender issues all at once. Furthermore, just as the joke cut across generations (Paula was younger than the other women), it also joined everyone in the room in appreciation of shared experience or, at least, a common understanding—Hispanos and Anglos alike. Its mixed effect of humor and truth is akin to the recitation of *dichos* by Isidora Flores de Madrid described in connection with the Villanueva Tapestry.

In 1990, during the first few months of the Sewing Circle's existence, there were a few residual funds from previous grants, and Economic Development Council allocations were still available as well. These were initially used to purchase yarn, muslin, drawing pens, and needles. A few of the stitchers who couldn't afford to purchase their own supplies found this arrangement particularly beneficial. However, when the funds were depleted, they dropped out of the sewing circle.

At the start of their workshops Sally Chavez and Evangeline Salazar purchased embroidery yarn through Paula Duggan. Later, when we first met, I asked if there was anything I could help them with since I lived closer to Denver and had access to a greater variety of resources. Soon after this they asked me to find a yarn distributor from whom they could order directly. Although the supplier I recommended after much research turned out to be the same as Paula Duggan's source, both women thanked me for my efforts and continued to mention my help for months afterward. This marked the onset of a tentative reciprocity that fluctuated between us throughout my time in the valley.

Evangeline Salazar shared Carmen Orrego-Salas's opinion concerning certain negative consequences of the indefinite extension or renewal of outside funding for these programs. Both felt that dependence on external financial sponsorship or grants eroded stitchers' self-confidence and individual responsibility. As head of the Ladies Sewing Circle, Evangeline believed the solution was for the women to seriously consider selling colcha embroideries. Carmen's interpretation of the problem was more complex. She went beyond the issues of self-responsibility and remuneration to the impact of economic dependency on the evanescent nature of creativity: "Stitchers must be responsible for the acquisition of their own materials. This way they can acquire a respect for the medium and a sense of responsibility toward the project and their own work. Otherwise an unhealthy attitude develops coupled with a dependent reliance on the funding institution ... an attitude which could ultimately curtail creativity."[28] Such attitudes represent a complicated mix of philosophy, aesthetics, economics, and individual political expectations. Evangeline's belief in the salability of colchas, however, was based on her own success at selling hers—despite prices which some consider high, but which are reasonable given the amount of materials and labor involved. During a telephone conversation in late 1991, Evangeline said that she had received one thousand dollars for a colcha depicting the picturesque health clinic building located just outside San Luis. She was deservedly proud and felt that her example of getting paid for her work gave everyone in the Sewing Circle "a shot in the arm."

Evangeline offered to take me to the clinic to view it and noted that people have commented that the glare from the windows upon the glass in the frame interferes with the impression that it is a colcha embroidery until one stands right next to it. She also mentioned her impulse "to show the other ladies the check" she received for it. She changed her mind after considering the impact this action might have on her friends coupled with the thought that her gesture might be misinterpreted as egotistic. Evangeline admitted that "they all know the price I received for it, anyway! The ladies drive out to the clinic to look at it."[29]

### *Los Recuerdos*: Pictorial Narratives

Continuity of art work is another form of connection between workshops and the Sewing Circle. Some colchas begun under Carmen Orrego-Salas were either finished later after the master/apprenticeships ended or the Ladies Sewing Circle started. Julia Valdez's *Adobe Plant* actually originated with the Virginia Neal Blue colcha embroidery project in the 1970s. At that time Julia put it aside for almost a decade until Carmen Orrego-Salas's stitching session in 1988. Once again it was brought out, but was superseded by her work on *Old San Acacio* (the embroidery Julia Valdez gave to Father Pat). So, in its final form this colcha was not completed until the 1989 master/apprenticeship experience with Sally Chavez.

Julia's pictorial narrative embroidery, which depicts her family cheerfully occupied with making adobe bricks, is representative of the cultural narrative category of colcha. On an aesthetic and iconographic level this interpretation acknowledges the symbolic program of such a work as consonant with the entrepreneurial concept of a picturesque ethnic scene, and thus its perceived "cultural appropriateness." As a visual and social picture of family industriousness and compatibility, it embodies important personal and community values. Finally, these very same inner values pictorially expressed in images of familial connection and pride also match the commercial marketing agent's and potential buyer's expectations of "life in San Luis." But it is also acknowledged among many townspeople of San Luis that these same values apply to them collectively and represent them as well.

*The Adobe Plant* shows the Valdez family making adobes on their land. The scene is angled toward the picture plane as if viewed from a distant overlook. The central action is framed on its lower side by the highway bisected by a middle row of distinct yellow dashes. This bold black band stretches across the bottom space on a slight diagonal. On the left, the driveway forms another lateral boundary and is balanced on the right side by the pond. Adobe manufacture itself is located in a zone divided into horizontal lines of adobe brick molds and figures preparing the bricks for transport. In the upper right-hand corner the mud-mixing operation involving the backhoe appears to suggest that something more is happening beyond the picture frame. Although this scene represents a typical day making adobes, its continuous narrative simultaneously depicts all stages of the process at once: from the massive dirt pile to mixing soil with straw, then from filling the molds to drying them in the sun, and finally to loading the flatbed truck.

This family endeavor stemmed from a project Julia Valdez's husband, Abie, originated to employ alcoholics from the local recovery center. Abie Valdez's former professional experience as county sheriff sensitized him to the need for constructive rehabilitative activity among recovering alcoholics. At the project's inception he donated dirt, labor, and expertise. When the dirt ran out the project transferred to another location, but Valdez continued to operate the adobe factory on his own land and made it a "family event."[30]

Julia Valdez's embroidered visualization of adobe making is not only an artistic *tour de force* but also a commemorative act honoring the ideals of harmonious family relationships and socially responsible community action. Moreover, Abie Valdez's personal background as an effective parent enabled him to externalize his value system by confidently initiating an innovative experiential social program for a segment of the community's emotionally (and economically) disadvantaged. In turn, when the actual alcoholic recovery program finally moved on, its essence of cooperative action reverted back to a private family venture. Thus, for Julia and Abie Valdez, parental conscientiousness informed successful social action, which reciprocally strengthened family ties. Further, *The Adobe Plant* visually signals to viewers that the artist, Julia, values intergenerational harmony and familial cohesiveness—enough to make them the focus of a particular art work. All of these factors are to some degree appreciated, even if downplayed for various personal reasons, in this Hispanic frontier community where little does not become public knowledge at some level.

In the manner of historical colcha manufacture of nineteenth-century wool-on-wool embroideries, Julia Valdez covers the entire piece, which measures approximately twenty-four by twenty-one inches, with densely stitched wool embroidery. There are no gaps where the ground fabric shows through. Her color scheme is inspired by the natural hues of the landscape in contrast with the bright primary accents of the earth-moving machines, the backhoe, the pickup, and the flatbed trucks.

The selection of varied stitches, from French knots to turkey clip (for vegetation), enhances the textural detail and the three-dimensional qualities of the embroidered composition. Shape, contour, and surface are both visual and tactile. Most intriguing of all is the way Julia met the spatial challenges of her piece. She solved her perceptual difficulty by creatively combining the perspective of a "bird's-eye view" (looking from above) with profile and three-quarter views as seen from the side at the same time and within the same space. The perpendicular sifting screen for the dirt, the pile of soil in the foreground, the fence, the vehicles, the people, and the ducks are all conceived in profile or three-quarter views, while the adobe brick molds, the highway, the pond, and the driveway leading up from the paved road along the left edge of the embroidery are flattened out and rendered as if one were flying over the scene.

Despite the resultant visual tension in the clash of two different perspective systems, there is a certain logic in arranging geographical features and landmarks as if on a map. That same visual logic extends to Julia Valdez's choice of profile to depict animated people and working machines in order to more easily and clearly suggest movement and lively action. Julia laughingly recalls her husband and son criticizing the concept of space in her colcha: "This highway—my husband said that I did it wrong. My son said, 'Mom, you could have just left it out and put in dirt. You would have had [a] third dimension.' I said, 'Well, that's *my* dimension, right there!' (Laughs) That's the way I see it . . . like a map."[31]

Julia Valdez credits Carmen Orrego-Salas with awakening her to the possibilities inherent in colcha embroidery as an art form. In formal language these possibilities extend from artistic conception to expression through refined craftsmanship. The artist works through a process of aesthetic and technical decisions, eventually achieving an art work faithful to the original conception, with which the viewer can empathize or at least understand. After Julia's extensive practice making colchas for sale through VNB, it was Señora Orrego-Salas's demonstration of how specialized stitches could be used to create different visual effects that really impressed her and convinced her that colcha was art:

> When I was making my picture [*The Adobe Plant*], Carmen gave me an idea of what to use for the water [of the pond] so it would look deep.... She says, "If you use this stitch a certain way, you can see that [the depth goes] way down." And, just different things—like the pile of dirt that we had there. She says, "just go around [and outline it] ... it will stick out a little better." But you do that in art, too, I think.[32]

Aesthetic decisions about formal elements such as perspective, shadow (to make the pond appear deep), texture (for a sense of dimension), and surface highlights (to heighten verisimilitude and visual interest) transform colcha making from replication into artistic action. The uneasy course of imaginative decision making is riddled with risk and experimentation, but ultimately tempered by the artist's creative engagement with the art work. Shape and artistic form emerge from an internal crossfire of questions and responses operating within the artist's mind and executed by her hand. As was explained earlier, the creation of complex artifacts requires an equally complex series of artistic decisions.[33]

In addition to the aesthetic underpinnings of the style of colchas like the one created by Julia Valdez, there is also the crucially important story line. Pictorial narratives by definition are based on stories but expressed nonverbally, through visual imagery. Unlike Tiva Trujillo, few of the San Luis women actually depict legends or folktales in their embroideries. Often, like Julia Valdez, they create entire scenes from memory fragments that artistically cohere into a story of autobiographical reminiscence.

Sostena Cleven—a stitcher who attended all Carmen Orrego-Salas's workshops and continues to stitch but is not a member of the Ladies Sewing Circle—has created several versions of her embroidery *El Rancho Grande*. In this rural scene of the farm where she lived for eight years on the New Mexico border, Cleven combined memories of her grandson (depicted as a lively stick figure) with images of her abundant truck garden. She enlivened the rest of the composition by scattering various caricature-like livestock over the remaining fields. In the center, Ute Mountain supports the sun on its summit, evocative of the local legend of the mountain as the sun's resting place. Sostena illustrated this by stitching the solar rays as if they were literally streaming down the mountain sides, but her use of a brilliant orange color distinguishes the sun's image from its geological pedestal.

Evidently the mixture of remembrance and whimsy in *El Rancho Grande* strongly appeals to the artist, since she has repeated it often and has even sold a few versions. The composition has enough personal power to retain Cleven's interest as well as sufficiently picturesque particulars which can be easily replicated in the stitcheries she offers for sale. Sostena's design is exemplary of the culturally conditioned colcha of the entrepreneurial dream. The character of her piece is colored by a few specific biographical details. However, the composition tends to be overshadowed by the universal scenic features rather than accentuating Sostena's individual circumstances. Thus, the piece is more immediately comprehensible, and appreciable, to a general audience influenced by certain preconceptions concerning rural lifestyles and the romanticization of self-sufficiency (truck gardens and animal husbandry). The picturesque, rather nonspecific quality of *El Rancho Grande* makes it more commercially viable than other embroidered pieces that are more densely packed with idiosyncratic autobiographical detail.

At first Sostena was not used to relying on her imagination, and she remembers her confusion over this. But once she started creating picturesque colchas and successfully selling them, she understood its significance:

> Carmen encouraged individual stories. I didn't know how to use my imagination. It was new to everyone [embroiderers]. I thought about the ranch near Costilla. The first one went to the [San Luis] Museum. Then I wanted one for me and made that one. I made some more and sold them all. I think I made about seven. Paula [Duggan] told me [imaginative themes] would bring more money and they were interesting because they were out of my mind. I never thought I could do anything. But I'm very proud of myself to have that one in the Museum.[34]

Daisy Ortega is about the only other stitcher in San Luis who repeats embroidery themes as Sostena does. She has duplicated her version of the Colorado State Seal, and will reproduce other themes that are not autobiographical or personal. *El Convento* is only one frame from the film of Daisy's life. The scene of the two sisters playing hopscotch is crystallized in a single moment from the past. However, the main culturally significant theme, the connection between family and church, is atemporally situated in the eternal present. Its meaning transcends a historical biographical cut to represent an alliance between the sacred and secular that is omnipresent in the San Luis community.

Embroideries by two parishioners, Teresa Vigil and Edicia Manzanares, are also "stories about ourselves" inspired by memory and cultural activities. These women participated in stitching sessions with Carmen Orrego-Salas but either did not continue or stayed only briefly when the group reorganized into the Ladies Sewing Circle. Teresa Vigil protests that someday she will finish her embroidery, but her life is consumed by running her own herbal business in addition to volunteer work at the parish. Edicia Manzanares was a sewing circle member at the beginning but stopped attending in the spring of 1990.

Despite its unfinished state, Teresa Vigil's as yet untitled embroidery eloquently embodies a *recuerdo,* a memory, of an outing with her grandparents, *sus abuelos,* on one of their seasonal trips to the local *Culebra* river. She has chosen an unusual but striking color-coordinated scheme of deep green, burgundy, and shades of purple, which heightens the mood of her piece. Its ambiance suggests the gravity of an impending summer storm and the watery presence of the river. In the midst of children playing, Teresa Vigil shows her grandmother cooking in a black bean pot, a utensil still used by Teresa. She uses this pot to make the herbal infusions that go into her *remedios* (cures). Teresa had learned about herbs and remedies from her grandmother. Thus, the pot not only represents a generational link, but also symbolizes their common interest and the great affection Teresa Vigil feels for the grandmother who raised her. By retelling her story in thread, Teresa Vigil sympathetically regenerates the presence of her grandparents and activates a series of tender memories.

Edicia Manzanares's embroidery portrays the annual procession of celebrants making their way to the mission church of St. Peter and St. Paul in San Pedro during the annual Saints' Day observance. She has created a festive mood of celebration enhanced by the expressive faces of the parishioners who not only worshipfully progress toward the church but also betray an eagerness anticipating the promise of a convivial post-service shared meal. In this scene of a popular cultural enactment, Edicia Manzanares has personified individual character and sentiment within a group setting.

Teresa Vigil's embroidered memories are a testimonial to a past era when the extended family was a vital unit of relationship. In this instance the act of embroidery symbolically rekindled cherished familial ties. Obviously, many of these embroidered themes still possess an immediacy for San Luis residents as well, since Teresa felt that such subject matter was worth representing and that it retained the kind of vigor that appeals to potential viewers. Through a sequence of creative decisions as part of the embroidery process, colcha making revitalizes memory. As Julia Valdez says, "You express and you remember." For viewers and artists alike, the creative act merges with the viewing act, simultaneously becoming the catalyst and the response—the product of memory and the stimulus for it.

Depicting the present era but also suggesting timelessness, Edicia Manzanares's pictorial conception portrays devotion and fellowship within a communal context. Similar to Teresa Vigil's need to express a subject that is personally and collectively meaningful, Edicia Manzanares has created a scene of public cultural enactment illustrative of a combined individual and group viewpoint with which most parishioners identify. As colcha artists, these women wield metaphoric elements that symbolize aspects of the collective identity of the San Luis community. In fact, colcha exhibitions and public displays are opportunities for members of the community to witness and respond to these artistic images. The colchas on view become both narrative portraits and representative verifications of viewers' own individual and collective selves. Even if people no longer practice these values or have left the church, they acknowledge the familiarity of these themes and their predominance in the past.

## Scenic Colchas

The pictorial narrative format is one variant within the culturally consistent or "appropriate" colcha category. Another class of colchas with similar symbolic significance is the set of embroideries depicting scenic subject matter. Evangeline Salazar's *La Vega* (fig. 7) depicts La Culebra mountain with the San Luis *vega* or common meadows extending into the foreground in front of it. The suggestion of space is so adroitly handled that the meadow appears to dip beneath the lower frame. In order to augment the impression that the viewer is about to step onto the grass, Evangeline Salazar has utilized French knot stitches that repeatedly circle and wrap around the yarn to create a cluster of tender-looking embroidered flowers. These project out of the embroidered background and drape gracefully over the edge of the inner mat board. This artistic device is both an illusory deceit and a genuine three-dimensional feature of her picture.

In the background the foothills recede into the higher snow-covered mountain peaks by means of a chiaroscuro effect created from scattered light and dark contrasts. This pattern delineates the successive alpine ridges and evokes the sensation of fast-moving cloud shadows scattered over the landscape.

The meaning of this composition derives from the landmark status of the San Luis vega as it extends to the base of the fourteen-thousand-foot La Culebra. The vega—meadow or pasture land—and the tree-covered mountain slopes symbolize a conjunction of topographical and cultural icons. The two land forms (the vega and its extension into the mountain tract) represent the loci of historic communitarian practices of communal grazing rights and access to lumber. Residents still cooperatively graze their cattle on the vega. But the wooded mountainous areas are now privately owned and fenced. This state of affairs has been a source of contention for the local Hispanic population since the land was acquired by outsiders in the 1960s. The curtailing of timber rights and access to historic hunting areas for people in San Luis are continually contested in courts, and have been challenged for decades by active and intentional trespassing.

Evangeline Salazar undoubtedly did not have all of this in mind when she conceived this embroidery. Because she is a descendant of one of the first families to settle San Luis, the vega is a vital element in her personal history. However, the tranquil springtime atmosphere of her embroidery suggests a possibly utopian ideal of peace and tranquility rather than the combativeness associated with a site of long-standing political controversy. Evangeline Salazar portrays the scene as if it were an Eden of promise and bounty in the shadow of sublime mountains and vast space. This was probably very much the way the original frontier settlers experienced this land in the spring—as a respite from the unceasing winter winds and heavy snowstorms.

To an outside viewer there are no visual clues to *La Vega*'s historical or cultural significance as contested land. There are no figures involved in narrative action. Salazar's primary interest is in competently rendering formal properties by means of technical virtuosity (e.g., the display of skill in the wildflowers and the interplay of light and shadow). It is easy for the viewer to respond in kind—to appreciate her embroidery for its vivid artistic touches but miss its cultural eloquence. Thus, although the scenic variant of this colcha type arises out of a rather specific historically and ethnically determined cultural context, in its visually expressive form it is less localized and more universal (mountain landscape) than examples of the pictorial narrative genre (family adobe factory or a particular religious procession).

Sally Chavez also creates scenic colchas. Two of her pieces are variations on the same scene. They are *La Casa de Piedra,* the house of stone (fig. 8), and an unfinished embroidery of a view of the Sangre de Cristo church tower seen through one of the ruined stone foundations of *La Casa de Piedra.* In her finished piece Chavez reconstructs the image of the stone building from the ruins that remain on her family's property in the center of San Luis. A century ago the parish priests used this multipurpose space to house their carriages, store grain, and shelter a dovecote—all within this structure. Sally Chavez recreates the solitary building in a bucolic setting beneath a blustery cloud-filled sky. The intricate mosaic pattern of the stone wall framing the door is offset by the barn's red planks and sienna bricks complemented by smooth green meadows extending beyond. The dense patterning of the stonework corresponds stylistically to the interlocked designs of cloud and sky overhead.

Both Evangeline Salazar and Sally Chavez are superb technicians and enjoy using as many stitches as they can remember in their pieces. A few years after working with Carmen Orrego-Salas, Evangeline described her fascination with the Palestrina stitch—the same one that attained a kind of symbolic status for the Villanueva stitchers: "It is one of the most beautiful of the stitches. It's a very beautiful stitch . . . and very simple to do. And if you asked me to do one right now, I wouldn't know how because it leaves you and you have to practice a little bit before [you] get going again. It's a very beautiful stitch. That's how my lilacs are made . . . nothing but Palestrinas."[35]

When Sally Chavez describes *La Casa de Piedra* she delights in enumerating the various stitches she included for textural effect, especially in the stonework and the delineation of the adobe bricks, which also triggers memories of Carmen:

> Every time I think of Carmen, I think of my *Casa de Piedra*. She left a kind of little fingerprint of hers on my *Casa de Piedra*. It's still there. I asked her, "How would moss look on grayish rock?" She says, "Well, you might try it." And so, she looked at it and picked it up. She tried the turkey clip stitch on one corner of one rock. It's still there [laughs]. It's still there. So, she left her fingerprint on mine.[36]

Sally's absorption in detail and enthusiasm for the mastery of complex stitching vocabulary was also remembered by Carmen Orrego-Salas in her letter to the sewing circle dated May 15, 1990: "[and] Sally, have you finished laying down the adobe? What have you turned to?"[37]

Without specific narrative elements to anchor it in space and time, Sally Chavez's picture is subject to the same sense of loss of locale as Evangeline's *La Vega*. Surrounded by a lush landscape, it could be an outbuilding anywhere in the Midwest. However, if one is familiar with the region, the local identity is very apparent in the cloud patterns, expansive sky, bright undifferentiated light, and particular style of stonework. In terms of thematic material, however, there is little autobiographical evidence of the building's significance for Sally Chavez's family, the Trujillos. It is only during discussions with family members that one discerns the additional importance of this structure (or its ruins) within the context of San Luis parish history.

## Bird, Animal, and Flower–Style Colchas

The next set of colchas share some correspondence with the scenic colchas, but deviate sharply from the pictorial narrative colcha category based on specific culturally inspired content. This group of embroideries is representative of the majority of work being created by members of the Ladies Sewing Circle. These artists are inspired by imagery of animals and flowers found in magazines and other popular sources. In selecting these images, some embroiderers have departed from Carmen Orrego-Salas's insistent advocacy of ethnically identified and historicized subject matter. Instead they have created pictures of single images usually isolated on a plain background. Although the subject matter is pictorial, in order to avoid confusion I prefer to use "decorative style" as a descriptive term for this category of Sewing Circle colchas. Decorative refers to the primacy of an image-based design without narrative accompaniment.

Pacífica La Combe has stitched two black-and-white compositions, one of a solitary magpie (fig. 9) and the other of a skunk, against carefully modulated pale blue backgrounds. These pieces are pleasant in their simplicity and restraint. She has also completed a cartoonlike raccoon emerging from a trash can with a characteristically quizzical expression.

Frances Martínez's repertoire includes a stag with its rack silhouetted against the moon and another embroidery of a single unicorn head. The stag was originally inspired by a design on her son's sweatshirt, and this colcha was intended for him. Among Cordy Valdez's favorite designs are a prowling tiger and a marsh scene with ducks and water lilies. Sally Chavez created a predominantly black image of a bald eagle on a black background, which presents an interesting perceptual exercise since the figure of the dark bird is barely distinguishable from the equally intense monochromatic background. Flowers are also favored by most of the women. Evangeline Salazar has created lilacs, carnations, roses, and a columbine, while Daisy Ortega likes to embroider her namesake, *las margaritas,* daisies.

Although many of the bird, animal, and flower designs are inspired by magazine illustrations, most of the images chosen by the women are regional. The San Luis Valley shelters raccoons, magpies, bald eagles, and a variety of flowers. Deer are also common to this area. It is tempting to attribute more symbolism to Frances Martínez's stag than was perhaps intended by the artist, and to view it as a personal icon of the local wilderness. The image of the hunted deer is central to San Luis society, in which many members depend upon subsistence hunting. But the quality of mystery and elusiveness associated with the buck's image could also at some level symbolize the incremental curtailment of free-range hunting over the years by the growing number of fenced parcels of private land.

By appropriating from commercial sources (sweatshirts and magazines) motifs that correlate with familiar native imagery, Sewing Circle stitchers are repeating a process of thematic localization similar to that enacted by colonial frontier embroiderers a century earlier. When they introduced local flora and fauna into their colcha designs, nineteenth-century embroiderers in the upper Rio Grande Valley localized decorative European patterns by substituting buffalo, deer, wild turkey, and pomegranates for such heraldic symbols as lions and griffins or shields and coronets.

Several of those San Luis stitchers in the Sewing Circle who normally choose contemporary popular images for their colcha designs publicly eschew historical and even autobiographical themes by verbally expressing their dislike of "[this kind of] old-fashioned thing." Father Pat, who still monitors artistic action in his spiritual community, attributes this aversion to the fact that most people in San Luis have always been immersed in the old and in the historical. Some stitchers appear to find it difficult to seek artistic inspiration in the familiar, especially if it is exemplary of hardship and outmoded lifestyles. As Father Pat says, "Old is what they've grown up with."[38]

Unlike Sally Chavez, who enjoys creating "cultural pictures," Evangeline Salazar has never really cared for colchas as cultural reconstructions of bygone eras. In monitoring the Ladies Sewing Circle, she encouraged the women to embroider subjects that appealed to their taste, ones that excited them. "[Instead of exclusively promoting] only cultural pictures—rather than turn people off, we just embroidered whatever. . . . If I was told that [I had] to do those [historical themes], they would have turned me off a long time ago."[39]

Flowers, still life designs, and animal pictures are essentially inspired by domestic imagery and affirm domestic practices of decoration. Embroideries become artistic vehicles through which women of the Sewing Circle are able to fashion themselves as artists and needle workers embellishing their homes with their handwork—i.e., embroidered objects, created from their newly acquired skills, which (they have also been told) buyers on the other side of the mountains covet. This generic domestic imagery of floral motifs and animal frolics is an outgrowth of aesthetic practices celebrating the mundane and the everyday. It has a limited appeal, however, for discerning consumers in search of the distinctive, the exotic—that is, ethnic art. On the contrary, decorative-style colchas fit the philosopher John Dewey's thoughts on art as experience. His remarks referring to the continuity between life experience and art support the interpretation of this set of domestic images (in opposition to cultural enactment themes) as "celebrations . . . of things of ordinary experience."[40]

## Local Folk Aesthetics

Many of the members of the Sewing Circle were apprentices of either Evangeline Salazar or Sally Chavez. The influence of these particular women is felt in the group's absorption in technique and complicated stitching patterns that utilize as many stitches as possible. It is true that certain figural designs can be enhanced by fancy embroidery stitches, as in the example of the wonderfully tactile stamens of stitcher Cordy Valdez's water lilies. But the inherent difficulty in such a situation pertains to what Carmen Orrego-Salas stated earlier: "[there is] a tendency to emphasize the technical aspects . . . the technique, and the spirit of the piece is sacrificed."[41] Her feeling is that creative expressiveness ("the spirit of the piece"), when overshadowed by technical concerns (virtuosity for its own sake), may result in the latter dominating the artistic nature or integrity of the embroidery. Furthermore, if technical skill is privileged over images of ethnic self-representation, then a certain type of cultural expressiveness, which is considered to be the hallmark of colcha embroidery, is lost.

Evangeline Salazar differs from Carmen. According to her the Ladies Sewing Circle definition of an authoritative colcha is based on technical features and a certain kind of perfection. In her view, the embroidery must be stitched tightly with no ground fabric showing through the spaces between the stitches. The predominant stitches used should be the long and the short rather than the traditional colcha stitch, which in the opinion of some Sewing Circle stitchers presents a clumsy appearance. For this reason few of the women use the traditional colcha stitch, instead relying almost exclusively on variations of the twenty-nine crewel work stitches introduced by Carmen. Daisy Ortega is the only embroiderer among the women to use a series of chain stitches for most of her colchas.

Another important aesthetic criterion is the neatness of the back of the embroidery. To Evangeline Salazar and Sally Chavez the appearance of the back is one way to judge the embroiderer's ability. Apparently Carmen Orrego-Salas considered the back of an embroidery to be negligible, but its importance to Evangeline extended all the way back to her grandmother's counsel.

> Carmen was not interested in the back . . . that was one of the things my mother and grandmother always said, "*Hijita*, the back always has to be nice and neat and don't . . ." They never used knots. No knots. So, the back always looked so

nice with their work.... Well, Pacífica's [La Combe] backs are fantastically well done. That's how she learned to embroider, you know. Like my grandmother said, "You have to be neat about your rows."[42]

The Carson colcha style is probably a close match to this idea of "finishing the backs." But Josie Lobato's technique, which she believes replicates nineteenth-century stitching practice in the valley, covers the back as densely as the front, so that the reverse image perfectly mirrors what is on the front of the piece. Sewing Circle members object to Josie's method because of the "waste" of yarn, since it requires large amounts to finish a colcha in this manner. These differences of opinion, again, determine and highlight dissenting aesthetic attitudes among San Luis stitchers, whose opinions also diverge with respect to authentic sources for artistic transmission of a craft (the grandmother/mother line or historical precedent?). Which are more genuine—those passed on from family members and accomplished stitchers, or those gleaned from careful examinations of historical references?

Another phenomenon perhaps particular to the Ladies Sewing Circle is that the majority of the stitching group opted for assistance in drawing their designs and choosing their colors from one particular person, Paula Cunningham, the single Anglo-American member of the circle. Independent embroiderers like Josie Lobato, Teresa Vigil, Sostena Cleven, and others usually coped with their own drawing skills. The practice of relying on someone else to assist with drawing and design goes against Carmen Orrego-Salas's belief that colcha as a medium for aesthetic communication "[has great potential] in the way spirit fills the work of an individual [so that] it is not just a matter of copying."[43] Nevertheless, some of these stitchers are inhibited by thoughts of the potential viewing audience, and feel intimidated because of their inability to draw. They prefer to seek help rather than create what a few embroiderers refer to as "kindergarten figures."

It is actually common practice for stitchers to seek help in drawing. Most women in this area who are adept at embroidery learned from preprinted stencils on muslin at a very early age. These experiences refined stitching skills, but did nothing to encourage the young stitchers to draw their own designs or even choose their own color combinations. In the tapestry at Villanueva, New Mexico, there are examples of collaboration between relatives or friends who drew the images for accomplished embroiderers such as Isidora Madrid de Flores or Filomena Gonzales (see fig. 5). Carmen Orrego-Salas also described a woman in one of her stitching workshops at Ninhue, Chile, who had difficulty drawing profiles and asked her children for help. Even in a recent church-sponsored embroidery project in Chile, she mentioned that women have sought help from a self-trained artist to aid them in "tricky visual problems." Carmen maintains that help of this kind facilitates the "realization of the vision but doesn't interfere with or direct that vision."[44] The Carson colcha women as well initially relied on male relatives like Wayne Graves to draw for them.

Soon after her arrival in San Luis in 1989, Paula Cunningham joined Sally Chavez's Master/Apprentice group, one of the immediate precursors to the Ladies Sewing Circle. When the women realized that Paula had some expertise in drawing and could assist them in their selection of the appropriate colors for their pieces, her status shifted from stitching apprentice to a type of "artist-in-residence" role for which she was modestly paid.

Paula Cunningham and her husband left teaching positions on the Navajo Reservation and came to San Luis with their young son because of Tim Cunningham's appointment at the local high school. Neither of the Cunninghams were Catholic in a town where one was considered Catholic from birth. As Father Pat states, despite religious affiliation, "the whole place is Catholic." But Paula's rapid acceptance by the Ladies Sewing Circle due to her artistic background, her willingness to advise the stitchers, and her friendshjip with Evangeline helped the Cunninghams to be more readily integrated into San Luis society than most Anglo-American outsiders.

It soon became apparent that Paula Cunningham's role as advisor to the stitchers was expanding, making greater demands on her time to the detriment of her own work. On realizing this, Evangeline instituted a pay scale. Rates were assessed according to the task, whether it was drawing, conferring about the composition, or recommending a color scheme with reference to choices of yarn. At first payments for Paula's efforts were made from funds remaining in the grant pool of the Ladies Sewing Circle. When these funds were depleted, payment became the responsibility of the individual stitcher seeking assistance.

Paula Cunningham's presence in the sewing circle had interesting consequences for the other members, though perhaps these were not immediately apparent. Because of her status as an Anglo and an outsider thought to have superior training, the women were more likely to defer to her knowledge, and to seek her recommendations, than if she were Hispanic. Moreover, since Paula drew a major number of images for the stitchers, her style tended to produce a certain similarity among the colchas. This uniformity was also compounded by her intervention concerning color choice. These tendencies toward sameness were further accentuated by the fact that Sally Chavez and Evangeline Salazar supplied yarn from a single distributor. Thus the work of the Ladies Sewing Circle became identifiably uniform in terms of color usage and style; i.e., the repeated use of a certain blue for backgrounds or skies and similar design strategies gave separate works by different women a fairly homogeneous appearance.

Despite the visual evidence that this process of consultation interfered with fostering individual inventiveness and creativity, an interesting byproduct of Paula Cunningham's interaction with the stitchers was the burgeoning aesthetic interest these women showed in the landscape. Consequently, during her residency, stitchers began to notice and talk about naturally occurring colors in the countryside. They started to observe nature for its artistic effects and intrinsic aesthetic merit. Evangeline Salazar describes her growing awareness of the presence and strength of color:

> I think it's made us more aware of colors. For in the past we were used to embroidering kits. Colors had been selected. Now we can sit and watch these beautiful mountains and beautiful skies. I've never been so aware of colors. Who had ever thought of a pink sky? When I made that picture—that sunset? I used to sit in my little den and look out that way.... I had never noticed a pink sky. Well, I was doing a pink sky. You don't think of that, but here was a sunset.... It's just made us more keen, [more aware] of all the beautiful mountains.[45]

In the summer of 1992 Paula Cunningham and her family moved to Alamosa, about forty-five miles northwest of San Luis. Without their resident artist, the Ladies Sewing Circle tried to find other ways around the problem of drawing their own compositions. Some women, like Sally Chavez, transferred their young grandchildren's drawings to muslin by using a method customarily associated with transferring images from commercial stencil designs. These pieces were then passed on to their families as keepsakes. Sally Chavez embroidered a drawing her five-year-old grandson gave her. He drew it from his perspective, standing outside his house and peeking in through the window at the backs of his grandmother's and mother's heads as they sat together on the living room couch. After she had finished her rendition of his drawing, Sally even embroidered her grandson's signature and the date on her piece.

As an artistic and cultural gesture, the idea of memorializing grandchildren's art is not confined to Hispanic ethnic practice; but Sally Chavez's embroidery does represent an inherent San Luis concern with family and with the belief in publicly promoting intergenerational compatibility. The metamorphosis of the child's fragile drawing on notebook paper into the richer, more substantial medium of embroidery by a grandmother's hand transcends the actual act of media transference to symbolize both emotionally and artistically the perpetuation of familial links and heritage.

It is interesting that stitchers like Sally Chavez who denigrate their own drawing skills as rudimentary and their sketches as awkward and unaesthetic enthusiastically adopt children's work for their embroideries. Apparently, grandmother-artists can appreciate childlike stylistic traits within what they consider to be the proper age bracket and artistic context. But the universality and appeal of these same characteristics as a foundation for their own styles does not interest them.

Encouraged by Evangeline Salazar, a core of women in the Ladies Sewing Circle insist on framing their embroideries under glass in elaborate frames by commercial framers. These often have color-coordinated double and triple mats embellished with small ornate openwork designs cut into one corner by the framer. Stitchers choose framing styles according to personal taste and to coordinate with their domestic decor. They also believe that their embroideries deserve the ultimate in ornamental treatment since these finished pieces represent long hours of involvement and hard work.

Framing colchas in this manner has been criticized by outsider art professionals arbitrating cultural and artistic authenticity; many feel that it detracts from the nature of the embroidery medium (soft, sensuous, opaque, and textural). Their view calls for framing the colchas in materials more consonant with locale—weathered barn wood or cholla cactus skeletons—rather than displaying them within a setting that broadcasts commercial glitter and modern decorativeness.

Carmen Orrego-Salas also objects to framing embroidery with glass, because without air circulation to remove trapped moisture (and for other reasons), the textile can suffer damage over time. She also observes that aesthetically the glass's reflective surface obscures the rich appearance of complex stitchery. Evangeline Salazar is a proponent of framing colchas but did mention that same problem of reflection, which detracted from the distinction or integrity of her framed piece depicting the Health Clinic as an intricate, meticulously done embroidery when it was hung next to a window.

Conflicting internal and external opinions concerning thematic subject matter and the pros and cons of framing underscore some of the issues first raised in the stitching workshops sponsored by outside entrepreneurs from Villanueva to San Luis. Neocolonial overtones have been identified within much of the dialogue between stitchers and those promoters who advocate pictorial themes that tend to reinforce outsiders' expectations of the timelessness of Hispanic village life rendered in a picturesquely "primitive" style.

The cast of this externally generated advocacy is significant when one observes that the fine art of the culture brokers is situated within a domain of fluid, ever-changing societal tastes. Furthermore, fine art is currently valued for its novelty, and is routinely framed as a way of displaying privilege, status, and cultivated sensitivity. It may also seem slightly paradoxical to members of the San Luis stitching group to be advised to choose a "primitive look" in framing materials that does not satisfy their personal taste or complement the decor of their own homes. Outsiders (according to San Luis stitchers) have the desire, the means, and the cosmopolitan imagination to integrate unusual art work into their decor. This is not the case in San Luis or Villanueva (areas of more conservative taste subject to certain rules of etiquette that privilege conformity over novelty). Obviously the work of the Ladies Sewing Circle demonstrates that this group too exists in a changeable artistic climate—one that can be mediated by individual interpretation and preference.[46]

## Cultural Politics

Another problematic set of dynamics within the configuration of colcha creation and cultural action comprises the marketing, exhibiting, and gift-giving strategies aimed at colcha making. Colcha display can fall within the sphere of the market. Or, in terms of traveling exhibitions and local shows in the San Luis region, it can subvert external marketing strategies by taking colcha objects out of commercial circulation for use in different venues. Also, gift-giving as a culturally determined action that reinforces social solidarity undermines outside marketing interests by simply depleting inventory for sale, never permitting the craft to become commercially viable in the first place.

Carmen Orrego-Salas's stitching workshops taught embroidery skills intended to be used to create and market art work from the San Luis community to tourists and to outside shops and galleries. Within a marketing context it was believed by entrepreneurs that after a relatively short developmental period for the local industry, colcha embroidery would become established as a commodity. However, Carmen Orrego-Salas verbally and by example promoted the stitching experience as a fundamentally creative and artistic act. For stitchers like Julia Valdez, Daisy Ortega, Teresa Vigil, and Josie Lobato this involved imaginatively entering their work on a deep, intensely personal level. The more the artists who were creating in the pictorial narrative mode responded to the entrepreneurial recommendations to stitch pictures replete with cultural emblems, autobiographical detail, and action, the deeper their individual artistic involvement became. Thus, as the intensity of personal expression increased, so did the market value, because of the enriched subject matter. At the same time these embroidered pictures became so inherently valuable to their creators, their personal worth was of such importance, that the artists could not sell them. Ironically, the spirit of creativity that generated the art work also tended to defy the aims of the marketplace.

Pride in their burgeoning talents as artists affected other embroiderers as well. Sally Chavez describes one of the most common reasons for holding on to a colcha once it has been completed: "and seeing that the end product is what you are after and once you see it framed, I mean you just want to keep it! You don't want to sell it! You put in so many hours and hours and hours. It does take a lot of time. And once you see the finished product, you don't want to sell it. Maybe others don't see it as beautiful . . . but we think it is. It's gorgeous!"[47]

The Ladies Sewing Circle arose from the 1988 stitching workshop with an agenda of fellowship plus the hope of marketing their work. The genre of pictorial narrative, which has such appeal to outside consumers, is practically nonexistent in the stitching repertoire of the Sewing Circle. Instead, some women embroider scenic landscapes or architectural monuments that are marketable principally as icons of locale. The majority of stitchers, however, prefer to create pictures from popular sources that reflect individual taste and their sense of aesthetic beauty. The choice of imagery (birds, flowers, animals) marginally connects these embroideries to the local geographic and cultural region. These are also highly personal statements, but without knowing or understanding the cultural context outsiders are unlikely to comprehend or appreciate this aspect of their creation.

As director of the Sewing Circle, Evangeline Salazar wants to sell these decorative-style colchas in order to augment personal revenues but also to increase the self-esteem of group members. When a collection of these colchas was exhibited during the San Luis Shrine Dedication Weekend in May 1990 (there were thousands of visitors), the Denver marketing agent/art consultant hired by the local Economic Development Council displayed them in an area away from the general flow of tourist traffic without advertising their location, and neglected to label the colchas with the names of the artists or list the prices. Pondering this "non-event," Evangeline expressed the ambivalence that seems to pervade San Luis: "And then, too, I don't know if there's ever been any real interest from anyone wanting to sell their pictures [laughs]. But I was hoping we could sell *one* to show that money could be made by selling one."[48]

Similar dynamics and problems have played out over the past decade with a collection of several colcha embroideries from the early-1970s Virginia Neal Blue Resource Center stitching workshops. These are on display in the San Luis Cultural Museum. The presence of these pieces is not common knowledge among San Luis citizens. They are not promoted as unique features within the San Luis artistic and cultural landscape; nor are tourists encouraged to view them, since the lights are usually turned off in the exhibit room of the Museum.

It is true that these embroideries have been given back to the community by the VNB stitching project and are not for sale. Yet their presence could be considered a powerful cultural statement for both San Luis insiders and visiting tourists. From a marketing perspective, making them more accessible to visitors could also generate outside interest in this medium and potentially result in a few commissions for Sewing Circle stitchers.

Evangeline Salazar has always been receptive to outside marketers and gallery owners. She also encourages other members of the Sewing Circle to seek public exposure for their work. However, in so doing she consistently promotes the scenic and decorative idioms of colcha over the pictorial narrative genre. Salazar's embroideries were featured in the traveling Colorado Council for the Arts and Humanities Folk Arts Master/Apprentice Exhibit. I also included her scenic colcha embroidery, *La Vega*, along with pieces by other San Luis embroiderers in the January 1992 National Center for Atmospheric Research (NCAR) exhibition in Boulder, just north of Denver on Colorado's Front Range. This event was followed by another showing of the same colcha collection the next month at the national corporate headquarters of Coors Corporation in Golden, Colorado.

In the NCAR exhibit I did not include any decorative-style colchas inspired by magazine reproductions. However, there were a couple of scenic colchas for sale. During the exhibition I received inquiries only about buying the pictorial narrative embroideries (including Julia Valdez's *Adobe Plant* and Daisy Ortega's *El Convento*). These items were from family collections and were therefore not for sale.

Although there is a polite eagerness to accommodate external requests to exhibit art work in situations that might lead to greater exposure and sales, many San Luis residents experience a feeling of loss of control over the fate of their prized possessions once their embroideries are taken to the other side of La Veta Pass (the point where the limits of the San Luis Valley meet the summit of Colorado's Front Range). I encountered this attitude when I asked to borrow a Virginia Neal Blue embroidery from the San Luis Cultural Museum for the exhibit I was installing at NCAR in Boulder. After much respectful negotiation with careful explanation, promises to obtain insurance coverage, and adherence to protocol on my part, the Museum Board refused my request on the grounds that they did not want the colcha to leave the area for fear of damage or loss. Also implicit in this refusal is a reluctance to allow an outsider (albeit a friend of the community) to remove a cultural item from their arena of power and control.

The Board's decision had repercussions for the stitcher whose work was involved. This individual really wanted to participate in the NCAR exhibit, believing that she might receive commissions if one of her embroideries was featured. At the time of exhibit planning, she had sold all her inventory, and had nothing left at home and inadequate time to create another colcha. We thought that at least we could borrow her piece from the Virginia Neal Blue collection in the Museum, which would give her work some public exposure. It would also be good publicity for the San Luis Museum's collection, and perhaps raise its profile as a repository for regional cultural treasures. Despite the initial setback, this stitcher managed to create a small-scale colcha for the exhibition in Boulder, and it was ultimately purchased.

The saying "creativity is a gift" sums up the final part of this analysis. No matter what the stylistic content is, by and large the San Luis stitchers are so engrossed in the creation of their embroideries that their emotional involvement inspires and sometimes compels them to give their colchas to family and friends rather than sell them. This also holds true for the women who start out with selling in mind—the stitchers who create the popularly based decorative-style pieces (fig. 9). The progressive personal and artistic engagement with their work makes it difficult for the stitchers to turn these items over to be marketed. For them it is like releasing an object brimming with memory into an appreciative but indifferent world.

Considering Father Pat's early discovery of rooms full of craft items languishing in parishioners' homes, a venerable history of hand craft production within the Hispanic household evidently persists in San Luis. For generations it was customary for that domestic center to be the scene of artistic action, and this same center served as the nexus for barter and exchange from frontier days to more contemporary times. Traditionally, cultural items circulated throughout San Luis as gifts. Within this context gifts are exchanged among equals—unlike the hierarchical structure of patron and artist that obtains within the commercial art world and marketplace. Domestic-centered exchange is (at least in this Hispanic context) essentially egalitarian.

Colcha gift-giving is private. By refusing to sell, stitchers can hold on to these objects as personal relics of solitary, contemplative moments, of memories stimulated by the act of stitching, and of their own artistic struggles to create these pieces. They keep them within the family for their exclusive appreciation. This private action resists the course of commoditization and reroutes the distribution of the art object from its intended external destination, the marketplace, to the internal circuit of relatives and friends. Thus, to retain an object many outsiders would like to buy, one that was produced with this intention, subverts commercial interests.

But gift exchange among friends and family is another very particular kind of circulation.⁴⁹ "The irony is that the very act of giving enhances the worth of the object given, because what is given [and received] is social as well as material."⁵⁰ Usually, the more a colcha is circulated among friends, the more it is viewed, commented upon, and passed along through a family's generations, the more it becomes both socially and economically valuable. Instead of losing value because of its removal from the world of commerce, colcha's worth is elevated by its increasing rarity and preciousness.

Accordingly, once disseminated through many hands in ever widening circles of cherished gift-giving, the colcha increases its intrinsic worth and extrinsic value until, by chance or circumstance (estate sales, auctions, or trade), it reaches the marketplace. In this rather circuitous manner, these art objects finally fit the original external conception of colcha embroidery as an art-brokered commodity. But by that point they are so removed in time (and space) that the original intended benefits as a community resource have either been postponed or never realized.

Most San Luis stitchers are reluctant to sell because of their personal involvement in their work. The power they derive from the process itself is another factor. These reasons contribute to the stitchers' desire to keep the colchas as heirlooms or only give them to friends and family. Sally Chavez describes the gift-giving momentum colcha making engenders: "The thing is, the ones who have made pictures, their children see them and say, 'Mom, I want that one. Will you make me one?' And the other ones say, 'Well, you gave him [or her] one, will you make me one, too?' And so they have been making them and giving them to their children."⁵¹ Father Pat views colchas in the same vein—more in terms of their destiny as family heirlooms: "Colchas are being made strictly for families—for children. They are heirloom quality. There is good money to be paid for them. But right now I see it as a hobby."⁵²

The San Luis Ladies Sewing Circle interacts with outsiders in a perpetual round of aesthetic, social, and cultural alteration. The tenor of this interaction is revealed in several apparently ambiguous, often contradictory series of events and anomalous circumstances subject to a mode of cultural inversion where the relations between cause and effect are upended, reversed, or even hindered. The idea of using cultural inversion to explain the connections among stitchers, parishioners, and entrepreneurs is particularly helpful in determining the nature and extent of San Luis's struggles with cultural and artistic autonomy, self-representation, and outside influence.

The way all these components fit together underscores a central issue affecting the linkage of power to community self-representation in San Luis. Throughout this chapter, power has been assessed, tracked, and teased through aesthetic factors, an analysis of creativity and observing memory's role in art and social relations. Ethnoaesthetics or folk aesthetics, which internally value and even monitor colcha creation in San Luis, constitute the yardstick by which creativity, symbolic action, and the power inherent in making art are measured against the impact of cultural institutions. In San Luis these "institutions" are represented by the Sangre de Cristo Catholic Church and various factions within the community, as well as by externally and internally organized programs of renewal and economic development. The dimensions of this yardstick are determined by the traditions embedded in the local aesthetic system, which are validated through practice and refinement by the stitchers themselves. These standards shape artistic decisions, either commanding conformity or—for some stitchers—setting a boundary to be transgressed.

Creativity, the meaning or significance of colcha making (to insiders and outsiders), and reflexivity as a form of meditative feedback flowing between art and life are also part of ethnoaesthetics. Much of our discussion emphasizes the creative process mobilizing different art worlds (individual stitchers, Sewing Circle, Father Pat's parish, and Carmen Orrego-Salas's workshops) rather than restricting ourselves to the divided and limited territories subsumed under an exclusive duality of art versus non-art.

Memory is activated by stitching, and stitching is motivated by memory. This circularity is implied in Julia Valdez's saying, "You express and you remember." In the study of colcha, particularly the San Luis styles, we can ascertain how art literally constructs and reconstructs history through remembrance (and forgetting) as these personal and collective forces are transformed into embroidery. This process is clearly visible in the pictorial narratives of women like Julia Valdez, Josie Lobato, Teresa Vigil, Sostena Cleven, and Daisy Ortega. Other Sewing Circle women, with their scenic and decorative-style colchas, actually demonstrate how the conscious act of forgetting can relate to choice of imagery.

These stitchers avoid heavily personalized subject matter that might reveal aspects of their individual or communal histories they would rather not revive. Earlier Father Pat sympathetically stated that many embroiderers are not interested in depicting historical themes that evoke bitter memories: "Old is what they've grown up with. Some of the ladies say, 'Well, it's old and I don't like *old*. I grew up with old all my life.'"[53] Evangeline reiterated the same thoughts in a different context when she described her attitude toward unilaterally advocating cultural themes for members of the Sewing Circle:

[The] Virginia Neal Blue group and even with Carmen at the time they were going in for cultural pictures and rather than turn people off we just, you know, sewed and embroidered whatever we liked. Now ... if I was told you just have to do that, they would have turned me off a long time ago and we would have turned off Pacífica with her black-and-whites and we would have turned off Frances with her deer and unicorn ... and Cordy with her beautiful flowers.[54]

Ever since the Santa Fe Trail brought manufactured goods overland from the eastern United States, generations of Hispanic women have tried to meld with, or have been assimilated by, the dominant Anglo culture by adapting to its materialism and pervasive aesthetic system. Later, modern San Luis stitchers learned or refined their embroidery skills in compliance with the aims of Anglo-dominated workshops. Along with the reappropriation of "traditional" techniques, Sewing Circle women interested in reproducing scenic or decorative-style colchas also appropriated patterns and the "look" of embroideries featured in craft magazines—popularly regarded as the acme of Anglo taste.

For as long as these women can remember, they aspired to imitate that taste and what they believed to be the goals of Anglo culture. Now they discover the rules have changed. Affluent and educated outsiders want ethnic art with all its awkwardness and "charming" imperfections, which are deemed examples of *pure* cultural expressiveness. To stitchers this dictum is a form of silence about their work—a silence that ignores current lifestyles and discounts their personal opinions of themselves. This amounts to just another form of erasure and consignment to "difference" enacted all over again. The climactic twist in forces of cultural inversion at work here is the fact that Hispanic stitchers want to sell these colchas, because they are proud and believe them to be cleverly done. But purely decorative-style colchas are unmarketable to discerning art brokers because of the apparent *absence* of the ethnic artist's touch and "cultural" sensibility.

Art making and colcha history in particular are notable for stalemates like this. Memory and forgetting (in terms of the decorative colcha style) are also susceptible to partisan forces. Clearly, the use of memory is selective and provocative. As the focus of visual narrative, memory intercedes between individual remembrance and the "prescriptive nature of social or 'official' memory." For example, the artistic intentions, the message of the embroidery, depends not only on which personal or individual memories are being recorded but on what cultural institution condones them as well. It was demonstrated with Josie Lobato's colchas that a "specific memory repertoire (religious, racial, or gendered) can be used to symbolically reinforce power and status of special interest groups (entrepreneurs, redevelopment projects); or, conversely, to underscore the absence of such power (embroiderers)."

The dominance of certain memories over others also emphasizes the intentionality of remembrance and forgetfulness. Some women stitch themes laced with positive recollections that appear buoyant and affirming. Others select designs inspired by mass media (images from sweatshirts, craft magazines, or catalogues) based on their own preferences and their sense of "cultural safety," which buffers them against too much personal exposure or risk. Deliberately or not, these patterns then become substitutes for memory-driven motifs dealing with topics that may have been expressly forgotten because they recall bleak periods of little money and the unease of discrimination and difference. Therefore, contemporary colcha embroidery together with its traditional variants is not a neutral medium; as discovered in earlier chapters, "it is populated—overpopulated—with the intentions of others."

# 6

## stitches of myth and memory

Colcha is a combination of the old and the new—the old that I remember and the new that was in my life at that period. So, it's a memory. It's absolutely a memory.
—Josephine Lobato

It may seem repetitive—possibly tautological—to restate how carefully colcha embroidery tracks life's actions, how closely it is intertwined with perception and experience. Colcha is a medium and an arena of creative action that certainly corroborates Kenneth Burke's idea that "[T]here are no forms of art which are not forms of experience outside art."[1] In fact, with much of colcha making it is difficult to determine where everyday experience ceases and threads of invention begin.

Occasionally, at different points in our discussion, "story" has been substituted for "study." This emphasis is attuned with the idea that the two foci of this work—art and life—are always variable. Story implies that what is being detailed in these pages is ongoing—that it is truthful but not finite. Future storytelling scholars may devise other endings or invent interpretations that more accurately assess the impact and quality or extent of human versatility and imagination at work here. For the time being, the main emphases on memory, ethnoaesthetics, and social critique enable art historical concerns (iconography, symbolism, and style) to align and integrate with cultural behavior in all its richness.

A strong force activating ethnoaesthetics (how a group judges their work and the value they assign to it) is the power inherent in creative and interpretive processes. Peripherally, the course of cultural power shapes the colcha object by ricocheting between external pressures or expectations and internal native cultural and aesthetic responses. These dynamics are forged from alternating rounds of adaptation and resistance. Despite the greater "official" authority of external art brokers, stitchers have the final word. For they must create colchas according to their own taste and pleasure; otherwise they feel their efforts are hollow. When Evangeline Salazar describes herself and her friends as being "very proud of our pictures. It's like Sally says—'we can't paint with a brush . . . but we can certainly do it with a needle,'" she expresses her belief in creative autonomy vis-à-vis her view of being an artist.

Deviations from outsiders' expectations of consistently "ethnic" embroideries occur throughout colcha history, from colonial nineteenth-century embroidered textiles that cut across genres to emulate contemporary weaving styles to Carson colcha stitchers' preference for narrative detail and nontraditional materials like acrylic yarn. Applied aesthetics, aesthetics at work, register the tenor of artistic engagement while concurrently measuring the impact of cultural institutions (church, government, and economic recovery programs) on social and cultural behavior.

External and internal forces spin around each other attempting to resolve and finalize slippery concepts such as tradition, authenticity, and change. This study opts for an interpretive space that is highly sensitive and responsive to the changeability of human nature and honors the transcendent character of making art as inherent in all artistic struggles and accomplishments. My primary intention in writing on ethnic art is to offer a notion of art making as a creative space where the continual negotiation and redefinition of boundaries occurs with respect to alterations between insiders and outsiders, shifts in tradition and change, and individual versus collective creative expression. Instead of outlining contours of separation, these boundaries can be perceived as mutable, or better yet as permeable—more like interlocking pathways than monolithic dividers or barriers.

Colchas as objects of memory are not only timeless but also time*full*. They are overlaid with memories of the past that are remembered in the present and signify future directions. Much reconstructing of memory also factors in what is forgotten. This is certainly evident in San Luis embroideries. Josie Lobato stitches her childhood memories from a transitional period in San Luis history when Anglo influences were quite strong. Other members of the community view visible reminders of that era negatively because many of these seemingly picturesque elements (or what they would regard as encroachments) recall the discomfort of assimilation. They feel that subject matter, those themes, are not suitable for art work and are best forgotten. External entrepreneurs have mixed feelings about these compositions because they prefer the picturesque unaffected by indications of change or compromised by hints of Anglo influence. Art brokers tend to favor romanticized scenes of remembrance minus the various subplots characteristic of life in the valley, thus perpetuating a kind of cultural amnesia.

To compose her Penitente colcha, Josie Lobato worked hard at reconstructing her husband Eugene's memories in order to depict accurately such a sensitive theme. A few people in San Luis were not pleased that Josie was featuring the Penitentes in an art work (although Father Pat was very encouraging). A member of the Brotherhood who is active in public affairs of the community was particularly displeased. He behaved as if he had proprietary interest in penitente observances, thus claiming sole ownership of all memory and information surrounding these clandestine practices. The way memory can be altered and the strength of collective memories that promote certain cultural values are also very important to the formulation of cultural and social identity. In San Luis this was expressed through the iconography of the main street mural and the maintenance (among a certain sector in town) of a common belief system espousing strong links with Baroque Spain, which in turn supports the notion of an abiding Catholic attitude as well. Colcha embroideries are also culture carriers—aesthetic objects that give meaning over time to the possible relationships of artist to society and memory to social and political realities.

Despite different agendas, we must not overlook the importance of each of these factors to people trying to cope with the evanescent present moment—whether they are embroiderers transmitting memories mixed with self-defining traditions or a reawakened community forging a vital identity. Art courts immortality; it also encapsulates memory. Josie Lobato is trying to ensure that her memories are not lost by transforming them into art. When she describes her method of recovering memory piecemeal and converting it into imagery, she is also creating a new cultural past: "This is my history, the history that I grew up with. So, it's coming out in bits and pieces in my mind as to what was important. But the point of the whole thing is . . . not to lose something that is going to be lost." Julia Valdez believes that stitching and thinking work together to activate memory: "You express and you remember." These ideas give a different emphasis to Tiva Trujillo's concept of visual memory as truth consigned only to the past: "My life—it's a true picture and a real picture. They were alive sometime . . . oh once upon a time." Memory thus triggered by art and creativity brings "once upon a time" into the present moment.

It is fitting that I finish with the theme of memory. I am far away from San Luis, but memory keeps me near. One of my last impressions of the San Luis Valley concerns the Holy Week reenactment of Las Tinieblas (Darkness) and the Penitente Brothers as memory-keepers. This ceremony, also called Tenebrae, recreates the tumult and confusion following Jesus' death, when the dead rose and walked the earth. In Penitente moradas it usually occurs on Holy Thursday, sometimes on Good Friday nights. When I was coming down the hill after the El Encuentro service on Good Friday afternoon one of the Hermanas invited me to return that evening for Tinieblas. I was honored but a little apprehensive because of the stories I had heard about sitting in a darkened chapel (in my case mainly with strangers) surrounded by noise and shouting.

Fortunately, Josie and our friend Pat Sloan were interested in accompanying me, so we all returned Friday night for the service. Before it began we sat in the chapel while other women talked among themselves and restless children roamed about the room. I could hear the Brothers praying and chanting in the next room. They abruptly entered and knelt at the altar to recite the Rosary. A Brother stood and after each *alabado* verse extinguished one of thirteen candles until only the top candle remained burning on the triangular candelabrum, just as Jesus was left after having been abandoned by the twelve Apostles. Then all the Brothers rose and left the chapel, taking the single candle with them and leaving us sitting together but alone in the darkness.

From within the sacristy a Brother shouted out "Ave Maria!" This was followed by chains clanking, sounds of rattles, pounding on the floor, clapping, and moaning. This commotion, intensifying the disorienting blackness, represented the chaos and shadow that enveloped the earth as Jesus died. The noise faded into the recitation of prayers for the souls of the dead, for the Brothers and their families, and for those of us present. During this litany we all became witnesses to the power of memory as the living commemorated the dead in the face of disorder and uncertainty. Our names were called out with the rest, thus firmly binding us together in a pledge of remembrance not only to the dead but to ourselves as well.

| *Adios todos los presentes* | Good-by, all those present, |
| *Que me van a acompanar* | All who accompany me . . . |
| *Adios todos mis proximos* | Good-by all my neighbors, |
| *No me vayan a olvidar.* | And do not forget me. |
| *Fin—Fin—Amen* | The End—The End—Amen[2] |

# notes

**Chapter 1. *Tierra Nueva***

1. Terry Mattingly, "San Luis Bears a Cross of Its Own," *Rocky Mountain News,* 14 April 1990, 10 col. 1.
2. James Coates, "Coloradoans Building a Mountain Shrine," *Chicago Tribune,* 20 October 1990, 23 col. 1.
3. Mattingly, "San Luis," 10 col. 1.
4. Solitude and geographical isolation in New Mexico, and consequently in Colorado, have also fostered independence and privacy vis-à-vis the cultural and religious politics of the establishment. Preference for this type of lifestyle is evident in the late eighteenth-century criticism directed at it by Spanish colonial administrators; e.g., Governor Fernando de la Concha complained of Santa Feans' "churlish nature" and condemned "the perfect freedom in which they have always lived." In 1778 Father Morfí indicted New Mexicans for being "undisciplined and for preferring to live on their own in remote areas rather than congregating in towns." See Marc Simmons, "Colonial New Mexico and Mexico: The Historical Relationship," in *Colonial Frontiers: Art and Life in Spanish New Mexico,* ed. Christine Mather (Santa Fe: Museum of New Mexico Press, 1983), 76.
5. Ron Sandoval, "The San Luis Vega," in *La Cultura Constante de San Luis,* ed. Randall Teeuwen (San Luis: The San Luis Museum Cultural and Commercial Center, 1985), 22.

6. Virginia Simmons, *The San Luis Valley: Land of the Six-Armed Cross* (Boulder, Colo.: Pruett Publishing Company, 1979), 13.
7. Evangeline Salazar and Sally T. Chavez, taped interview by author, San Luis, Colorado, 18 January 1991.
8. Father Patricio Valdez, taped interview by author, Sangre de Cristo Rectory, San Luis, Colorado, 18 January 1991.
9. Terry Mattingly, "Higher Ground: Father Patrick Valdez Has San Luis on the Rise," *Rocky Mountain News*, 3 June 1990, 14M–17M.
10. "Sangre de Cristo Parish Newsletter" 4, no. 2 (summer 1991): 7.
11. Coates, 23 col. 1.

## Chapter 2. Josephine Lobato as Cultural Commentator

1. Josephine Lobato, taped interview by author, Fort Garland Museum, Fort Garland, Colorado, 20 July 1990.
2. J. Lobato, interview, 1990.
3. Henry Glassie, Exhibition catalogue, *Turkish Traditional Art Today* (Santa Fe: Museum of New Mexico, 1991), 5.
4. J. Lobato, interview, 1990.
5. J. Lobato, interview, 1990.
6. J. Lobato, interview, 1990.
7. J. Lobato, interview, 1990.
8. This concept appears in Janet Berlo's article on the Inuit graphic artist as cultural commentator. See Janet Catherine Berlo, "Portraits of Dispossession in Plains Indian and Inuit Graphic Arts," *Art Journal* 49, no. 2 (summer 1990): 133–41.
9. J. Lobato, interview, 1990.
10. J. Lobato, taped interview by author, Fort Garland Museum, Fort Garland, Colorado, 24 February 1993.
11. J. Lobato, interview, 1990.
12. J. Lobato, interview, 1990.
13. J. Lobato, interview, 1990.
14. J. Lobato, telephone conversation with author, 15 January 1991.
15. J. Lobato, interview, 1990.
16. J. Lobato, interview, 1990.
17. Maria Lugones and Elizabeth Spelman, "Have We Got a Theory for You! Feminist Theory, Cultural Imperialism, and the Demand for the 'Woman's Voice,'" *Women's Studies International Forum* 6, no. 6 (1983): 593.
18. J. Lobato, interview, 1990.
19. J. Lobato, interview, 1990.
20. Similar allegorical themes appear in Carlos Sandoval's San Luis mural. Refer to chapter 1.

21. J. Lobato, interview, 1990.
22. J. Lobato, interview, 1990.
23. *Chorreras* originally formed fortifications around the frontier village plazas as a defense against Indian raids.
24. J. Lobato, interview, 1990.
25. J. Lobato, interview, 1990.
26. Nelson H. H. Graburn, "'I Like Things to Look More Different than That Stuff Did': An Experiment in Cross-Cultural Art Appreciation," in *Art and Society: Studies in Style, Culture and Aesthetics,* ed. Michael Greenhalgh and Vincent Megaw (New York: St. Martin's Press, 1978), 66.
27. J. Lobato, interview, 1990.
28. J. Lobato, interview, 1990.
29. During a visit to Josie in February 1991, I met a woman from Pueblo on Colorado's Front Range who was planning to include *La Entriega* as part of her daughter's wedding ceremony. This could indicate that cultural memory or cultural interest lingered longer in urban communities where Latinos conscientiously maintained or retrieved (revitalized) certain customs.
30. J. Lobato, interview, 1990.
31. J. Lobato, interview, 1990.
32. Cleofas Jaramillo, *Shadows of the Past* (Santa Fe: Ancient City Press, 1941), 34.
33. J. Lobato, interview, 1990.
34. J. Lobato, interview, 1990.
35. J. Lobato, interview, 1990.
36. J. Lobato, interview, 1990.
37. J. Lobato, interview, 1990.
38. Juan Estevan Medina, taped interview by author, Fort Garland Morada, Fort Garland, Colorado, 23 September 1993.
39. J. Lobato, telephone conversation with author, 18 November 1991.
40. J. Lobato, letter to author, 15 September 1991.
41. J. Lobato, telephone conversation with author, 22 August 1991.
42. J. Lobato, telephone conversation with author, 15 September 1991.
43. J. Lobato, telephone conversation with author, 18 August 1991.
44. Eugene Lobato, conversation with author, Chama, Colorado, 19 January 1991.
45. E. Lobato, taped interview by author, Chama, Colorado, 29 March 1991.
46. Mary Taylor, conversation with author, El Rito Morada, El Rito, Colorado, 17 April 1992.
47. J. Lobato, taped interview by author, Fort Garland Museum, Fort Garland, Colorado, 23 February 1993.
48. J. Lobato, interview, 1993.
49. J. Lobato, interview, 1993.
50. J. Lobato, interview, 1993.

51. J. Lobato, interview, 1993.
52. J. Lobato, interview, 1993.
53. J. Lobato, interview, 1993.
54. J. Lobato, interview, 1993.
55. J. Lobato, interview, 1993.
56. J. Lobato, telephone conversation, 12 February 1992.
57. Tiva Trujillo, quoted in *Las Artistas del Valle de San Luis* (Arvada, Colo.: Arvada Center for the Arts and Humanities, 1982), 8.
58. Trujillo, in *Las Artistas,* 21.
59. Paula Hamilton, "The Knife Edge: Debates about Memory and History," in *Memory and History in Twentieth-Century Australia,* ed. Kate Darian-Smith and Paula Hamilton (Oxford: Oxford University Press, 1994), 20.
60. J. Lobato, interview, 1993.
61. Carmen Orrego-Salas, letter to San Luis Sewing Circle, 15 May 1990.
62. J. Lobato, interview, 1990.
63. J. Lobato, interview, 1990.

## Chapter 3. Change and Tradition in Historical Colcha Making

1. M. A. Wilder and Herman Schweitzer, correspondence 23–26 December 1936, Taylor Museum Archives, Colorado Springs Fine Arts Center. Wilder was Director of the Taylor Museum at that time. Schweitzer collected for the Fred Harvey Company in Santa Fe from 1902 until 1940.
2. Robert Blair St. George, "Bawns and Beliefs: Architecture, Commerce, and Conversion in Early New England," *Winterthur Portfolio* 25 (1990), 246.
3. St. George, 247.
4. Susan Stewart, *On Longing* (Baltimore, Md.: Johns Hopkins University Press, 1984), 48.
5. Nora Fisher, "Colcha Embroidery," in *Spanish Textile Tradition of New Mexico and Colorado,* ed. Nora Fisher (Santa Fe: Museum of New Mexico Press, 1979), 161.
6. E. Boyd, *Popular Arts of Spanish New Mexico* (Santa Fe: Museum of New Mexico Press, 1974), 210.
7. Marc Simmons, 74.
8. Christine Mather, "Works of Art in Frontier New Mexico," in *Colonial Frontiers: Art and Life in Spanish New Mexico,* ed. Christine Mather (Santa Fe, N.M.: Ancient City Press, 1983), 12.
9. A convent connected to the Mission of Santa Ana could imply either a nunnery or a monastery. Since there is no evidence of nuns in the area at this time, it was probably the latter. Although no information was found in the New Mexico State Records Center and Archives regarding the existence of early nunneries in colonial New Mexico, I am grateful to Dr. Helen Lucero, former Curator of New Mexican Hispanic Crafts and Textiles, Museum of International Folk Art in Santa Fe, for suggesting I investigate the linkage between cloisters and wool-on-wool colcha making. For more information see: Fray

Angelico Chavez, *Archives of the Archdiocese of Santa Fe* (Washington: Academy of American Franciscan History, 1957), 25, 117–18; and Sisters of Loretto Microfilm Collection, New Mexico State Records Center and Archives.

10. Finely executed Mexican embroidered textiles, distinct from Rio Grande Hispanic colchas in terms of materials and variety of stitches, are found in local collections; e.g., the Taylor Museum, the Millicent Rogers Museum, and the Museum of International Folk Art.

11. Shirley Ortega, taped interview by author, Alamosa, Colorado, 14 August 1991.

12. Jane Schneider, "The Anthropology of Cloth," *Annual Review of Anthropology* 16 (1987): 424.

13. Jules David Prown, "Mind in Matter: An Introduction to Material Culture Theory and Method," *Winterthur Portfolio* 17 (1982): 1–19.

14. Henry Glassie, "Folkloristic Study of the American Artifact: Objects and Objectives," in *Handbook of American Folklore,* ed. Richard M. Dorson (Bloomington: Indiana University Press, 1983), 377.

15. Glassie, "Folkloristic Study," 377–78.

16. Fisher, "Colcha Embroidery," 153.

17. Boyd, 209–10.

18. Phyllis C. Kane, "Foreword," in *Portugal and the East through Embroidery* (Washington, D.C.: International Exhibitions Foundation, 1981), 6.

19. T. S. Eliot, "Notes towards the Definition of Culture." Quoted in Homi Bhabha, "Culture's In-Between," in *Questions of Cultural Identity,* ed. Stuart Hall and Paul du Gay (London: Sage Pubs., Ltd., 1996), 54.

20. Mather, "Works of Art," 7.

21. Edward Said, "Reflections on Exile," in *Out There: Marginalization and Contemporary Cultures,* ed. Russell Ferguson et al. (Cambridge: MIT Press, 1990), 364.

22. Under the name "Oriental Stitch," nineteenth-century scholars chart its early transmission from China and Japan through India to Persia and ultimately, into the Iberian peninsula via North African Muslims, the Moors.

23. Spain never had such a flourishing embroidery industry as that of Castelo Branco in Portugal. The huge collection of Spanish popular embroidery in Madrid's Museum of Decorative Arts includes no quilts similar to the colchas of the Portuguese region—see Maria ClementinaCarneiro Moura, "Castelo Branco Coverlets," in *Portugal and the East through Embroidery* (Washington, D.C.: International Exhibitions Foundation, 1981), 11. In western Spain, Extremadura, the area adjacent to Portugal, is renowned for handiwork. A Spanish friend recently showed me a bedspread from there, which she referred to as *colcha*. It was covered with subtle monochromatic diamond designs executed in series of running and satin stitches. I could not discern any stylistic correspondence between this piece and Rio Grande Hispanic colchas.

24. Other scholars have not emphasized the connection between Portuguese textiles and Rio Grande colchas. When Nora Fisher was researching extant colchas and investigating their origins worldwide in preparation for the *Spanish Textile Tradition* exhibit at the Museum

of International Folk Art in Santa Fe, she was informed by David King, the curator of textiles at the Victoria and Albert Museum in London, that there was a slight resemblance between the photographs she had sent him of New Mexican colchas and seventeenth- and eighteenth-century Portuguese examples in his collection. According to Mr. King's response, this tenuous similarity was based on a few limited designs: "small, strutting birds" and "to a lesser extent, the curving leaf-shapes." More importantly, however, at the end of his letter King differentiates between the wool embroidered Portuguese carpets typically worked in cross-stitch and the eighteenth-century silk embroidered coverlets from Castelo Branco, where the laid silk was "secured with conventional surface couching stitches." David King, Keeper, Department of Textiles and Dress, Victoria and Albert Museum, letter to Nora Fisher, Museum of International Folk Art, 25 November 1977, Library Archives, Museum of International Folk Art, Santa Fe, New Mexico.

25. From 1600 to 1800, India exported fabrics to countries around the world, including England, from whence these fabrics were transported to the eastern United States, where they influenced crewel embroidery work. In the early nineteenth century New England embroideries were ultimately disseminated along the Santa Fe Trail to the Southwest. Prior to this eastern trade, *indianas* and *pintados* had been commonly listed on New Mexico import inventories from Spain and Mexico—see Fisher, "Colcha Embroidery," 159–61.

26. John Baxter, *Las Carneradas: Sheep Trade in New Mexico, 1700–1860* (Albuquerque: University of New Mexico Press, 1987), 45.

27. I credit Dr. Helen Lucero with enthusiastically drawing my attention to this rare citation.

28. Boyd, 313.

29. *Jerga* or *xerga* refers to a twill-woven fabric used primarily as a floor covering and also under mattresses and for packing material.

30. Material from transcripts of interviews with Isidora Madrid de Flores and Rosabel Garcia de Gallegos from the Villanueva Project, 15 July 1976. Library Archives, Museum of International Folk Art, Santa Fe, New Mexico.

31. The accession cards at the Taylor Museum describe this fabric as *cotonilla*, which is probably *cotonia*, "a cotton twill similar to cotton flannel." See Ruben Cobos, *A Dictionary of New Mexico and Southern Colorado Spanish,* 3d printing (Santa Fe: Museum of New Mexico Press, 1987), 37.

32. The religious sector was liberated as well. In Santa Fe on June 26, 1833, Bishop Zubiría declared an end to Spanish religious domination with "the happy emancipation of this Republic from the Kingdoms of Spain." Fray Angelico Chavez, *Archives of the Archdiocese of Santa Fe* (Washington, D.C.: Academy of American Franciscan History, 1957), 212.

33. William Wroth, conversation with author, 12 May 1990.

34. After 1821, Mexico's assumption of political control over New Mexico did not have much cultural impact. As Mather suggests, once the parameters of the "internal artistic dialogue" had been established, external forces had little effect (Mather, "Works of Art," 25–

26). This period of artistic *laissez faire* ended at mid-century when Anglo trade influences introduced commercial materials and new styles.
35. George Kubler, "The Arts Fine and Plain," in *Perspectives on American Folk Art*, ed. Ian M. G. Quimby and Scott T. Swank (New York and London: W. W. Norton & Company, 1980), 238–39.
36. Richard R. Flores, "The *Corrido* and the Emergence of Texas-Mexican Social Identity," *Journal of American Folklore* 105 (spring 1992): 194.
37. Frances Varos Graves, interview by author and Helen Lucero, Taos, New Mexico, 19 November 1991.

**Chapter 4. Embroidery Revivals**

1. Baxter, 50.
2. Carmen Orrego-Salas, telephone conversation with author, 22 May 1990.
3. Venetia Newall, "Folklorismus," *Folklore* 98 (1987): 136.
4. Richard Handler and Joyce Linnekin, "Tradition, Genuine or Spurious," in *Folk Groups and Folklore Genres*, ed. Elliott Oring (Logan: Utah State University Press, 1989), 40.
5. Suzanne Forrest, *The Preservation of the Village* (Albuquerque: University of New Mexico Press, 1989), 52.
6. Forrest, 71.
7. Sarah Nestor, *The Native Market of the Spanish New Mexican Craftsmen: Santa Fe, 1933–1940* (Santa Fe: The Colonial New Mexico Foundation, 1978), 11.
8. Deirdre Evans-Pritchard, "The Portal Case: Authenticity, Tourism, Traditions, and the Law," in *Folk Groups and Folklore Genres: A Reader*, ed. Elliott Oring (Logan: Utah State University Press, 1989), 50.
9. S. Ortega, interview, 1991.
10. Sarah Deutsch, *No Separate Refuge: Culture, Class, and Gender on an Anglo-Hispanic Frontier in the American Southwest, 1880–1940* (New York: Oxford University Press, 1987), 192–93.
11. William Wroth, ed., *Weaving and Colcha from the Hispanic Southwest* (Santa Fe, N.M.: Ancient City Press, 1985), 2.
12. Beth Morgan, "Sewing Circle with a Difference," Española, N.M., *Rio Grande Sun*, 1 October 1987, D4.
13. Morgan, D6.
14. Deutsch, 192.
15. Forrest, 75.
16. David E. Whisnant, *All That Is Native and Fine* (Chapel Hill: University of North Carolina Press, 1983), 7.
17. H. H. Garnett, Correspondence and Notebooks, Garnett Collection, Taylor Museum of Southwestern Studies, Colorado Springs Fine Arts Center, Colorado Springs, Colorado, 1951.
18. H. H. Garnett, Correspondence and Notebooks.

19. F. Graves, interview, 1991.
20. F. Graves, interview, 1991.
21. *Denver Post* Clipping files, Archives of the Henderson Museum, University of Colorado, Boulder, Colorado, undated.
22. F. Graves, interview, 1991.
23. Maria Graves, taped interview by author, Taos, New Mexico, 15 August 1991.
24. F. Graves, interview, 1991.
25. Roland Dickey, *New Mexico Village Arts* (Albuquerque: University of New Mexico Press, 1949), 122.
26. Garnett, 1951.
27. Garnett, 1951.
28. Marta Weigle, ed., *Hispanic Arts and Ethnohistory in the Southwest*, 2d printing (Santa Fe, N.M.: Ancient City Press, 1983), 193, 201.
29. See Jaramillo, *Shadows of the Past,* and Lorenzo de Córdova [Lorin W. Brown], *Echoes of the Flute* (Santa Fe: Ancient City Press, 1972).
30. These pieces are classified as TM 1671 and TM 1672 in the Taylor Museum system. Taylor Museum, Colorado Springs, Colorado.
31. Roland Dickey, "Catalogue Essay," in *The Spanish Southwest* (Boston: The Museum of Fine Arts, 1974), no pagination.
32. This photo postcard was found among the uncatalogued Garnett papers in the Taylor Museum archives, Colorado Springs Fine Arts Center, Colorado Springs, Colorado. I thank Kathy Reynolds, Registrar, for her assistance in making this material available to me.
33. This workshop took place on July 18, 1992, in Del Norte, Colorado, and was sponsored by the Colorado Council of the Arts in conjunction with the Museum of Western Colorado and the Arvada Center for the Arts and Humanities.
34. Dickey, Catalogue Essay.
35. M. Simmons, 76.
36. Carole Rinard and Ann Roeder, "Heritage of Hispanic and Pueblo Indian Embroidery in New Mexico," The Embroiderers' Guild of America, Inc. Study Box, 1991.
37. Nelson H. H. Graburn, ed., *Ethnic and Tourist Arts: Cultural Expressions from the Fourth World* (Berkeley: University of California Press, 1976), 6.
38. F. Graves, interview, 1991.
39. Opening text from a handout circulated through parishes and craft groups of northern New Mexico, distributed by the Museum of International Folk Art in 1973.
40. Carmen Orrego-Salas, telephone conversation, 22 May 1990.
41. Transcripts of interview as part of Villanueva Project, Archives, Library of the Museum of International Folk Art, Santa Fe, New Mexico, 15 July 1976.
42. Transcripts, Villanueva Project, 15 July 1976.
43. Transcripts, Villanueva Project, 15 July 1976.
44. Isidora Madrid de Flores, taped interview by author, Villanueva, New Mexico, 19 July

1991. I interviewed Señora Madrid de Flores at her home. There was a dramatic thunderstorm raging outside that caused lights to flicker; this combined with the remoteness of Villanueva added a bit of a *frisson* to the experience for both of us.
45. Transcripts, Villanueva Project, 15 July 1976.
46. C. Orrego-Salas, telephone conversation, 22 May 1990.
47. C. Orrego-Salas, telephone conversation, 24 May 1990.
48. Carmen Orrego-Salas, "The Villanueva Tapestry," *Needle Arts* 8, no. 4 (1977): 8–9.
49. Madrid de Flores, interview, 1991.
50. Madrid de Flores, interview, 1991.
51. Madrid de Flores, interview, 1991.
52. Orrego-Salas, telephone conversation, 24 May 1990.
53. Madrid de Flores, interview, 1991.
54. Lilo Markrich, "The Ultimate Embroidery Teacher," *Threads* (October–November 1989): 58–61.
55. Refer to the treatment of antimodernist nostalgia in T. J. Jackson Lears, *No Place of Grace: Antimodernism and the Transformation of American Culture 1880–1920* (New York: Pantheon Books, 1981). See also Whisnant, *All That Is Native and Fine*.
56. Schneider, 415.
57. Barbara Kirshenblatt-Gimblett, "Mistaken Dichotomies," *Journal of American Folklore* 101 (1988): 140–55.
58. Forrest, 71.
59. Madrid de Flores, interview, 1991.
60. Trujillo, in *Las Artistas,* 21.
61. Victoria Mascareñas, conversation with author, Santa Fe, New Mexico, 15 February 1992.
62. Newall, 138.
63. C. Orrego-Salas, telephone conversation, 22 May 1990.
64. Madrid de Flores, interview, 1991.

## Chapter 5. The Ladies Sewing Circle of San Luis

1. Julia Valdez, taped interview by author, San Luis, Colorado, 12 April 1990.
2. J. Valdez, interview, 1990.
3. J. Valdez, interview, 1990.
4. Daisy Ortega, taped interview by author, San Luis, Colorado, 12 March 1991.
5. D. Ortega, interview, 1991.
6. Josephine Lobato, taped interview with author, Fort Garland, Colorado, 24 February 1993.
7. Susanne Kuchler and Walter Melion, *Images of Memory: On Remembering and Representation* (Washington, D.C.: Smithsonian Institution Press, 1991), 4.
8. See Sylvia Lobato, "Crime-Torn Weekend Shakes San Luis," Alamosa, Colo., *Valley Courier,* 30 May 1990, 1; and Erin Smith, "Weekend Uprising Pits Sheriff against San Luis Throng," *The Pueblo [Colo.] Chieftain,* 30 May 1990, 1.

9. Evangeline Salazar, conversation with author, San Luis, Colorado, 29 May 1990.
10. Charles Manzanares, taped interview by author, San Luis, Colorado, 18 January 1991.
11. Manzanares, interview, 1991.
12. Bella Saenz [pseud.], interview by author, San Luis, Colorado, 20 July 1991.
13. Sally T. Chavez, taped interview by author, San Luis, Colorado, 18 January 1991.
14. Sostena Cleven, taped interview by author, San Luis, Colorado, 22 February 1991.
15. Father Patricio [Patrick] Valdez, taped interview by author, San Luis, Colorado, 18 January 1991.
16. Father P. Valdez, interview, 1991.
17. C. Orrego-Salas, telephone conversation, 24 May 1990. See chapter 3 with reference to the historical discontinuity of colcha embroidery after the last quarter of the nineteenth century. Also, Marianne Stoller, "A Study of Nineteenth-Century Hispanic Arts and Crafts in the American Southwest: Appearances and Processes" (Ph.D. dissertation, University of Pennsylvania, 1979), 441.
18. Sally T. Chavez, telephone conversation with author, 15 September 1992.
19. Refer to Shifra M. Goldman, "The Iconography of Chicano Self-Determination: Race, Ethnicity, and Class," Art Journal 49, no. 2 (summer 1990): 167–73, for the political implications of ethnic labeling.
20. C. Orrego-Salas, telephone conversation, 22 May 1990.
21. C. Orrego-Salas, telephone conversation, 22 May 1990.
22. San Luis embroideries are in a pictorial format with dimensions that easily conform to "fine art" presentation. When framed they measured on the average twenty-three inches high by nineteen to twenty inches wide.
23. C. Orrego-Salas, telephone conversation, 22 May 1990.
24. C. Orrego-Salas, telephone conversation, 24 May 1990.
25. John Berger's Pig Earth provided a literary model for this discussion. See Berger, Pig Earth (New York: Pantheon Books, 1979), 5–11.
26. C. Orrego-Salas, telephone conversation, 24 May 1990.
27. Salazar and Chavez, 18 January 1991.
28. C. Orrego-Salas, telephone conversation, 24 May 1990.
29. Salazar, telephone conversation, 14 November 1991.
30. J. Valdez, interview, 1990.
31. J. Valdez, interview, 1990.
32. J. Valdez, interview, 1990.
33. Refer to the discussion in chapter 3 on creativity and the mid-nineteenth century colcha embroideries in the Taylor Museum collection.
34. S. Cleven, interview, 1991.
35. Salazar and Chavez, interview, 1991.
36. Salazar and Chavez, interview, 1991.
37. C. Orrego-Salas, letter to Ladies Sewing Circle, 15 May 1990.
38. Father P. Valdez, interview, 1991.

39. Salazar and Chavez, interview, 1991.
40. John Dewey, *Art as Experience* (New York: Capricorn Books, 1934), 11.
41. C. Orrego-Salas, telephone conversation, 22 May 1990.
42. Salazar and Chavez, interview, 1991.
43. C. Orrego-Salas, telephone conversation, 22 May 1990.
44. C. Orrego-Salas, telephone conversation, 22 May 1990.
45. Salazar and Chavez, interview, 1991.
46. See Sally Price, *Primitive Art in Civilized Places* (Chicago: The University of Chicago Press, 1989) for a discussion of fine art world practices as a yardstick for various art-related interactions.
47. Salazar and Chavez, interview, 1991.
48. Salazar and Chavez, interview, 1991.
49. Schneider, 416.
50. Virginia R. Dominguez, "The Marketing of Heritage," *American Ethnologist* 13 (1986): 553.
51. Salazar and Chavez, interview, 1991.
52. Father P. Valdez, interview, 1991.
53. Father P. Valdez, interview, 1991.
54. Salazar and Chavez, interview, 1991.

## Chapter 6. Stitches of Myth and Memory

1. Kenneth Burke, *Counter-Statement* (Berkeley: University of California Press, 1968); quoted in Suzanne P. Blier, *African Vodun: Art, Psychology and Power* (Chicago: University of Chicago Press, 1995), 1.
2. "*Adios al mundo*," transcribed and translated by Alice Corbin Henderson, as cited in William Wroth, *Images of Penance, Images of Mercy* (Norman: University of Oklahoma Press, 1991), 62.

# bibliography

Ahlborn, Richard E. "Frontier Possessions: The Evidence from Colonial Documents." In *Colonial Frontiers: Art and Life in Spanish New Mexico,* ed. Christine Mather. Santa Fe: Ancient City Press, 1983.

Armstrong, Robert Plant. *The Affecting Presence: An Essay in Humanistic Anthropology*. Urbana: University of Illinois Press, 1971.

———. *Forms and Processes of African Sculpture*. Occasional Publication. Austin: African and Afro-American Research Institute, The University of Texas at Austin, 1970.

Babcock, Barbara A. "Modeled Selves: Helen Cordero's 'Little People.'" In *The Anthropology of Experience,* ed. Victor W. Turner and Edward M. Bruner. Urbana: University of Illinois Press, 1986.

Babcock, Barbara A., and Guy and Doris Monthan. *The Pueblo Storyteller: Development of a Figurative Ceramic Tradition*. Tucson: University of Arizona Press, 1986.

Bausinger, Hermann. *Folk Culture in a World of Technology*. Translated by Elke Dettmer. Bloomington: Indiana University Press, 1990.

Baxter, John. *Las Carneradas: Sheep Trade in New Mexico, 1700–1860*. Albuquerque: University of New Mexico Press, 1987.

Bendix, Regina. "Folklorism: The Challenge of a Concept." *International Folklore Review* 6 (1988): 5–15.

———. "Tourism and Cultural Displays—Inventing Traditions for Whom?" *Journal of American Folklore* 102, no. 404 (1989): 131–46.

Berger, John. *Pig Earth*. New York: Pantheon Books, 1979.

Berlo, Janet Catherine. "Portraits of Dispossession in Plains Indian and Inuit Graphic Arts." *Art Journal* 49, no.2 (summer 1990): 133–41.

Bhabha, Homi. "Culture's In-Between." In *Questions of Cultural Identity*, ed. Stuart Hall and Paul du Gay. London: Sage Publications, 1996.

Biebuyck, Daniel P., ed. *Tradition and Creativity in Tribal Art*. Berkeley: University of California Press, 1969.

Blier, Suzanne P. *African Vodun: Art, Psychology and Power*. Chicago: University of Chicago Press, 1995.

Boas, Franz. *Primitive Art*. 1927. Reprint, New York: Dover, 1955.

Bowen, Dorothy Boyd. "A Brief History of Spanish Textile Production in the Southwest." In *Spanish Textile Tradition of New Mexico and Colorado*, ed. Nora Fisher, 5–7. Santa Fe: Museum of New Mexico Press, 1979.

Boyd, E. *Popular Arts of Spanish New Mexico*. Santa Fe: Museum of New Mexico Press, 1974.

Briggs, Charles L. *Competence in Performance*. Philadelphia: University of Pennsylvania Press, 1988.

———. *The Wood Carvers of Cordova, New Mexico*. Albuquerque: The University of New Mexico Press, 1980.

Bunzel, Ruth L. *The Pueblo Potter*. 1929. Reprint, New York: Dover, 1972.

Burke, Kenneth. *Counter-Statement*. Berkeley: University of California Press, 1968.

Caitlin, Amy. *Textiles as Texts: Arts of Hmong Women from Laos*. Los Angeles: The Woman's Building, 1987.

Campa, Arthur L. *Hispanic Culture in the Southwest*. Norman: University of Oklahoma Press, 1979.

Cerny, Charlene, and Christine Mather. "Textile Production in Twentieth-Century New Mexico." In *Spanish Textile Tradition of New Mexico and Colorado*, ed. Nora Fisher, 168–90. Santa Fe: Museum of New Mexico Press, 1979.

Chavez, Fray Angelico. *Archives of the Archdiocese of Santa Fe*. Washington, D.C.: Academy of American Franciscan History, 1957.

Christian, William A. Jr. *Person and God in a Spanish Valley*. Studies in Social Discontinuity. New York: Seminar Press, 1972.

Clifford, James. *The Predicament of Culture: Twentieth-Century Ethnography, Literature and Art*. Cambridge: Harvard University Press, 1988.

———, and George E. Marcus, eds. *Writing Culture*. Berkeley: University of California Press, 1986.

Coates, James. "Coloradoans Building a Mountain Shrine." *Chicago Tribune*, 20 October 1990, 23 col. 1.

Cobos, Ruben. *A Dictionary of New Mexico and Southern Colorado Spanish*. 3d printing. Santa Fe: Museum of New Mexico Press, 1987.

Coe, Ralph T. *Lost and Found Traditions: Native American, 1965–1985.* New York: American Federation of Arts, 1986.

Coles, Robert. *The Call of Stories: Teaching and the Moral Imagination.* Boston: Houghton Mifflin Company, 1989.

———. *Doing Documentary Work.* New York: Oxford University Press, 1997.

Córdova, Lorenzo de [Lorin W. Brown]. *Echoes of the Flute.* Santa Fe: Ancient City Press, 1972.

Crawford, Stanley. *Mayordomo.* Albuquerque: University of New Mexico Press, 1988.

Cruikshank, Julie, with Angela Sidney, Kitty Smith, and Annie Ned. *Life Lived Like a Story.* Lincoln: University of Nebraska Press, 1990.

Darian-Smith, Kate, and Paula Hamilton, eds. *Memory and History in Twentieth-Century Australia.* Melbourne: Oxford University Press, 1994.

Deutsch, Sarah. *No Separate Refuge: Culture, Class, and Gender on an Anglo-Hispanic Frontier in the American Southwest, 1880–1940.* New York: Oxford University Press, 1987.

Dewey, John. *Art as Experience.* New York: Capricorn Books, 1934.

Dewhurst, C. Kurt, Betty MacDowell, and Marsha MacDowell. *Artists in Aprons: Folk Art by American Women.* New York: E. P. Dutton, 1979.

Dickey, Roland. Catalogue Essay. *The Spanish Southwest.* Boston: Museum of Fine Arts, 1974.

———. *New Mexico Village Arts.* Albuquerque: University of New Mexico Press, 1949.

Dominguez, Virginia R. "The Marketing of Heritage." *American Ethnologist* 13 (1986): 546–55.

Dunton, Nellie. *The Spanish Colonial Ornament and the Motifs Depicted in the Textiles of the Period of the American Southwest.* Philadelphia: H. C. Perleberg, 1935.

Enthoven, Jacqueline. "The Bokhara Stitch and Colcha Embroidery." *Needle Arts* 7, no. 3 (1976): 27–28.

Evans-Pritchard, Deirdre. "The Portal Case: Authenticity, Tourism, Traditions, and the Law." In *Folk Groups and Folklore Genres: A Reader,* ed. Elliott Oring, 43–51. Logan: Utah State University Press, 1989.

Fisher, Nora. "Colcha Embroidery." In *Spanish Textile Tradition of New Mexico and Colorado,* ed. Nora Fisher, 153–67. Santa Fe: Museum of New Mexico Press, 1979.

———, ed. *Spanish Textile Tradition of New Mexico and Colorado.* Santa Fe: Museum of New Mexico Press, 1979.

Flores, Richard R. "The *Corrido* and the Emergence of Texas-Mexican Social Identity." *Journal of American Folklore* 105, no. 416 (spring 1992): 166–82.

Forrest, Suzanne. *The Preservation of the Village.* Albuquerque: University of New Mexico Press, 1989.

Garnett, H. H. Correspondence and Notebooks. Garnett Collection. Taylor Museum of Southwestern Studies. Colorado Springs Fine Arts Center. Colorado Springs, Colorado.

Geertz, Clifford. "Art as a Cultural System." In *Local Knowledge.* New York: Basic Books, 1983.

Glassie, Henry. Exhibition catalogue. *Turkish Traditional Art Today.* Santa Fe: Museum of New Mexico, 1991.

———. "Folkloristic Study of the American Artifact: Objects and Objectives." In *Handbook of American Folklore*, ed. Richard M. Dorson, 376–83. Bloomington: Indiana University Press, 1983.

———. *The Spirit of Folk Art*. New York: Harry N. Abrams, 1989.

———. *Turkish Traditional Art Today*. Bloomington: Indiana University Press, 1993.

Goldman, Shifra M. "The Iconography of Chicano Self-Determination: Race, Ethnicity, and Class." *Art Journal* 49, no.2 (summer 1990): 167–73.

Gowans, Alan. *Learning to See: Historical Perspectives on Modern Popular/Commercial Arts*. Bowling Green, Ohio: Bowling Green State University Popular Press, 1981.

Graburn, Nelson H. H. "'I Like Things to Look More Different than That Stuff Did': An Experiment in Cross-Cultural Art Appreciation." In *Art and Society: Studies in Style, Culture and Aesthetics*, ed. Michael Greenhalgh and Vincent Megaw, 51–70. New York: St. Martin's Press, 1978.

———. "Tourism: The Sacred Journey." In *Hosts and Guests*, ed. Valene L. Smith, 21–36. 2d ed. Philadelphia: University of Pennsylvania Press, 1989.

———, ed. *Ethnic and Tourist Arts: Cultural Expressions from the Fourth World*. Berkeley: University of California Press, 1976.

Greenhalgh, Michael, and Vincent Megaw, eds. *Art in Society: Studies in Style, Culture and Aesthetics*. New York: St. Martin's Press, 1978.

Hamilton, Paula. "The Knife Edge: Debates about Memory and History." In *Memory and History in Twentieth-Century Australia*, ed. Kate Darian-Smith and Paula Hamilton, 9–32. Oxford: Oxford University Press, 1994.

Handler, Richard, and Joyce Linnekin. "Tradition, Genuine or Spurious." In *Folk Groups and Folklore Genres: A Reader*, ed. Elliott Oring, 38–42. Logan: Utah State University Press, 1989.

Hebdige, Dick. *Subculture: The Meaning of Style*. London and New York: Methuen, 1979.

Henderson Museum. Archives. Clipping Files. University of Colorado. Boulder, Colorado.

Hood, Adrienne D., and David Thiery Ruddel. "Artifacts and Documents in the History of Quebec Textiles." In *Living in a Material World*, ed. Gerald L. Pocius, 55–91. St. John's, Newfoundland: Institute of Social and Economic Research, 1991.

Isaacs, Susan L. F. "Redware Revival and Re-presentation: A Pennsylvania Pottery Tradition." In *Craft and Community*, ed. Shalom D. Staub, 127–30. Philadelphia: The Balch Institute for Ethnic Studies and the Pennsylvania Heritage Affairs Commission, 1988.

Jaramillo, Cleofas M. *Shadows of the Past*. Santa Fe: Ancient City Press, 1941.

Jouve, Nicole Ward. *White Woman Speaks with a Forked Tongue*. London: Routledge, 1991.

Kane, Phyllis C. "Foreword." In *Portugal and the East through Embroidery*. Washington, D.C.: International Exhibitions Foundation, 1981.

Kirshenblatt-Gimblett, Barbara. "Mistaken Dichotomies." *Journal of American Folklore* 101 (1988): 140–55.

Kubler, George. "The Arts Fine and Plain." In *Perspectives on American Folk Art*, ed. Ian M. G.

Quimby and Scott T. Swank, 234–46. New York and London: W. W. Norton & Company, 1980.

———. "On the Colonial Extinction of the Motifs of Pre-Columbian Art." In *Anthropology and Art,* ed. Charlotte M. Otten, 212–26. Austin: University of Texas Press, 1961.

Kuchler, Susanne, and Walter Melion. *Images of Memory: On Remembering and Representation.* Washington, D.C.: Smithsonian Institution Press, 1991.

Kutsche, Paul, and John R. Van Ness. *Cañones, Values, Crisis, and Survival in a Northern New Mexico Village.* Albuquerque: University of New Mexico Press, 1981.

Kutsche, Paul, ed. *The Survival of Spanish American Villages.* The Colorado College Studies 15. Colorado Springs: The Research Committee, 1979.

*Las Artistas del Valle de San Luis.* Exhibition Catalogue. Arvada, Colo.: Arvada Center for the Arts and Humanities, 1982.

Lears, T. J. Jackson. *No Place of Grace: Antimodernism and the Transformation of American Culture 1880–1920.* New York: Pantheon Books, 1981.

Lippard, Lucy. "Up, Down, and Across: A New Frame for New Quilts." In *The Artist and the Quilt,* ed. Charlotte Robinson, 32–43. New York: Alfred A. Knopf, 1983.

Lobato, Sylvia. "Crime-Torn Weekend Shakes San Luis." Alamosa, Colorado, *Valley Courier,* 30 May 1990, 1.

Lugones, Maria, and Elizabeth Spelman. "Have We Got a Theory for You! Feminist Theory, Cultural Imperialism, and the Demand for 'The Woman's Voice.'" *Women's Studies International Forum* 6, no. 6 (1983): 590–611.

MacAulay, Suzanne. "Colcha Embroidery along the Northern Rio Grande: The Aesthetics of Cultural Inversion in San Luis, Colorado." Ph.D. dissertation, University of Pennsylvania, 1992.

———. "The Eloquent Colcha: Traditional Hispanic Embroidery," and "Josephine Lobato: Embroidering a Story." *Piecework* 1, no. 3 (November–December 1993): 52–60.

———. 1991. "Hispanic *Colcha* Embroidery: Stitches in Time." In *Master Apprentice: Colorado Folk Arts and Artists, 1986–1990.* Arvada, Colo.: Arvada Center for the Arts and Humanities, 1991.

MacCannell, Dean. "Reconstructed Ethnicity: Tourism and Cultural Identity in Third World Communities." *Annals of Tourism Research* 11 (1984): 375–91.

———. *The Tourist.* New York: Schocken Books, 1976.

MacDowell, Marsha. *Stories in Thread: Hmong Pictorial Embroidery.* East Lansing: Michigan Traditional Arts Program, Michigan State University Museum, 1989.

MacNair, Peter L., Alan L. Hoover, and Kevin Neary. *The Legacy: Tradition and Innovation in Northwest Coast Indian Art.* Seattle: University of Washington Press, 1984.

Manning, Frank E. *The Celebration of Society: Perspectives on Contemporary Cultural Performance.* Bowling Green, Ohio: Bowling Green State University Popular Press, 1983.

Manzanares, Mary Jo. "Interview." *Rocky Mountain News,* 29 May 1990, 38.

Marcus, George E., and Michael M. J. Fischer. *Anthropology as Cultural Critique.* Chicago: University of Chicago Press, 1986.

Marin, Gerardo, and Barbara VanOss Marin. *Research with Hispanic Populations.* Applied Social Research Methods Series 23. Newbury Park, Calif.: Sage Publications, 1991.

Markrich, Lilo. "The Ultimate Embroidery Teacher." *Threads* (October–November 1989): 58–61.

Martin, Charles E. "Creative Constraints in the Folk Arts of Appalachia." In *Sense of Place: American Regional Cultures,* ed. Barbara Allen and Thomas J. Schlereth, 138–51. Lexington: The University Press of Kentucky, 1990.

Martínez, Maclovio. "The Penitente." In *La Cultura Constante de San Luis,* ed. Randall Teeuwen, 26–33. San Luis, Colo.: The San Luis Museum and Commercial Center, 1985.

Mather, Christine. "Introduction." In *Colonial Frontiers: Art and Life in Spanish New Mexico,* ed. Christine Mather, 1–7. Santa Fe, N.M.: Ancient City Press, 1983.

———. "Works of Art in Frontier New Mexico." In *Colonial Frontiers: Art and Life in Spanish New Mexico,* ed. Christine Mather, 7–26. Santa Fe, N.M.: Ancient City Press, 1983.

Mattingly, Terry. "Higher Ground: Father Patrick Valdez Has San Luis on the Rise." Denver, Colo., *Rocky Mountain News,* 3 June 1990, 14M–17M.

———. "San Luis Bears a Cross of Its Own." Denver, Colo., *Rocky Mountain News,* 14 April 1990, 10 col. 1.

McLaren, Peter. "Field Relations and the Discourse of the Other." In *Experiencing Fieldwork,* ed. William B. Shaffir and Robert A. Stebbins, 149–63. Newbury Park, Calif.: Sage Publications, 1991.

McWilliams, Carey. *North from Mexico: The Spanish-Speaking People of the United States.* New York: Greenwood Press, 1968.

Morgan, Beth. "Sewing Circle with a Difference." Española, N.M., *Rio Grande Sun,* 1 October 1987, D3–D7.

Moura, Maria Clementina Carneiro. "Castelo Branco Coverlets." In *Portugal and the East through Embroidery.* Washington, D.C.: International Exhibitions Foundation, 1981.

Munro, Eleanor. "Breaking Stars: A Collaboration in Quilts." In *The Artist and the Quilt,* ed. Charlotte Robinson, 44–47. New York: Alfred A. Knopf, 1983.

Myerhoff, Barbara. *Number Our Days.* New York: Simon and Schuster, 1978.

Nestor, Sarah. *The Native Market of the Spanish New Mexican Craftsmen: Santa Fe, 1933–1940.* Santa Fe: The Colonial New Mexico Foundation, 1978.

Newall, Venetia. "Folklorismus." *Folklore* 98 (1987): 133–39.

Orrego-Salas, Carmen. "The Villanueva Tapestry." *Needle Arts* 8, no. 4 (1977): 8–9.

Otten, Charlotte M., ed. *Anthropology and Art.* Austin: University of Texas Press, 1971.

Parker, Rozsika. *The Subversive Stitch: Embroidery and the Making of the Feminine.* London: The Women's Press, 1984.

Patai, Daphne. "U.S. Academics and Third World Women: Is Ethical Research Possible?" In *Women's Worlds: The Feminist Practice of Oral History,* ed. Sherna Berger Gluck and Daphne Patai, 137—53. New York: Routledge, 1991.

Personal Narratives Group, ed. *Interpreting Women's Lives: Feminist Theory and Personal Narratives.* Bloomington: Indiana University Press, 1989.

Peterson, Sally. "From the Heart and the Mind: Creating Paj Ntaub in the Context of Community." Ph.D. dissertation, University of Pennsylvania, 1990.

Phillips, Ruth B. "Why Not Tourist Art? Significant Silences in Native American Museum Representations." In *After Colonialism: Imperial Histories and Post Colonial Displacement,* ed. G. Prakesh. Princeton, N.J.: Princeton University Press, 1994.

Pinto, Maria Helena Mendes. 1981. "Indo-Portuguese Coverlets." In *Portugal and the East through Embroidery,* ed. Phyllis C. Kane, 9–10. Washington, D.C.: International Exhibitions Foundation, 1981.

Pocius, Gerald L., ed. *Living in a Material World.* St. John's, Newfoundland: Institute of Social and Economic Research, 1991.

Price, Sally. *Primitive Art in Civilized Places.* Chicago and London: The University of Chicago Press, 1989.

Prown, Jules David. "Mind in Matter: An Introduction to Material Culture Theory and Method." *Winterthur Portfolio* 17 (1982): 1–19.

———. "Style as Evidence." *Winterthur Portfolio* 15 (1980): 197–210.

Pye, David. *The Nature of Design.* New York: Reinhold Book Corporation, 1964.

Redfield, Robert. "Art and Icon." In *Anthropology and Art,* ed. Charlotte Otten, 39–65. Austin: University of Texas Press, 1971.

Reich, Alice H. "Spanish American Village Culture: Barrier to Assimilation or Integrative Force?" In *The Survival of Spanish American Villages,* ed. Paul Kutsche. Colorado Springs: The Colorado College Studies Research Committee, 1979.

Reichard, Gladys A. *Navajo Shepherd and Weaver.* 1936. Rev. ed. Glorieta, New Mexico: The Rio Grande Press, 1984.

Rickman, H. P., ed. *Meaning in History: W. Dilthey's Thoughts on History and Society.* London: George Allen & Unwin, 1961.

Rinard, Carole, and Ann Roeder. "Heritage of Hispanic and Pueblo Indian Embroidery in New Mexico." The Embroiderers' Guild of America, Inc. Study Box, 1991.

Robinson, Charlotte, ed. *The Artist and the Quilt.* New York: Alfred A. Knopf, 1983.

Rosaldo, Renato. *Culture and Truth.* Boston: Beacon Press, 1989.

Said, Edward. "Reflections on Exile." In *Out There: Marginalization and Contemporary Cultures,* ed. Russell Ferguson et al. Cambridge, Mass.: MIT Press, 1990.

St. George, Robert Blair. "Bawns and Beliefs: Architecture, Commerce, and Conversion in Early New England." *Winterthur Portfolio* 25 (1990): 241–87.

Sandoval, Ron. "The San Luis Vega." In *La Cultura Constante de San Luis,* ed. Randall Teeuwen, 18–25. San Luis, Colo.: The San Luis Museum Cultural and Commercial Center, 1985.

"Sangre de Cristo Parish Newsletter." Vol. 4, no. 2 (summer 1991). Sangre de Cristo Parish, San Luis, Colorado.

Sayer, Chloe. *Costumes of Mexico.* Austin: University of Texas Press, 1985.

Schlereth, Thomas J. "Material Culture or Material Life." In *Living in a Material World,* ed. Gerald L. Pocius, 231–40. St. John's, Newfoundland: ISER Press, 1991.

Schneider, Jane. "The Anthropology of Cloth." *Annual Review of Anthropology* 16 (1987): 409–48.
Shaffir, William B., and Robert A. Stebbins, eds. *Experiencing Fieldwork: An Inside View of Qualitative Research*. Newbury Park, Calif.: Sage Publications, 1991.
Simmons, Marc. "Colonial New Mexico and Mexico: The Historical Relationship." In *Colonial Frontiers: Art and Life in Spanish New Mexico*, ed. Christine Mather, 71–89. Santa Fe, N.M.: Ancient City Press, 1983.
Simmons, Virginia McConnell. *The San Luis Valley: Land of the Six-Armed Cross*. Boulder, Colo.: Pruett Publishing Company, 1979.
Smith, Erin. "Weekend Uprising Pits Sheriff against San Luis Throng." *The Pueblo [Colo.] Chieftain*, 30 May 1990, 1.
Smith, Valene L., ed. *Hosts and Guests*. 2d ed. Philadelphia: University of Pennsylvania Press, 1989.
Sommers, Laurie Kay. 1991. "Inventing Latinisimo: The Creation of 'Hispanic' Panethnicity in the United States." *Journal of American Folklore* 104, no. 411 (1991): 32–53.
Stacey, Judith. "Can There Be a Feminist Ethnography?" In *Women's Words: The Feminist Practice of Oral History*, ed. Sherna Berger Gluck and Daphne Patai, 111–20. New York and London: Routledge, 1991.
Staub, Shalom D., ed. *Craft and Community: Traditional Arts in Contemporary Society*. Philadelphia: The Balch Institute for Ethnic Studies and The Pennsylvania Heritage Affairs Commission, 1988.
Steele, Thomas J. *Santos and Saints*. Rev. ed., 3d printing. Santa Fe, N.M.: Ancient City Press, 1982.
Stephen, Lynn. *Zapotec Women*. Austin: University of Texas Press, 1991.
Stern, Stephen, and John Allan Cicala, eds. *Creative Ethnicity*. Logan: Utah State University Press, 1991.
Stewart, Susan. *On Longing*. Baltimore, Md.: Johns Hopkins University Press, 1984.
Stoller, Marianne L. "Determining the Feasibility of Developing a Craft Business Enterprise for Rural Low-Income United States Citizens Living in the San Luis Valley." Final Report. Submitted to the Four Corners Regional Commission by the Virginia Neal Blue Resource Centers for Colorado Women, 1974.
―――. "A Study of Nineteenth Century Hispanic Arts and Crafts in the American Southwest: Appearances and Processes." Ph.D. dissertation, University of Pennsylvania, 1979.
―――. "La Tierra y La Merced." In *La Cultura Constante de San Luis*, ed. Randall Teeuwen, 12–17. San Luis, Colo.: The San Luis Museum Cultural and Commercial Center, 1985.
Teeuwen, Randall. "La Gente de la Tierra." In *La Cultura Constante de San Luis*, ed. Randall Teeuwen, 9–11. San Luis, Colo.: The San Luis Museum Cultural and Commercial Center, 1985.
―――, ed. *La Cultura Constante de San Luis*. San Luis, Colo.: The San Luis Museum Cultural and Commercial Center, 1985.

Tsing, Anna Lowenhaupt. *In the Realm of the Diamond Queen.* Princeton, N.J.: Princeton University Press, 1993.

Turner, Victor W., and Edward M. Bruner, eds. *The Anthropology of Experience.* Urbana: University of Illinois Press, 1986.

Upton, Dell. "Form and User: Style, Mode, Fashion, and the Artifact." In *Living in a Material World,* ed. Gerald L. Pocius, 156–69. St. John's, Newfoundland: ISER Press, 1991.

Valdez, Father Pat. "Interview." *Rocky Mountain News,* 14 April 1990, 10.

Van Maanen, John. "Playing Back the Tape: Early Days in the Field." In *Experiencing Fieldwork,* ed. W. B. Shaffir and R. A. Stebbins, 31–42. Newbury Park, Calif.: Sage Publications, 1991.

Washburn, Dorothy K. *Style Classification and Ethnicity: Design Categories on Bakuba Raffia Cloth.* Transactions, American Philosophical Society, Vol. 80, Part 3. Philadelphia: American Philosophical Society, 1990.

Waterbury, Ronald. "Embroidery for Tourists: A Contemporary Putting-Out System in Oaxaca." In *Cloth and Human Experience,* ed. Annette B. Weiner and Jane Schneider, 243–71. Washington, D.C.: Smithsonian Institution Press, 1989.

Weigle, Marta. *Brothers of Light, Brothers of Blood: The Penitentes of the Southwest.* Santa Fe, N.M.: Ancient City Press, 1976.

———, ed. *Hispanic Arts and Ethnohistory in the Southwest.* 2d printing. Santa Fe, N.M.: Ancient City Press, 1983.

Weiner, Annette B., and Jane Schneider, eds. *Cloth and Human Experience.* Washington, D.C.: Smithsonian Institution Press, 1989.

Whisnant, David E. *All That Is Native and Fine.* Chapel Hill: University of North Carolina Press, 1983.

Whitten, Dorothea S., and Norman E. Whitten, eds. *Imagery & Creativity: Ethnoaesthetics and Art Worlds in the Americas.* Tucson: University of Arizona Press, 1993.

Wilson, Chris, and David Kammer. *Community and Continuity: The History, Architecture and Cultural Landscape of La Tierra Amarilla.* Santa Fe: New Mexico Historic Preservation Division, 1989.

Wroth, William. *Images of Penance, Images of Mercy.* Norman: University of Oklahoma Press, 1991.

———, ed. *Hispanic Crafts of the Southwest.* Colorado Springs: Taylor Museum of the Colorado Springs Fine Arts Center, 1977.

———, ed. *Weaving and Colcha from the Hispanic Southwest.* Santa Fe, N.M.: Ancient City Press, 1985.

Zeleny, Carolyn. *Relations between the Spanish-Americans and Anglo-Americans in New Mexico.* New York: Arno Press, 1974.

Zolberg, Vera L. *Constructing a Sociology of the Arts.* New York: Cambridge University Press, 1990.

# index

*Note:* The phrase "fol. p. 46" indicates the location of illustrations.

*abuelos*, 23–24
*Adobe Plant* (Valdez), 128, 129, 130, 131, 146
alchoholism, 32, 129
altarpieces, 59, 70, 119
Anglo-American influences, 21–22, 39; in embroidery motifs, 70–71, 150; and revitalization, 78, 82–83, 106; in San Luis, 26, 39, 141, 155; Santa Fe Trade and, 72, 164n. 34
Applegate, Frank, 78
art, 59, 64, 78, 80, 115, 130–31, 168n. 22; change in, 154–55; creativity in, 62–63, 123–24, 149; and culture, 143–44; and ethnicity, 18–19; folk, 106–7; grandchildren's, 142–43; and life experiences, 138–39, 155–56; regional, 67–68; signed, 26–27; stichery as, 103–4; values of, 144–45
Arte Antiguo, El, 82, 83–84, 107

*Artistas del Valle de San Luis*, 117
artists, 18, 22, 79, 104–5, 123; Carson Revival, 89–90; and gift-giving, 115–16; identity as, 144–45; and marketplace, 80–81; as storytellers, 27–28
Arvada Center for the Arts and Humanities, 116–17, 166n. 33
Austin, Mary, 78, 79, 91, 105
authenticity, 73–74, 154; defining, 4, 5, 63–64, 95; revivals and, 79, 86, 88, 93, 96

Bayeux Tapestry, 101
Beaubien Deed, 7
Ben-Amos, Paula, 96
Boston Musem of Fine Arts, 93, 94
Boyd, E., 63, 65, 80

Capulin, 85, 116, 121
Carson Revival colchas, fol. p. 46, 84, 107, 140; production of, 85–87, 94–97; scenes in, 88–

91; structure of, 87–88, 122; in Taylor Museum, 92–93
*Casa de Piedra, La* (Chavéz), fol. p. 46, 135–36
Castelo Branco, 66, 67, 163nn. 23, 24
Catholicism, Catholic church, 10, 42, 43, 50, 68, 76, 141; iconography and, 110–13, 134; influence and role of, 88–89, 102, 113–16, 118–19, 124. *See also* Penitente Brotherhood
Chavez, Arnold: *Haciendo Ristras,* fol. p. 46, 103
Chavez, Sally T., 9, 118, 119–20, 124–25, 126, 127, 128, 138, 141, 142, 145, 148; *La Casa de Piedra,* fol. p. 46, 135–36; on technique, 139, 143
Chile, 97–98, 140–41
China: textiles from, 58–59, 73
chintz: East Indian, 66, 67
Christmas, 23–24
Cleven, Sostena, 118, 119, 140, 149; *El Rancho Grande,* fol. p. 46, 131–32
colchas: cultural context of, 73–74; defining, 5, 54, 55, 63–64; mending, 68–69, 87–88; nineteenth-century, 56–58, 71–72; religious use of, 59–60; wool-on-cotton, 100–101
Colonial Arts Shop, 78
colonial era, 8, 9, 60, 65, 159n. 4
Colorado, 77–78, 80, 81, 159n. 4. *See also* San Luis
Colorado Council for the Arts and Humanities, 124–25, 146, 166n. 33
Colorado Historical Society, 67
Colorado University Board of Regents' Distinguished Service Award, 114
community, 96–97, 115, 135; guardianship of, 33–34; kinship in, 42–43; San Luis as, 123–24; self-representation of, 148–49; values of, 129–30

*Convento, El* (Ortega), 111, 113, 132, 146
convents, 59–60, 162n. 9
Coors Corporation exhibit, 146
Cordoba, Lorenzo de (Lorin W. Brown), 92
Costilla County, 5, 6, 81, 116
crafts. *See* hand crafts
creative process, 62–63, 99–100, 105–6, 149; identity and, 122, 123–24; intensity of, 49–50, 148; J. Lobato's, 13, 14, 16–17, 21–22, 24, 35–36, 49–50; and memory, 133–34, 150–51; self-identity and, 107–8; social context of, 126–27; stitchery and, 105–6; J. Valdez's, 130, 131
crewel work, 70–71, 97, 103, 122, 164n. 25
Culebra River, 6, 133
culture, 19, 64, 67–68, 70, 71, 150; legitimacy of, 73–74
culture brokers, 83, 106–7, 143–44
Cunningham, Paula, 126, 127, 140, 141
Cunningham, Tim, 141
Curtin Paloheimo, Leonora, 79, 81, 106

decorative style, 137, 138–39
Depression, 81, 97, 111
Deutsch, Sarah, 83
Dewey, John, 138–39
*dichos,* 101–2, 127
Dickey, Roland, 78, 90, 93, 94
dowries, 60, 65
drawing, 140–41, 142, 143
Duggan, Paula, 116, 117, 127, 132
economic development, 84, 112, 113–14, 117; funding and, 127–28; and gift-giving, 115–16
Economic Development Council, 115, 116, 145
elites, 83. *See also* social class
El Pueblo Museum, 67
El Rancho de Las Golondrinas, 106
El Rito, 36–37
embroidery: Chinese silk, 58–59; Indo-

Portuguese, 65–66; J. Lobato's, 19–23, 25, 32; manuals for, 81–82; signing, 26–27; traditional, 57–58; vs. weaving, 61–62; wool on cotton, 69–70, 100–101. *See also plates and figures fol. p. 46*
*Encuentro, El,* 36–37, 156
*Entriega, La,* 28–30, 33, 161 n. 29
*Entriega de los Novios, La* (Lobato), 13, 28, fol. p. 46; composition of, 30–33
Escandon, Irene, 60
Espinosa, Carmen, 81, 82
Espinoza, Emma, 111
ethnicity, 27–28, 110, 154; art and, 18–19, 26; Hispanic, 71–72, 105; of San Luis, 121, 155; Spanish, 7, 8–10
ethnoaesthetics, 149, 154
exhibitions, 116–17, 144, 145, 146–47

families, 17, 42–43, 86, 129–30, 142–43
Fernandez, Agnes Varos, 86
Fisher, Nora, 63, 263n. 24
floral designs, fol. p. 46, 137
Folk Arts Master/Apprentice grants, 124–26
folktales, 41–42
formats: bird, animal, flower, 137–39; pictorial, 27, 103–4, 129–30, 131–34; scenic, 134–36
Fort Garland Museum, 15, 18; bed cover at, 19–20, 46, 54, 67, 68, 95; embroidery portrayal of, 21–22, 73
frontier society, 64–65, 68, 71
funding, 127–28, 141

Gallegos, Rosabel: *Mi Fogoncito,* 103
Garnett, Harry H., 84–85, 86, 90, 92
gender, 40–41
gift-giving, 115–16, 147–48
godparents, 28, 29
Gonzales, Filomena, 140; *Haciendo Ristras,* fol. p. 46, 103

Good Friday, 36–37, 92, 156–57
government projects, 81–84
Governor's Prize for Excellence in the Arts, 114
grandparents, 17–18
Graves, Buddy, 86
Graves, Frances Varos, 73, 85–86, 87, 88, 91, 94–95, 96, 118; as artist, 89–90
Graves, Frank, 86
Graves, John, 85, 86
Graves, Mary (María) Fernandez, 86, 87, 89, 95–96, 118
Graves, Richard Claude, 86, 88
Graves, Sophie Varos, 86, 88, 94–95
Graves, Wayne, 91, 141; colchas made by, fol. p. 46, 92–94
Graves, Winnie, 86
Guadalupe-Hidalgo, Treaty of, 70
Guadalupita, 97
*Haciendo Ristras* (Gonzales and Chavez), fol. p. 46, 103
hand crafts, 72, 97, 163n. 23; as art, 103–4; as gifts, 115-16; government and, 81–84; marketing, 76–77, 84–85, 105, 147; reviving, 78–81
Hassenfuss, Louis, 98
heirlooms, 56, 147–48
*Hermanas Piadosas,* 34
Hermandad de Nuestro Padre Jesús Nazareno. *See* Penitente Brotherhood
Hispano-Mauresque style, 66
Hispanos, 7, 78; as artists, 104–5; and Carson Revival, 84, 96; as culture brokers, 82–83, 106–7; identity of, 8–10, 71–72, 73, 80, 120, 121; traditions of, 17, 18–19, 23–24, 28–30, 33–34, 36–37
history: portraying, 20–21, 23, 27–28
Holy Week, 33–34, 36–37, 39, 91, 156–57
hunting rights, 135, 138

iconography, 67, 89–90, 94, 134; Catholic, 110–16; in *Mis Crismes,* 23–28; penitente, 91–92
identity, 107–8, 122; Hispanic, 8–10, 18, 71–72, 73, 80, 120, 121, 155
India: textiles from, 65, 66, 67, 73, 164n. 25
*indianas, indianillas,* 66, 264n. 25
insider/outsider perspectives, 18, 40

Jacquez family, 42
Jaramillo, Cleofas, 92
John Paul II, Pope, 11

La Combe, Pacifica, 126, 137, 140, 150; *Magpie,* fol. p. 46
La Culebra mountain, 134, 135
Ladies Sewing Circle, 4, 95, 114, 116, 145; aesthetics of, 139–40, 141–42, 144, 150; creativity and, 123–24, 142–43; formation of, 120, 121, 125; funding for, 127–28; motifs and styles of, 137–39, 143–44; social context of, 126–27, 128–29, 148–49
Lamy, Jean, 60
land grants, 6, 8–9
landscapes, 134–36, 142
Lange, Yvonne, 97
Las Animas County, 81
La Veta Pass, 5
legends, 41–42
Lobato, Eugene, 24, 29, 33, 34, 38–39, 42–43, 155
Lobato, Josephine (Josie), 15, 29, 49–50, 54, 63, 87, 95, 117, 121, 126, 140, 144, 149; artwork of, 14, 23–27, 28, 30–41, 43–47, fol. p. 46, 64–65, 73, 89, 112–13, 118, 155, 156; creativity of, 13, 16–17, 50–51, 150–51; family of, 17–18, 42–43; techniques of, 19–23, 56–57; themes used by, 47–48
Lobato, Ursula, 118
luxury goods, 60, 64, 65, 68

Madrid, Stella, 105
Madrid de Flores, Isidora, 69, 75, 103, 105, 106, 107, 108; and Villanueva Tapestry, 98–99, 101–2, 127, 140
Maestas, Huberto, 10–11
*Magpie* (La Combe), fol. p. 46, 137
Manzanares, Charles, 115
Manzanares, Edicia, 118, 126, 133, 134
Manzanares, Mary Jo, 10
marketing, 90, 102–3, 105, 116, 128, 144, 145, 146, 147; Carson colchas, 95–96; and craft revival, 79, 84–85, 106; power brokerage in, 80–81
Martínez, Frances, 126, 137, 150
Martínez, Mary, 111–12, 113, 118
Mascareñas, Victoria, 106
Medina, Juan Estévan, 34
memory, 48, 49, 113, 119–20, 149, 155, 156, 157; and creativity, 150–51; and pictorial narrative, 131, 132–34
Mera, H. P., 90
Mercedarian nuns: sampler by, 59–60
*Mi Fogoncito* (Gallegos), 103
*Milagro de San Acacio, El* (Lobato), 14, 41, fol. p. 46, 47; composition of, 43–46
Millicent Rogers Museum, 88, 93–94, 103, 163n. 10
military, 20–21, 43
miracle at San Acacio, 41–42
*Misa del Gallo, La,* 23
*Mis Crismes* (Lobato), 19, 33, fol. p. 46; iconography of, 23–27
*Misiones, Los* (Lobato), 14, fol. p. 46, 112–13
Moorish influence, 66, 93, 94
*moradas,* 33–34, 91; Holy Week and, 36–37; portrayals of, 35–36
Morfi, Father, 76, 159n. 4
Mormons, 17, 84, 89, 90, 93, 96
Mortarell, Father, 30–31, 110; depictions of, 111–13

## index

motifs, 66, 81, 105–6; on Carson colchas, 86–87, 88–89, 90–91, 92, 93, 94, 96; choosing, 150–51; diamond, 60–61; floral, 58–59, 67; religious, 70, 118; on Villanueva Tapestry, 101–2. *See also* formats
*mudejar* style, 66, 94
Museum of International Folk Art, 59–60, 90–91, 97, 98, 163n. 10

narrative: pictorial, 27, 88, 103–4, 129–30, 131–34, 149
National Center for Atmospheric Research (NCAR), 146–47
National Youth Administration, 81
Native Americans, 8, 69, 87, 96. *See also* Utes
Native Market, 78, 79, 80, 81, 106
NCAR. *See* National Center for Atmospheric Research
New England, 70–71, 164n. 25
New Mexico, 58, 59, 64–65, 68, 71, 159n. 4, 164nn. 32, 34; revival movements in, 77–81. *See also* Carson Revival colchas; Villanueva Tapestry
*Nuestra Señora de Guadalupe*, 101

Ojo Caliente, 86, 95
*Old San Acacio* (Valdez), fol. p. 46, 110, 128
*Old San Acacio in 1925* (Trujillo), 111
Olivas, Mary, 126, 127
Orrego-Salas, Carmen Benavente de, 15, 22, 26–27, 49–50, 84, 139, 143, 149; on creativity, 105–6, 132; on revitalization, 97–98, 103, 115, 144; and San Luis, 116–17, 118, 123–24, 133, 136, 150; on self-identity, 107–8; on stitchery as art, 104, 130–31; on tradition, 76–77; and Villanueva, 99–100, 101, 102; workshops by, 104, 120–23
Ortega, Daisy, 31, 118, 126, 137, 139, 144, 149; *El Convento*, 111, 113, 132, 146
Ortega, Prax, 111

Ortega, Shirley, 61, 80
Otero-Warren, Nina, 82, 83
Our Lady of Guadalupe Church, 101

padrinos, 28–29
Pat, Father. *See* Valdez, Patricio
Penitente Brotherhood, 10, 33–34, 91–92; Holy Week and, 36–37, 156–57; portraying, 39–41, 88, 89, 90, 155
*Penitentes, Los* (Lobato), 14, fol. p. 46; composition of, 34–41
pictorial themes, 27, 88, 103–4, 129–30, 131–34, 149
*pintados*, 66, 164n. 25
politics: cultural, 14–15, 80, 82–83, 154, 159n. 4
Portal Case, 79
Portugal, 163n. 23; textiles from, 65–66, 67, 73, 163n. 24
power brokerage, 80–81, 83, 148–49, 154

*Rancho Grande, El* (Cleven), fol. p. 46, 131–32
Reano II, Joseph de, 68
recycling in Carson colchas, 85, 95
regeneration: art as, 64–65
religion: as theme, 110–12, 118–19, 164n. 32. *See also* Catholicism
reproductions: Carson, 85–86
resistance, 154
*retablos*, 70, 88
revival, revitalization movements, 76, 106–7, 120; Carson, 84–85; early-twentieth-century, 77–81; local and government, 81–84; and San Luis, 117, 144; in Villanueva, 97–108
Rio Grande, 8, 60–61, 68, 138. *See also various towns, locales*
Romero, Esther, 3, 111–12, 113, 118, 125, 126
Romero, Joyce, 118

*sabanilla*, 61, 67, 70, 85
St. Peter and Paul Church, 112, 133
saints, 14, 50, 88, 89, 118–19
Salazar, David, 106
Salazar, Evangeline, 118, 124–25, 126, 136, 138, 141, 142, 143, 145; ethnic identity of, 9–10; on funding, 127–28; *La Vega*, fol. p. 46, 134–35, 146; on technique, 139–40
Saltillo style, fol. p. 46, 60–61, 68
samplers, 59–60
San Acacio, 41–42, 43, 47, 110
Sánchez, Eva, 118, 126
Sandoval, Carlos, 7
Sangre de Cristo Church, Parish, 10–11, 15, 110, 112, 117, 149
Sangre de Cristo Land Grant, 7–8
San Luis, 2, 3, 4–5, 6, 7, 17, 36, 49, 80, 119, 120, 125, 144, 147, 155, 168n. 22; Catholicism in, 10–11; as corporate community, 123–24; economic development in, 112, 127–28; ethnicity in, 8–10; Father Pat and, 113–15; portraying, 25–26; social context in, 126–27, 128–29; workshops in, 116, 117–18, 121–23
San Luis Cultural Museum, 145–47
San Luis Valley, 5–6, 8, 20–21, fol. p. 46, 78
San Pedro, 112, 133
Santa Ana, 8–9, 162n. 9
Santa Claus in *Mis Crismes*, 24, 26
Santa Fe, 159n. 4, 164n. 32; Spanish arts and crafts revival in, 78–81
Santa Fe–Chihuahua Trail, 68, 70–71, 72, 150, 164nn. 25, 34
*Santa Rita* (Lobato), 14, 50, 118
Santistevan, Tina, 126
scenery as theme, 134–36
Schweitzer, H., 55–56, 162n. 1
SDVE. *See* State Department of Vocational Education
Semana Santa, 33–34. *See also* Holy Week

Senior Center, 125–26
Serna, Aggie, 82
Sewell, Brice, 81
shawls: Chinese silk, 58–59, 73
shrine: San Luis, 10–11, 111, 114, 145
Shumate, John "Shorty," 90
Shupe, Elmer, 85, 86, 88, 90
Shupe, W. K., 85
silk: Chinese embroidery in, 58–59
Sloan, Pat, 156
Smith-Hughes Vocational Training, 81
social class, 68, 69, 83, 117–18, 120–21
social context, 32, 130, 147–49
Society of the Brotherhood. *See* Penitente Brotherhood
Spain, 65–66, 70, 163n. 23; ethnic heritage of, 8–10, 43, 68, 121, 155
Spanish Colonial Arts Society, 91, 105; founding and function of, 78–81
Spanish Market, 80, 82, 95
*Spanish Southwest, The* (exhibit catalogue), 93
State Department of Vocational Education (SDVE), 81
status symbols: colchas as, 68, 72, 73
storytelling, 38–39, 42, 132–33
Suaso, Juan Antonio, 68
symbolism, 133–34, 137–38; in *Mis Crismes*, 24–25

tapestries: colchas as, 57–58, 122. *See also* Villanueva Tapestry
Taylor Museum, 55, 58, 59, 60–61, 62, 70, 163n. 10; and Carson revival, 84–85, 92–93, 162n. 1
technique(s), 56–57, 102, 136; as aesthetic, 139–40; and foundation cloth, 61–62; J. Lobato's, 19–23, 25, 32, 34–35
*Tierra Benedita*, 101
Tinieblas, Las (Tenebrae), 91, 156–57

tourism, 27, 107, 144, 145–46
Trade and Industrial Bulletins (Bluebooks), 81–82
trade fairs, 60
tradition(s), 17, 18, 76–77
Trujillo, Tiva, 15, 16, 24, 28, 46, 50, 51, 117; *Old San Acacio in 1925*, 110–11
Trujillo family, 136

Utes, 41–42, 43, 45

Valdez, Abie, 129, 130
Valdez, Cordy, 126, 137, 139, 150
Valdez, Julia, 31, 111, 113, 117, 118, 125, 126, 144, 149; *Adobe Plant*, 128, 129, 130, 131, 146; *Old San Acacia*, fol. p. 46, 110, 128
Valdez, Luisa, 126
Valdez, Patricio, 3, 4, 24, 26, 110, 112, 118, 147, 148, 149, 155; and San Luis, 10–11, 113–15, 117, 119, 138

Varos, Jose Manuel, 88
Varos family, 86
*Vega, La* (Salazar), fol. p. 46, 134–35, 146
Vigil, Julia, 118
Vigil, Teresa, 118, 133–34, 140, 144, 149
Villanueva, 69, 80, 84, 97, 122, 144
Villanueva Tapestry, 98, 107, 127, 140; composition of, 99–102
Villanueva Tapestry Corporation, 102–3
Virginia Neal Blue (VNB) Resource Center workshops, 116, 118, 120, 125, 128, 145, 146, 147, 150

weddings, 28–30, 161n. 29
Wheelwright, Mary Cabot, 91, 92, 105
Wilder, M. A., 53, 54–55, 56, 60, 162n. 1
workshops, 97–98, 104, 112, 126, 166n. 33; in San Luis, 116–18, 122–23, 128, 133, 145; social context of, 120–21, 125
Works Progress Administration, 81

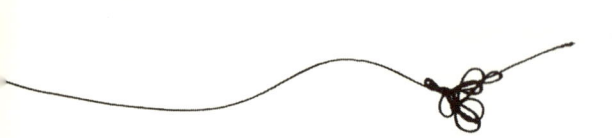

## about the author

Suzanne MacAulay, an art historian and folklorist, heads the School of Fine Arts at the Wanganui Polytechnic, located on the shore of the Tasman Sea in New Zealand. Her expertise is in material culture, specifically textiles and vernacular architecture, with emphasis on the liveliness of folk aesthetics, social critique, and memory. She has published articles on colcha embroidery, art revivals, pedagogy, and cultural politics.

MacAulay received her M.A. in art history from the University of Colorado, and her Ph.D. in folklore and ethnography from the University of Pennsylvania. She has taught art history, was Division Head of Fine Arts at Colorado Women's College, owned a gallery in Denver, and served as folklorist-in-residence for the Arizona Commission on the Arts. In 1994 she was hired by the Fine Arts Department at Wanganui to develop and coordinate a culturally based art history and liberal arts program. Her current research involves fieldwork with "professional" exiles, highly trained individuals like her who have come from other countries to work in the academic or medical sectors in Wanganui. She is particularly interested in the symbolic role material culture plays as these people reconstruct their identity via lifelines to their past through art objects and ritual behavior.

While living in Colorado, MacAulay also produced and aired her own radio program, "The Family of Man and Other Animals," on Boulder, Colorado community radio, which broadcast throughout Colorado's Front Range.